A Green River Reader

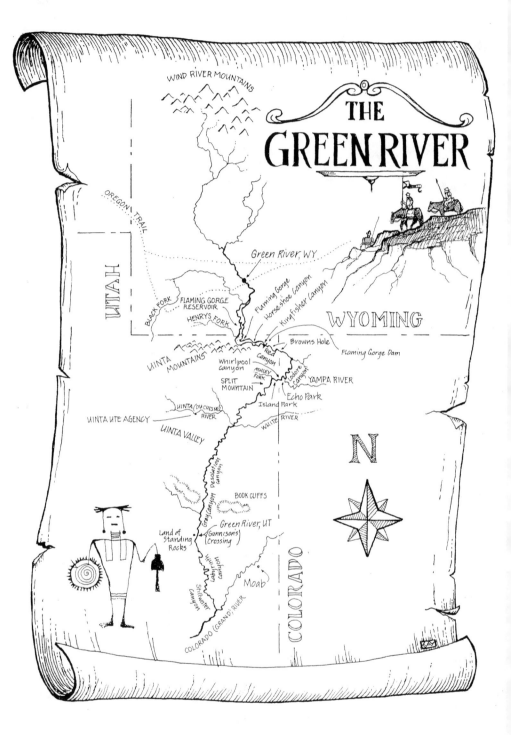

A Green River Reader

Edited by

Alan Blackstock

THE UNIVERSITY OF UTAH PRESS
Salt Lake City

The Defiance House Man colophon is a registered trademark of the University of Utah Press. It is based upon a four-foot-tall, Ancient Puebloan pictograph (late PIII) near Glen Canyon, Utah.

LIBRARY OF CONGRESS CATALOGING-IN-PUBLICATION DATA

A Green River reader / edited by Alan Blackstock.
    p. cm.
 ISBN-13: 978-0-87480-837-7 (pbk. : alk. paper)
 ISBN-10: 0-87480-837-5 (pbk. : alk. paper)
 1. Green River (Wyo.-Utah)—Description and travel—Anecdotes. 2. Green River (Wyo.-Utah)—Discovery and exploration—Anecdotes. 3. Natural history—Green River (Wyo.-Utah)—Anecdotes. 4. Green River (Wyo.-Utah)—History—Anecdotes. 5. Explorers—Green River (Wyo.-Utah)—Biography—Anecdotes. 6. Travelers—Green River (Wyo.-Utah)—Biography—Anecdotes. I. Blackstock, Alan, 1956-
 F767.G7G74 2005
 917.92'5—dc22

                    2005024621

Frontispiece: Map by Charles Aldrich

Contents

Acknowledgments

Among the many people who assisted in bringing this project to completion, the following deserve special recognition: John Barton, senior lecturer in history at Utah State University (USU)-Uintah Basin, for his invaluable guidance in pinning down the locations of the mountain-men rendezvous and the early forts and trading posts along the Green; Charlie Aldrich, for the many laborious hours he spent creating the Green River map that graces the frontispiece; Dr. Guy Denton and the USU-Uintah Basin management team for their support, both for the Writing on Rivers course that inspired this anthology and for the anthology itself; and the staffs of the Uintah County Library, the Utah Historical Society, the Colorado Historical Society, the Special Collections division of the Marriott Library of the University of Utah, and the University of Michigan Digital Library, for their assistance in locating and reproducing many of the documents included here. I would also like to thank Roy Webb and the heirs of David Brower for granting permission to reprint their work in this anthology, along with Ann Zwinger for her all-around graciousness. Finally, I am indebted to all the students and colleagues at USU-Uintah Basin who have participated in Writing on Rivers over the years, and to Wendy Hatch and the boatmen and women of Hatch River Expeditions, along with Sue Watson and the interpretive staff at Dinosaur National Monument, who have helped ensure its continued success.

Introduction

Alan Blackstock

RED CANYON, GREEN RIVER, FIVE MILES BELOW FLAMING GORGE
DAM. AN OSPREY CIRCLES OVERHEAD, GRASPING IN ITS TALONS AN
ENORMOUS TROUT, SEARCHING FOR THE UPDRAFT THAT WILL CARRY
IT OUT OF THE CANYON AND TO A PLACE WHERE IT CAN CONSUME
ITS MEAL WITHOUT FEAR OF ATTACK BY A RIVAL. AS THE BIRD
WHEELS ABOVE, WE DRIFT IN AN EDDY, WATCHING TRANSFIXED AS
SKY, CLOUDS, RED CLIFFS, AND LODGEPOLE PINES REVOLVE IN THE
STILLNESS.

The seven-mile stretch of the Green from the dam to Little Hole is certainly the most heavily traveled on the river, since no permit is required to run this section, and it offers some of the best fly-fishing in the country. Behind the dam, jet boats and Sea-Doos roar from one end of flooded Flaming Gorge to the other. Downstream, though, a float trip can be made in perfect tranquility, on weekdays at least, when the only other humans one is likely to encounter are trout fishermen who maintain a reverential silence between the towering walls. On summer weekends, however, the river becomes a floating amusement park for mass excursions of youth groups and extended families—dozens of rafts congregated at the put-in point, waiting for the signal from the group leader to push off, jostling for position like the crowd at the start of a 5k race. And even the sections of the river requiring permits, such as the popular Split Mountain Canyon run, see hundreds of rafters a day during June and July, most taking advantage of day trips offered by several commercial rafting companies.

Like the Colorado River of which it is the largest tributary, the Green in its history has been seen as a force to be respected, an enigma to be explored, an obstacle to be conquered, a resource for irrigation and hydroelectric power, a remnant of wilderness in need of preservation, a sportsman's reserve, and a playground for recreation enthusiasts. And as with the Colorado, this variety of attitudes toward the river has inspired an equally varied range of written responses, representative samples of which are collected in this anthology. Why a reader devoted exclusively to the Green River? For several reasons: among them its geographical and historical significance, its prominence in the work of several of our preeminent American naturalist writers, and perhaps most practically, as a sort of interpretive guide to the river for the thousands who follow its course each summer in kayaks, canoes, jet skis, baloney boats, or even, mirabile dictu, on foot. Ever since John Wesley Powell, those who have attempted to "run the Colorado" have set out not at the headwaters of the Colorado (known as the Grand River above its confluence with the Green until 1921), but as close to the headwaters of the Green, in Wyoming's Wind River Range, as practical. Why? On the first page of *The Exploration of the Colorado River and Its Canyons,* Powell flatly asserts, "The Green River is larger than the Grand and is the upper continuation of the Colorado." And in *River: One Man's Journey Down the Colorado, Source to Sea,* Colin Fletcher writes, "because the Green is 300 miles longer than the former Grand (it also drains a larger area), geographers regard it as the 'master stream'" (9). Fletcher doesn't specify which geographers so regard it, but Philip L. Fradkin, in *A River No More: The Colorado River and the West,* cites U.S. government hydrologist E. C. LaRue's 1916 survey as evidence for his claim that "[t]he longer stem of a river…is usually considered its main branch, and that clearly is the Green River" (36). Powell and those who came after him—Julius Stone, the Kolb Brothers, Barry Goldwater, Fradkin, and Fletcher, to name a few—chose the Green as their point of origin, and both Ann Zwinger and Ellen Meloy have devoted entire books to the Green. Furthermore, the Green has figured as prominently in the history of the exploration and conquest of the American West, along with the political and economic disputes resulting from that conquest, as the Colorado—perhaps on a smaller scale, but therefore allowing for more detailed and nuanced inspection of some of these concerns. A sacred stream to the Native Americans who dwell along its banks and tributaries, an obstacle to the Spanish priests Domínguez and Escalante; a means of travel to mountain men, trappers, and prospectors like William H. Ashley and William Manley, a scientific puzzle to be solved for Major Powell, a pivotal factor in David Brower's losing battle to save Glen Canyon, and a storehouse of natural marvels to be celebrated in images and words by some of our most prominent photographers and writers, the Green River has generated a surprising amount of historical and artistic representation for a waterway that has never been in the forefront of the national consciousness the way the Colorado, the Mississippi, or the Columbia have been. All the more reason, then, for an anthology that surveys the chronological, thematic, and stylistic range of writing that the human encounter with the Green River has produced.

The idea for this anthology grew out of two recent educational endeavors in which I was privileged to take part. The first was a course called "Writing on Rivers" that I developed for Utah State University-Uintah Basin and taught along with Vini Exton, a colleague in the English department who also happens to be an experienced river guide. Browsing through the stacks at the Uintah County Public Library in Vernal while compiling readings for the course, I was surprised at the number of books I found that dealt largely or wholly with the Green River. Then, in the summer of 2002, I was invited by the library to lead a series of discussions of Richard F. Fleck's *A Colorado River Reader* as part of the National Endowment for the Humanities' *Moving Waters* exhibit. It was then that I conceived the idea of putting together a complementary anthology focusing on the Green River, both for use in my Writing on Rivers course and for the pleasure of anyone who enjoys reading about rivers. Since this collection is intended not to compete with but to complement Fleck's fine anthology, I have purposely avoided duplicating any of the material in his book. Several authors are represented in both collections, but I have selected different passages to excerpt, in the cases of Domínguez-Escalante, Powell, Dellenbaugh, and Meloy, or entirely different works, in the cases of Fradkin, Zwinger, and Abbey. It is my hope that anyone who has enjoyed *A Colorado River Reader* will equally enjoy *A Green River Reader,* and vice-versa.

Many of the writers represented in this anthology have noted distinct differences between the upper and lower reaches of the Green/Colorado river system. Powell's introduction to *The Exploration of the Colorado River and Its Canyons* notes how the Green and Grand rivers, "born in the cold, gloomy solitudes of the upper mountain region, have a strange, eventful history as they pass down through gorges, tumbling in cascades and cataracts, until they reach the hot, arid plains of the Lower Colorado, where the waters that were so clear above empty as turbid floods into the Gulf of California" (17). In *Run, River, Run*, Ann Zwinger identifies the geographical boundary as Split Mountain, the southernmost extension of the Uinta Range that laterally bisects the Green River: "Split Mountain is an end: the river cuts through no more mountains. The change from mountain to basin is sudden and complete. The river enters the Uinta Basin, the topmost province of the 150,000-square-mile Colorado Plateau, through which it continues until its confluence with the Colorado River" (191). And as Philip Fradkin points out in the preface to *Sagebrush Country: Land and the American West,*

> the Uintas serve as a line of demarcation not only geographically but historically and culturally: the mountains mark the dividing line between the hot Colorado Plateau country to the south and the cold Wyoming plains to the north. Not only does the topography differ on the north and south slopes, but also the fauna and the flora. The crest is a cultural divide, there having been different Indian tribes on each side of the range who were followed by disparate, transient whites on the north and homogenous, rooted Mormons to the south. (xvi)

The selections in this anthology have been arranged to reflect such differences both geographically and chronologically to the extent possible: that is, they move down the river as they move up in time. The earliest accounts, however—the journals of Domínguez-Escalante and Ashley, and the published reports of Kit Carson, Thomas J. Farnham, William Lewis Manley, John C. Frémont, and J. S. Newberry—are given priority in time rather than place, since they focus on specific locations rather than systematic attempts to chart the course of the river. The selections from the Domínguez-Escalante journals describe the crossing of the Green in 1776, just outside what is now Dinosaur National Monument, during the Spanish missionaries' abortive attempt to reach California by crossing the Utah mountains. The authors were keenly interested in the possibilities for Spanish colonization of the lands they explored, and the journal thus takes special note of the abundance of pasturage and the potential for irrigation in the area, but it also betrays the authors' anxiety about the river's reputation as the boundary between Ute and Comanche lands and their fear of attack by one or the other. But economic difficulties in Spain prevented the Spanish government from carrying out its plans for settlement of the area, and it was left largely undisturbed by Europeans until the advent of the Anglo- and French-American fur trade at the beginning of the nineteenth century.

The first Anglo-Americans known to have visited the Green were a party of fur trappers led by Wilson P. Hunt in the employ of John Jacob Astor's Pacific Fur Company. Hunt's party camped near the source of the Green, then known as "Spanish River," in August 1811. But it was not until 1823 that the first concerted effort was undertaken to exploit the possibilities the river offered to satisfy the European demand for beaver pelts. Members of an expedition launched by William Ashley and Andrew Henry trapped along the Green from 1823 to 1824, and in 1824 Etienne Provot and Antoine Robidoux led independent trapping expeditions on the Green. The excerpts from Ashley's own narrative reproduced here recount his 1825 descent through several of the Green River canyons in "bullboats" constructed of buffalo hide stretched over frames of willow or cottonwood poles, the first documented attempt at navigation of the Green. In the summer of 1825, along Henry's Fork near present-day Flaming Gorge Reservoir, Ashley organized the first great rendezvous of mountain men and fur trappers to be held west of the Continental Divide.

With this influx of trappers and, soon after, emigrants passing through the Green River region on their way to California, a number of enterprising mountain men quickly realized that investment in the construction of trading posts and forts could be as lucrative as trapping. In 1828 William Reed and Denis Julien established the Reed Trading Post at the confluence of the Whiterocks and Uinta rivers, two Green River tributaries on the south slope of the Uinta Mountains. Antoine Robidoux bought the trading post in 1832 and expanded it by building a fort nearby, known variously as Fort Uinta or Fort Wintey—variant spellings of the Ute word from which "Uinta" is derived. (Fort Uinta is not to be confused with Fort Robidoux, which Robidoux built in 1837 where the Duchesne River empties into the Green, as shown on maps from the period.) Other important forts along the Green were Fort Davy Crockett, established in 1836 in Brown's Hole near Vermilion Creek and commonly referred to as "Fort Misery" by travelers who had the misfortune of staying there for extended periods (see the excerpts in this volume from Thomas Farnham's 1839 account of his visit), and Fort Bridger, built by mountain man Jim Bridger in 1842 to sell supplies to emigrants traveling west on the Oregon Trail. Famed wilderness explorers Kit Carson and John C. Frémont spent extended periods along the Green River in the 1830s and 1840s, as the excerpts included here from Carson's autobiography and the journals of Frémont illustrate.

The gold rush of 1849 of dramatically increased the already considerable traffic along the Oregon Trail. Captain William Manley and his men duplicated Ashley's feat in 1849, using the river as a shortcut to the California goldfields, employing not bullboats but an old ferryboat and two handmade canoes. Manley provides the first detailed account of a trip through the canyons, along with an intriguing rendition of his party's encounter with Ute war chief Wakara (the same chief who would later lead the series of skirmishes known as Walker's War). Like Manley, most pioneers saw the inhospitable environs of the Green as little more than an obstacle, or at best a source of water and game, on their way west. As John Strong Newberry, official geologist for Captain J. N. Macomb, concluded after their unsuccessful 1859 attempt to reach the confluence of the Green and Colorado overland, "Perhaps no portion of the earth's surface is more irremediably sterile, none more hopelessly lost to human habitation, and yet it is but the wreck and ruin of a region rich and beautiful" (54). Likewise, when Brigham Young sent a party of scouts to the Uinta Basin to investigate its potential for Mormon settlement, they returned to report, as summarized in the 1861 Desert News article reproduced here, that "all that section of country…was 'one vast contiguity of waste,' and measurably valueless, excepting for nomadic purposes, hunting grounds for Indians and to hold the world together." And though Ashley had already proven that the Green was navigable, both Manley's and Farnham's accounts demonstrate vividly the sense of mystery and dread that the canyons of the Green and Colorado continued to inspire in the popular mythology of the time, a mythos that it was Powell's perceived destiny to dispel.

Powell and his expedition are well known to almost everyone with an interest in the history of the American West, the Grand Canyon, or river-running, but he was not the only one to keep records of his journey. In this collection, excerpts from Powell's journals are accompanied by those of his companions John Colton Sumner, George Y. Bradley, and Frederick Dellenbaugh, who provided sometimes conflicting accounts of the same incidents, as well as a human perspective of the major, a perspective often obscured by the more objective and scientific—though still susceptible to romantic embellishment—style of Powell's own writing. This section of the anthology is introduced with a passage from Wallace Stegner's masterful biography of Powell, *Beyond the Hundredth Meridian,* which efficiently and eloquently places Powell's 1869 expedition in its historical context. Powell's own account, *The Exploration of the Colorado and Its Canyons,* conflates the 1869 expedition with the repeat trip he and several of his companions made in 1871 to replace the scientific data lost as a result of the various mishaps the party suffered on the first expedition. The lessons learned from these disasters allowed for a much smoother and safer second expedition, suggesting that with proper preparation the river could be run without loss of life, although the expedition mounted by Frank Brown to chart a railroad route following the Colorado River from Grand Junction, Colorado, to San Diego, California, took the lives of three members, including Brown himself. Frank Brown's dream of a railroad through the Grand Canyon ended with his drowning in Soap Creek Rapid (where the inscription noting his death remains visible today), however, and it was not long thereafter that river-running purely for the sake of adventure began.

Although Ohio millionaire Julius Stone is often credited with being the first person to run the Green and Colorado solely for the thrill of it, he was actually preceded in that feat by George Flavell and Ramón Montés in 1896. Flavell died three years after completing the trip, however, and his journal was not discovered until the late 1940s and not published until 1987. But in 1909 Stone, after being rebuffed by Powell when he sought his assistance in retracing his trip, employed Vernal boatman Nathaniel Galloway to build him one of his "Galloway boats," expressly designed for river-running, and hired Galloway to guide him along Powell's route. Unlike Flavell, Stone published his journal, which he admits is written in a "telegraphic style," though in certain passages the style heightens to verge on the lyrical. Stone's book *Canyon Country* provides a more extensive photographic than narrative record of the trip, however, and in both respects it is surpassed by Ellsworth Kolb's *Through the Grand Canyon from Wyoming to Mexico*, which records the 1911 expedition of pioneering Grand Canyon photographers Ellsworth and Emory Kolb.

Like Stone, the Kolbs used Galloway boats to make the trip, and also like Stone, the purpose of their trip was primarily adventure, but also to create what they called the first "pictorial record of the entire series of canyons on the Green and Colorado." It might be argued that Powell, who brought photographer E. O. Beaman along on his second expedition, and Stone had already achieved that record, but the Kolbs did succeed in making the first motion pictures of anyone running the rapids. Both Stone and Kolb also describe encounters with the inhabitants of Brown's Hole (later known as Brown's Park), the infamous outlaw hideout where Butch Cassidy and the Wild Bunch sought refuge from the law. In "Queen Ann of Brown's Park," Ann Bassett Willis, who claimed to be the "original cowgirl" and earned the sobriquet "Queen Ann" with her innate sense of dignity and (according to her sister Josie) short temper, relates her memories of Butch and other gang members, as well as her great respect for the Ute Indians who befriended her family and her bitter resentment of their treatment at the hands of the U.S. government.

But it was not only governmental policies that would permanently alter life along the river: newspaper accounts of Powell's heroic deeds and the Kolbs' motion pictures would soon create a national appetite for river-running as a recreational pastime. First to capitalize on this appetite was Bus Hatch, profiled in Roy Webb's "Now We're Safe, Now We're on the River." Hatch and his brothers, cousins, and sons turned a rafting hobby into a commercial empire, Hatch River Expeditions, which today holds the dominant share of permits for trips on the Green and Yampa, as well as a sizable portion of those for the Grand Canyon. The birth of the commercial rafting industry, along with the advancements in technology that made it possible to harness the rivers of the West for irrigation and hydroelectric power, would bring about conflicts over the fate of the Green River that would come to a head in the battle for the preservation of Echo Park, a labyrinth of canyons at the confluence of the Green and Yampa rivers in the heart of Dinosaur National Monument.

The middle section of the anthology focuses on the controversy over the proposed Echo Park dam. As a part of the effort to block construction of the dam, Wallace Stegner edited a book entitled *This Is Dinosaur: Echo Park Country and Its Magic Rivers,* in which "The Marks of Human Passage" first appeared. The essay and the book as a whole were designed to acquaint the American public with the historical, geological, and ecological significance of the monument and to enlist their aid in the struggle for its preservation in its natural state. As Stegner points out, the name of the monument is somewhat misleading, for though it was originally created as a result of Earl Douglass's efforts to protect the dinosaur quarry he discovered, the park was later greatly expanded to include the wildest parts of the Green-Yampa river system, considered by many its chief glory. A previously unpublished article by Douglass, narrating his discovery of the dinosaur quarry and calling for the establishment of a monument to protect it, is included here, as are Bernard De Voto's *Saturday Evening Post* article "Shall We Let Them Ruin Our National Parks?" and David Brower's "Dinosaurs, Parks, and Dams," first published in 1954. Brower, the executive director of the Sierra Club at the time, led the fight in Congress against the Echo Park dam, but prevailed against it only by agreeing as a compromise not to oppose the remaining dams proposed for the upper Colorado water storage project, of which Glen Canyon Dam was the linchpin. Brower and other Sierra Club members who initially supported the compromise decision would later come to deeply regret it. The difference was that Brower had rafted through Echo Park and knew what stood to be lost; he did not make the trip through Glen Canyon until construction of the dam was nearly complete, and though he did mount a last-minute attempt to stop the filling of the reservoir, by then it was clearly too late. Though De Voto's and Brower's articles are dated, they make a still relevant appeal for the preservation of the national park system as it was originally envisioned, in the face of continued pressure for development, while Russell Martin's "The Battle for Echo Park" gives a detailed historical account of the complex political conflicts and tradeoffs that led to the eventual compromise. But the resolution of the Echo Park controversy did not end the political disputes surrounding the monument, as Philip Fradkin demonstrates in his account of a 1985 trip down the Yampa in the midst of a debate over changing the name from Dinosaur National Monument to Dinosaur National Park, a proposal of far more than merely semantic significance, and one that rekindled the same controversies that had swirled around Echo Park a generation earlier.

Although Echo Park was spared from inundation, the Flaming Gorge Dam was completed in 1962, and many of the most recent selections mention its effect on the quality of the river below the dam, often drawing contrasts between Powell's experience of the river and that of the modern-day river-runner. Another selection by Roy Webb, "The Other 'Place No One Knew,'" compares the loss of Flaming Gorge with that of Glen Canyon, and suggests that the gorge was even more obscure than the canyon, since its loss has never sparked the kind of national mourning or calls for decommission that the Glen Canyon Dam has inspired. And both Ann Zwinger and Ellen Meloy lament the diminution of experience the dam has imposed upon the river, yet celebrate the wildness that remains, as does Edward Abbey in "Terra Incognita: Into the Maze" from his classic *Desert Solitaire,* which leaves us with a view of the confluence of the Green and Colorado rivers as seen from above. Though some of this recent writing takes the form of day-to-day accounts of a linear progression along the river, most tends to be recursive, ranging the entire length of the river's course through space and time, alighting here and there whenever a pause is in order, occasionally circling and circling, waiting to catch that updraft that will allow for an ascent out of the canyon and a perspective of the river against the complex and convoluted landscape through which it flows.

Beginnings: Four Streams
in Search of a River

Philip L. Fradkin

In this excerpt from *A River No More: The Colorado River and the West,* Philip Fradkin recounts his pilgrimage to the source of the Green River, high in Wyoming's Wind River Range, and explains why hydrologists regard the Green as the "master stream" of the Colorado River system, although political machinations in 1921 resulted in the Grand River, rather than the Green, receiving official recognition as the upper section of the Colorado.

I t was the last night of August and the wind-driven snow was being slammed furiously against the rattling tent. The lightning would have had all the intensity and surprise value of a giant strobe set off randomly before the naked eye, had not the light been filtered by the two layers of orange fabric that formed the mountain tent. The thunder felt as though it was squatting directly over the campsite huddled beside a clump of subalpine fir permanently bowed by the wind. For a while the scene had all the ingredients of a *Walpurgisnacht*; then the fury tapered off to the steady slap of wet snow falling on the tent fly. This snow falling year after year and consolidated into glaciers formed the source of the Colorado River within two miles of the tent, pitched at 10,700 feet, between Peak Lake, the first gathering of the waters in Wyoming, and Knapsack Col.

In the morning there was a feeling of emergence. The clouds, in the aptly named Wind River Range, drifted apart and then formed again in random patterns outlined by the sun rising behind the saddlelike depression that marks the Continental Divide. It was as if with strokes of thunder and lightning and behind a curtain of swirling snow and dark the gods had created a river; like a pilgrim, I set off alone in the morning to the source. That there was a single source, a

learned river historian had told me, was a nineteenth-century concept, one that generated all those searches for the beginning of the
Nile.

The Green River, whose headwaters I was about to trace, has
undergone a number of interesting name changes. The Indian name
for the river was Seedskeedee (spelled variously), after the prairie
chickens that inhabited the high desert area. Its first European name
was the San Buenaventura, named after a thirteenth-century theolo-
gian by Silvestre Velez de Escalante, a Franciscan missionary who
stumbled on the river while looking for a route from Sante Fe, New
Mexico, to California. The Spanish who came after Escalante called it
the Rio Verde. This was translated to Green River by the fur trappers
in the early nineteenth century. Others simply called it the Colorado
River, since what is now known as the Colorado above the confluence
of the two streams was then known as the Grand River.

The appellation Green, perhaps derived from the reflection of the
surrounding vegetation or from the cast of glacial silt, stuck. But it
nearly became unglued sixty years ago when politics, combined with
local boosterism, invaded the realm of geographical nomenclature.
That politics should play a part in this process is appropriate, since so
much of what has happened to this river system has had a political
derivation. The Utah legislature started it off in early 1921 by introducing and then defeating a measure to change the name of the Green
to the Colorado River. This proposed action, at least, had some historical and hydrologic validity. The Utah lawmakers were not to meet
again for another two years, so the Colorado legislature acted quickly
on the prodding of Congressman Edward F. Taylor of Glenwood
Springs, who first as a state senator and then as a congressman had
campaigned to change the name of the Grand to the Colorado. The
Colorado legislature acted promptly, as did Congress, and on July 25,
1921, President Warren G. Harding signed the bill and gave the pen to
Taylor, who could now claim that his Colorado congressional district
was at the headwaters of the Colorado River. Throughout the process
the Board of Geographical Names, which is supposed to rule on such
matters, maintained a low profile.

Before the name change, it was commonly thought the Colorado
River began at the headwaters of the Green, which was longer and
drained a larger area than the Grand, whose average annual flow was

greater than the Green. When the hydrologist E. C. La Rue made the first comprehensive report for the U.S. Geological Survey on the Colorado River system in 1916, he wrote, "Colorado River is formed by the junction of the Grand and the Green. Green River drains a larger area than the Grand and is considered the upper continuation of the Colorado. Including the Green, the river is about 1,700 miles long." Since the name change, clearly an exercise of the chamber-of-commerce mentality, it has commonly been assumed that the upper Colorado River in Rocky Mountain National Park is the source; and official literature distributed by the Bureau of Reclamation and National Park Service, among others, has reflected this misapprehension. The longer stem of a river, termed the master stream, is usually considered its main branch, and that clearly is the Green River. Besides, the headwaters of the Green is a more proper setting for the start of such a great river system.

I walked east up the unnamed cirque valley, the first to go that way in the undisturbed snow that now, under the rising sun, was beginning to melt. The stream, also unnamed at this point, widened a few times into what could almost be called a series of small, thin lakes: paternoster lakes, so called because of their resemblance to the beads of a rosary. A coyote howled and its cries blended with the many different sounds of running water. It was as if the mountains were weeping. There were countless glints of warm light on water and ice as I walked toward the rising sun. To the right was a waterfall splashing down in stages from the small tarn holding the meltwater from Stroud Glacier. The minute, intense reflection of the sun in the tarn almost brought my perception of the source down to a single radiant drop. But on this day there were many sources.

The climb toward the col was tedious. The rocks buried by the snow could not be seen, but were slippery underfoot. As I went higher and neared the 12,000-foot-high ridge, the snow got deeper. My struggles were mocked by a rough-legged hawk that glided effortlessly over the saddle. The only other wildlife I saw were spiders trapped in the snow. At times the snow was to my hips, and I was glad I had brought an ice ax to probe with and gaiters to keep the snow out of my boots. It was hot, yet new clouds were piling up to the west. I stopped a few hundred feet short of my goal at the base of a steep slope that looked avalanche-prone. This was far enough. I no longer heard the sound of running water.

Although I was alone this day, I did have a companion of sorts, the guidebook for the mountains, written by Finis Mitchell. I have never met Mr. Mitchell, but by all accounts he is an unusual person. He arrived at the foot of the Wind River Range in a mule-drawn wagon in 1906 and has made the mountains his abiding interest ever since. Mitchell began climbing the mountains in 1909 and began photographing them in 1920. In 1977, at the age of seventy-five, Mitchell commented to an interviewer, "I'll be climbing for another ten or fifteen years. There are about fifty-eight more peaks I want pictures from." Up to that point the indefatigable Mitchell had climbed 220 peaks and taken 101,345 pictures, all properly filed and indexed. He used to carry a seventy-five-pound pack, but has whittled that weight down to fifty pounds over the years. Mitchell's regimen is simple. He does not smoke or drink liquor, coffee, or soft drinks. In the mountains he does not eat food warmer than his body temperature and wraps himself in a piece of plastic rather than seeking shelter in a $200 tent. Mitchell likes being alone in the mountains and, although he has had some close calls, told a local undertaker, "I'm going to put daisies on top of you before I leave." He follows in the tradition of William J. Stroud, known also as Rocky Mountain Bill, who first climbed Stroud Peak above my campsite and many other mountains in the same suit he wore to transact business and visit friends in Rock Springs. Somehow these earlier travelers make us Vibram-soled, Gore-Tex-clad late arrivals seem overprotected from the elements.

That more of us are arriving in numbers that can be considered a crowd became evident two days later when I packed my gear and headed down to the parking lot at the edge of the Bridger Wilderness Area. It was the start of the long Labor Day weekend, and a steady stream of backpackers and horseback riders was heading up the trail. It would be the same at the other headwaters of the Colorado River system, all located in officially designated wilderness areas, as it would be at the end of the river and any intermediate spot I visited. The West is not an empty region. In terms of what it can support, it is already crowded; the promises being made to future arrivals should be regarded with great care, since many cannot be fulfilled.

As I descended from the col I had a feeling of accomplishment, since I had tried once before to reach the source but had been turned back far below by the deep snows of early June. That I did not quite make it to the top, as I was not going to quite make it to the end of the river, left me with the satisfaction of retaining some small sense of mystery and wonder. I felt exuberant because of the nature of the day, and as I carefully picked my way down I sang. One of the songs that spilled out unconsciously was *Cry Me a River*—a tune, it occurred to me, that fit the surroundings. The mountains were weeping this day; the river's growing salinity, like tears, threatened to stifle its life-giving force; and my overall feeling of what had happened to the world's most-used river was one of muted sadness. It was a sadness tempered by the reality of the West, an arid land where the first impulse was to make water work for man's needs. This was an accepted national policy that had gone unchallenged for a half century. That the policy had outlived its usefulness—had, indeed, gone awry at times—was to become apparent in my travels through the lands the river nurtured. On such a day, though, these thoughts did not last long. There was more a feeling of birth than of death.

I was reluctant to leave my campsite and descend into the real world. It had been a restful place, and I had spent enough time there to feel some harmony between my rhythms and those of the mountains and falling water. Peak Lake, just below the campsite, was a friendly presence. Late in the afternoon I usually sat with my back against a boulder, facing this first gathering of the waters and the warm sun. Silver streaks of wind would flash across the dark-turquoise water. The streaks and trailing wisps gave the wind a tangible substance, yet the deep water remained undisturbed after their ephemeral passage. The taste of water was also insubstantial, perhaps because it was too pure or my palate had been spoiled by coarser water available below. The lake in its rock-encrusted setting was a scene of utmost purity and clarity, to a degree that was not to be repeated as I followed the river toward the ocean. Yet I was glad, at least, to have had this experience at the start.

The Domínguez-Escalante Journal

Fray Francisco Silvestre Vélez de Escalante

SPANISH PRIESTS FRANCISCO ATANASIO DOMÍNGUEZ AND FRANCISCO SILVESTRE VÉLEZ DE ESCALANTE MADE THE FIRST DOCUMENTED JOURNEY THROUGH THE GREEN RIVER REGION IN 1776 IN AN ATTEMPT TO FIND A ROUTE FROM SANTA FE, NEW MEXICO, TO MONTEREY, CALIFORNIA. DOMÍNGUEZ LED THE EXPEDITION WHILE ESCALANTE SERVED AS THE RECORD KEEPER, THOUGH IT IS ESCALANTE'S NAME THAT IS MEMORIALIZED IN THE NAMES OF NUMEROUS GEOGRAPHICAL FEATURES ALONG THEIR ROUTE.

≈≈ SEPTEMBER 13

On the 13th about eleven in the morning, we set out from El Arroyo del Cíbolo over a plain lying at the foot of a small sierra which the Yutas and Lagunas call Sabuagari; it extends from east to west, and its white cliffs can be seen from the high hills which come before El Cañon Pintado. After going west two leagues and three quarters, we arrived at the water source which the guide knew; it is a scanty spring and lies at the sierra's base almost at its western point. We continued for a quarter of a league in the same direction along a well-beaten path near which, toward the south, two copious springs of the finest water rise, a musket shot apart from each other, which we named Las Fuentes de Santa Clara. The small plain over which they flow and are absorbed produces an abundance of good pasturage from their moisture to which we descended and the horses consumed. From here we went a league northwest over the trail mentioned and crossed an arroyo which was coming down from the plain of Las Fuentes, and in which there were large waterholes. From here downstream there is a lot of good pasturage in its box channel bed, which is wide and level. We crossed it again, went up some low hills with finely ground rock in spots, and after going two leagues northwest came to a large river which we named San Buenaventura.[1] Today six leagues.

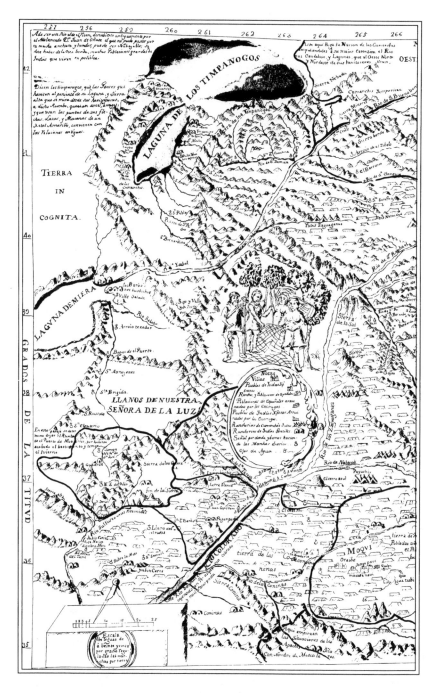

Map showing Utah Lake and the Great Salt Lake and the area to the
south and east, drawn by Don Bernardo Miera y Pacheco in 1778.

This river is the most copious one we have come by, and the same one which Fray Alonso de Posada, Custos of this [Custody] of New Mexico in the century gone by, relates in his report as separating the Yuta nation from the Comanche according to the indications he gives in it and the distance at which he locates it with respect to Santa Fe. And in fact it is the boundary between these two nations, along the northeast and the north. Its course along here is to the west-southwest but, ahead and down to here, to the west. It comes together with the San Clemente, but we do not know if it does with the preceding ones. Here it has a meadow abounding in pasturage and good land for farming with the help of irrigation, which in width might be more than a league and in length could reach five. It flows into it between two lofty stone hogbacks which, after forming a sort of corral, come so closely together that one can barely make out the gorge through which the river comes.[2]

According to our guide, one cannot cross anywhere else than by the single ford it has in this vicinity, which lies on the side west of the hogback on the north, very near to a chain of small bluffs of loose dirt, some lead colored and others of a yellow hue. It consists of finely ground rock, and there the water does not reach the mounts' shoulder blades, whereas everywhere else that we saw they cannot cross without swimming. We halted by its southern edge about a mile from the ford; we called the site La Vega de Santa Cruz. The latitude was taken by the North Star, and we found ourselves at 41° 19' N latitude.

≋ SEPTEMBER 14

On the 14th we made no day's march, holding back here so that the horse herd, which was quite weak by now, could regain its strength. Before noon the quadrant was set up to check the observation by the sun, and we found no more than 40° 59' 24". We concluded that this discrepancy could perhaps result because the needle deviated here, and to find this out we left the fixed quadrant set toward the north, along the needle's meridian, until night time. As soon as the North, or polar Star was sighted, the quadrant being on the meridian mentioned, we observed that the needle was swinging northeast. We again took the latitude bearings by the North Star and again came up with the same 41° 19' N of the previous night.

At this place there are six big black poplars which have grown in pairs attached to one another, and they are the ones closest to the river. Near them is another one by itself; on its trunk, on the side facing northwest, Don Joaquín Laín dug out a small piece with an adze in the shape of a rectangular window, and with a chisel carved on it the inscription letters and numbers "Year of 1776," and lower down in a different hand "Laín" with two crosses at the sides, the larger one above the inscription and the other one beneath it.[3]

Here we were lucky to catch another bison smaller than the first one, although we enjoyed little meat because it had been overtaken late and very far from the king's camp. It happened also this morning that Joaquin the Laguna prankishly mounted an exceedingly spirited horse, and while racing over the meadow the horse stuck its forefeet in a hole and fell, discharging the horse-breaker a long distance off. We feared that the Laguna had been badly hurt by the thump; he, after having recovered from the surprise, was shedding a flood of tears. But God was pleased that all the damage was borne by the horse, which got its neck completely broken and was no longer useful.

≋ SEPTEMBER 15

On the 15th we made no day's march either, for the reasons given.

≋ SEPTEMBER 16

On the 16th we set out from La Vega de Santa Cruz (on El Río de San Buenaventura), went up about a mile to the north, arrived at the ford, and crossed the river. We took to the west and, after going one league along the northern side and meadow of the river, crossed another smaller one which comes down from the northwest, and we entered it. Over the same meadow we turned south-southwest for a league and crossed another rivulet, a little larger than the first, which comes down from the same northwesterly direction and enters the river. From both of them irrigation ditches could be dug for watering the land on this side, which is likewise good for farming even when they could not be conducted from the large river.[4] We continued toward the southwest, getting away from the river, which swings to the south among hills and ravines of finely ground stone in spots. We descended to a dry arroyo down a long and very stony grade, its ascent on the other side being not as bad.

As soon as we reached the top we found tracks of one or two days' imprint, of about twelve horses and some people on foot; and after a close study of the surroundings, indications were found that they had been lying in wait or spying for some time on the ridge's highest part without letting go of the horses. We suspected that they might be some Sabuaganas who could have followed us to deprive us of the animal herd at this place, where we would likely attribute the deed to the Comanches instead of the Yutas, since we were no longer in the latters' country but the formers'.

What is more, Silvestre the guide gave us a strong basis for the suspicion the night before when casually and without being noticed he went off a short distance from the king's camp to sleep. All through the trip he had not worn the blanket we gave him, and today he left the place with it on, without taking it off all day, and we suspected that, for his having an understanding with the Sabuaganas, he wore it so as to be recognized in case they attacked us. He increased our suspicion all the more when he lagged behind for a while, pensive and confused, before reaching the ridge where we found the tracks—now wanting to go along the river's edge, now to lead us along this route. We gave him no sign whatsoever of our suspicion by dissembling it altogether, but as our journey progressed he gave us convincing proofs of his innocence.

We continued exactly where the tracks led, descended once more to El Río de San Buenaventura, and saw that the ones making the tracks had stayed for a long while in the leafy poplar grove and meadow which it has. We kept on following it over the meadow by the river's edge, naming the site Las Llagas de Nuestro Padre San Francisco—after having gone over the broken hills and slopes, and the meadow mentioned, six leagues to the southwest, and in the whole day's march eight leagues.

As soon as we halted, two companions went southwest along the trail to explore the terrain roundabout and concluded that they had been Comanches.

≈≈ Notes

1. The Green River

2. The mouth of Split Mountain Canyon.

3. The Spanish *alamo*, here translated "poplar," can also mean "aspen" or "cottonwood." A large stand of cottonwoods still exists at the spot where Laín carved his inscription, but since cottonwoods live only around one hundred years, these trees can only be the descendants of those mentioned here, and therefore the inscription no longer exists. But in 1871 Frederick Dellenbaugh found in the same area a large cottonwood tree marked with many names and dates, which he unfortunately failed to record but speculated that Escalante "may have camped under this very tree."

4. The rivulets mentioned here are Brush Creek and Ashley Creek, respectively, and both are still used to irrigate farmland.

Explorations of William H. Ashley and Jedediah Smith, 1822–29

William H. Ashley

This excerpt from Ashley's narrative relates his arrival at Black's Fork of the Green River, near the Utah-Wyoming border, on April 25, 1825, and his trip by bullboat down the Green to the mouth of the Uinta River (which Ashley calls the Tewinty).

Monday, 25th: the country today under our observation is mountainous on either side of the river for twenty miles, then it resumes its former appearance of elevated and broken heights. A beautiful bold running stream about fifty yards wide empties itself on the west side of the river bearing N.W. and S.E. Below this junction the river is one hundred and fifty yards wide, the valley narrow and thinly timbered. We encamped on an island after making about twenty-five miles. Thence we departed on the succeeding morning and progressed slowly without observing any remarkable difference in the appearance of the river or surrounding country until the 30th inst., when we arrived at the base of a lofty rugged mountain, the summit of which was covered with snow and bearing east and west. Here also a creek sixty feet wide discharges itself on the west side.[1] This spot I selected as a place of general rendezvous, which I designated by marks in accordance with the instruction given to my men. So far, the navigation of this river is without the least obstruction. The channel in the most shallow places affords not less than four feet water. Game continues abundant, particularly buffaloe. There is no appearance of these animals wintering on the river; but they are at this time travelling from the west in great numbers.

Saturday, May 2d: we continued our voyage about half a mile below our camp, when we entered between the walls of this range of mountains, which approach at this point to the waters' edge on either side of the river and rise almost perpendicular to an immense height. The channel of the river is here contracted to the width of sixty or seventy yards, and the current (much increased in velocity) as it rolled along in angry submission to the serpentine walls that direct it, seemed constantly to threaten us with danger as we advanced.[2] We, however, succeeded in descending about ten miles without any difficulty or material change in the aspect of things and encamped for the night. About two miles from camp, we passed the mouth of a creek on the west side some fifteen yards wide, which discharged its water with great violence.

SUNDAY, 3RD: after progressing two miles, the navigation became difficult and dangerous, the river being remarkably crooked with more or less rapids every mile caused by rocks which had fallen from the sides of the mountain, many of which rise above the surface of the water and required our greatest exertions to avoid them. At twenty miles from our last camp, the roaring and agitated state of the water a short distance before us indicated a fall or some other obstruction of considerable magnitude. Our boats were consequently rowed to shore, along which we cautiously descended to the place from whence the danger was to be apprehended. It proved to be a perpendicular fall of ten or twelve feet produced by large fragments of rock which had fallen from the mountain, and settled in the river extending entirely across its channel and forming an impregnable barrier to the passage of loaded watercraft.[3] We were therefore obliged to unload our boats of their cargoes and pass them empty over the falls by means of long cords which we had provided for such purposes. At sunset, our boats were reloaded and we descended a mile lower down and encamped.

MONDAY 4TH: this day we made about forty miles. The navigation and mountains by which the river is bounded continues pretty much the same as yesterday. These mountains appear to be almost entirely composed of stratas of rock of various colours (mostly red) and are partially covered with a dwarfish growth of pine and cedar, which are the only species of timber to be seen.

TUESDAY, 5TH: after descending six miles, the mountains gradually recede from the water's edge, and the river expands to the width of two hundred and fifty yards, leaving the river bottoms on each side from one to three hundred yards wide interspersed with clusters of small willows. We remained at our encampment of this day until the morning of the 7th, when we descended ten miles lower down and encamped on a spot of ground where several thousand Indians had wintered during the past season.[4] Their camp had been judiciously selected for defence, and the remains of their work around it accorded with the judgment exercised in the selection. Many of their lodges remained as perfect as when occupied. They were made of poles two or three inches in diameter, set up in circular form, and covered with cedar bark.

FRIDAY, THE 8TH: We proceeded down the river about two miles, where it again enters between two mountains and affording a channel even more contracted than before. As we passed along between these massy walls, which in a great degree exclude from us the rays of heaven and presented a surface as impassable as their body was impregnable, I was forcibly struck with the gloom which spread over the countenances of my men; they seemed to anticipate (and not far distant, too) a dreadful termination of our voyage, and I must confess that I partook in some degree of what I supposed to be their feelings, for things around us had truly an awful appearance. We soon came to a dangerous rapid which we passed over with a slight injury to our boats.[5] A mile lower down, the channel becomes so obstructed by the intervention of large rocks over and between which the water dashed with such violence as to render our passage in safety impracticable. The cargoes of our boats were therefore a second time taken out and carried about two hundred yards, to which place, after much labor, our boats were descended by means of cords.[6] Thence we descended fifty (50) miles to the mouth of a beautiful river emptying on each side, to which I gave the name of Mary's river.[7] The navigation continued dangerous and difficult the whole way; the mountains equally lofty and rugged with their summits entirely covered with snow. Mary's river is one hundred yards wide, has a rapid current, and from every appearance very much confined between lofty mountains. A valley about two hundred yards wide extends one mile below the confluence of these rivers, then the mountain again on that side advances to the water's edge.[8] Two miles lower down is a very dangerous rapid, and eight miles further the mountain withdraws from the river on the west side about a half mile. Here we found a luxurious growth of sweet-bark or round-leaf cottonwood and a number of buffaloe, and succeeded by narrow river bottoms and hills. The former, as well as several islands, are partly clothed with a luxuriant growth of round-leaf cottonwood and extend four miles down the river, where the mountains again close to the water's edge and are in appearance more terrific than any we had seen during the whole voyage.[9] They immediately produce bad rapids, which follow in quick succession for twenty miles, below which, as far as I descended, the river is without obstruction. In the course of our passage through the several ranges of mountains, we performed sixteen portages, the most of which were attended with the utmost difficulty and labor.[10] At the termination of the rapids, the mountains on each side of the river gradually recede, leaving in their retreat a hilly space of five or six miles, through which the river meanders in a west direction about (70) seventy miles, receiving in that distance several contributions from small streams on each side, the last of which is called by the Indians Tewinty river. It empties on the north side, is about (60) sixty yards wide, several feet deep, with a bold current.

I concluded to ascend this river on my route returning, therefore deposited the cargoes of my boats in the ground near it, and continued my descent of the main river fifty miles to the point marked 5 on the topographical sketch sent you.[11] The whole of that distance the river is bounded by lofty mountains heaped together in the greatest disorder, exhibiting a surface as barren as can be imagined. This part of the country is almost entirely without game. We saw a few mountain-sheep and some elk, but they were so wild, and the country so rugged that we found it impossible to approach them. On my way returning to Tewinty river, I met a part of the Eutau tribe of Indians, who appeared very glad to see us and treated us in the most respectful and friendly manner. These people were well dressed in skins, had some guns, but armed generally with bows and arrows and such other instruments of war as are common among the Indians of the Missouri. Their horses were better than Indian horses generally are east of the mountains and more numerous in proportion to the number of persons. I understood (by signs) from them that the river which I had descended, and which I supposed to be the Rio Colorado of the West, continued its course as far as they had any knowledge of it, southwest through a mountainous country.

≋ NOTES

1. Henry's Fork.

2. Flaming Gorge.

3. Ashley Falls in Red Canyon.

4. Brown's Hole.

5. The first rapid in Lodore Canyon (now called Winnie's Rapid, at Winnie's Grotto).

6. Disaster Falls, so named by Powell after his boat *No-name* was lost there.

7. The Yampa.

8. Echo Park.

9. Whirlpool Canyon.

10. In Split Mountain Canyon.

11. The topographical sketch Ashley presumably submitted to the War Department, to which his report was addressed, has never been located.

Kit Carson's Autobiography

Kit Carson

THIS EXCERPT FROM CARSON'S AUTOBIOGRAPHY COVERS HIS TRAD-
ING AND TRAPPING EXPEDITIONS TO THE GREEN RIVER FROM 1833
TO 1835. IN 1833, CARSON AND STEPHEN LEE SET OUT FROM TAOS
TO TRADE WITH THE UTE INDIANS IN THE UINTA BASIN, ONLY TO
FIND THAT ANTOINE ROBIDOUX HAD PRECEDED THEM. AT THE
CONFLUENCE OF THE GREEN AND WHITE RIVERS, CARSON AND LEE
BUILT THREE CABINS, LATER KNOWN AS FORT KIT CARSON. CAR-
SON ALSO DESCRIBES HERE HIS MEETING WITH JIM BRIDGER, THE
SUMMER RENDEZVOUS OF 1834 AND 1835, AND HIS ENCOUNTERS
WITH HOSTILE INDIANS AND FRENCHMEN.

In Taos, I met Captain Lee of the U.S.A., who was a partner of
Bent and St. Vrain and had purchased goods to trade with the
trappers. I joined him, and in the latter part of October we started
for the mountains to find them. We followed the Spanish trail that
leads to California till we struck White River, went down it till we
struck Green River, and crossed from Green to the Winty,[1] one of its
tributaries, where we found Mr. Robidoux. He had a party of some
twenty men that were trapping and trading. The snow was now com-
mencing to fall and we concluded to go into winter quarters. We found
a place at the mouth of the Winty that answered every purpose. During the winter a California Indian of Mr. Robidoux's party ran off
with six animals, some of them being worth two hundred dollars per
head. Robidoux came to me and requested that I should pursue him. I
spoke to Captain Lee and he informed me that I might use my pleasure. There was a Utah village close by, and I got one of the Indians to
accompany me. We were furnished with two fine animals and took
the trail of the runaway, who had gone down the river, his object
being to reach California.

After traveling about one hundred miles the animal of the Indian
gave out and he would not accompany me any farther. I was determined

not to give up the chase and continued the pursuit and in thirty miles overtook the Indian and the horses. Seeing me by myself, he showed fight and I was under the necessity of killing him. I recovered the horses, and returned to our camp, arriving in a few days without any further trouble.

Some trappers came to our camp and informed us that Fitzpatrick and Bridger were encamped on the Snake River. In March, 1834, we struck out for the purpose of finding their camp, and in fifteen days succeeded. Captain Lee sold his goods to Fitzpatrick and agreed to accept his pay in beaver. Lee then started for Taos, and I joined Fitzpatrick and remained with him one month. He had a great many men in his employ, and I thought it best to take three of them and go on a hunt by ourselves. We passed the summer trapping on the head of the Laramie and its tributaries, keeping to the mountains, our party being too weak to venture on the plains.

One evening, when we were en route to rejoin Bridger's party, after I had selected the camp for the night, I gave my horse to one of the men and started on foot to kill something for supper, not having a particle of anything eatable on hand. I had gone about a mile when I discovered some elk on the side of a ridge. I shot one and immediately after the discharge of my gun I heard a noise in my rear. I turned around and saw two very large grizzly bears making for me. My gun was unloaded and I could not possibly reload in time to fire. There were some trees at a short distance, and I made for them, the bears after me. As I got to one of them, I had to drop my gun, and make all haste to ascend it. I got up some ten or fifteen feet, where I had to remain till the bears found it convenient to leave. One remained but a short while, the other stayed for some time and with his paws nearly uprooted the small aspen trees that grew around the tree which I had ascended. He made several attempts at the tree in which I was perched, but as he could do no damage, he finally concluded to leave. I was heartily pleased at this, never having been so badly scared in all my life. I remained in the tree for some time longer, and when I considered the bears far enough off, I descended and made for my camp as rapidly as possible. It was dark when I arrived and I could not send for the elk which I had killed, so we had to pass the night without anything to eat. During the night we trapped some beaver, so we had something for breakfast.

We remained in this place some ten or fifteen days, when Bridger appeared, on his way to the summer rendezvous. We joined him and went to Green River, the place of rendezvous, where two camps were established.[2] I think there were two hundred trappers encamped, awaiting the arrival of supplies from St. Louis. We had to dispose of our beaver to procure the necessities of life. Coffee and sugar were two dollars a pint, powder the same, lead one dollar a bar, and common blankets from fifteen to twenty-five dollars apiece.[3]

We remained in the rendezvous during the month of August, 1834. In September, camp was broken up and we divided into parties of convenient size and started on our fall hunt. The party of which I was a member consisted of fifty men. We set out for the country of the Blackfoot Indians, on the headwaters of the Missouri. We made a very poor hunt as the Indians were very troublesome. Five of our men were killed. A trapper could hardly go a mile from camp without being fired upon. As we found that we could do but little in this country, we started for winter quarters.

In November we got to the Big Snake River, where we again encamped. Nothing of moment transpired till February, 1835, when the Blackfeet came and stole eighteen of our horses. Twelve of us followed them about fifty miles before we caught up with them. They had traveled as far as they could, being delayed by the snow. In endeavoring to get the horses we fired some shots at them but could not approach near enough to do any great damage. They had snow shoes, we had none; they could travel over the snow without difficulty, while we would sink in it up to our waists.

The horses were on the side of a hill where there was but little snow, and our only object now was to get them. We asked for a parley, and the Indians agreed. One man from each side was to proceed half of the distance that separated us and have a talk. This was done, and we talked for some time, the Indians saying that they thought we were Snake Indians and that they did not want to steal from the Whites. We replied that if they were friendly they would lay down their arms and have a friendly talk and smoke with us. They agreed to do this, and each party left one man to guard the arms. We then met at the place where the first two men were talking, and talked and smoked.

The Indians were thirty strong. They sent for our horses, but returned with only five of the worst and said they would not give up any more. We broke for our arms and they for theirs, and the fight commenced. A man named Markhead and I were in the advance, and overtook two Indians who had remained in the rear of the party, concealed behind two trees. I approached one, and Markhead the other. Markhead was not paying sufficient attention to his Indian who, I noticed, raised his gun to fire. I forgot entirely the danger in which I myself was and neglected my Indian for Markhead's opponent. As the latter was about to fire on Markhead, I raised my gun and took sight. He saw me and endeavored to conceal himself, but he was too late. I fired and he fell. The moment I fired I remembered the Indian that I was after. I looked and saw him sighting for my breast. As I could not load in time, I commenced dodging as well as I could. He fired, and the ball grazed my neck and passed through my shoulder.

We then drew off for about a mile and encamped for the night. It was very cold and we could not make any fires for fear the Indians might approach and fire on us. We had no covering but our saddle blankets, and I passed a miserable night from the pain of the wound, it having bled freely and the blood having frozen. In the morning we found that the Indians were in the same place. We were not strong enough to attack them, so we started for camp. On our arrival Bridger took thirty men and started for the place where we had left the Indians, but when he got there they had gone to the plains. So we only recovered the five stolen animals which they had given us.

In a few days we set out on our spring hunt. We trapped the waters of the Snake and Green rivers, made a very good hunt, and then went into summer quarters on Green River. Shortly after we reached the rendezvous our equipment arrived.[4] We disposed of our beaver to the traders that came up with it, remaining in summer quarters till September, 1835. There was a large Frenchman in the party of Captain Drips,[5] an overbearing kind of man, and very strong. He made a practice of whipping every man that he was displeased with—and that was nearly all. One day, after he had beaten two or three men, he said he had no trouble to flog French men, and as for Americans, he would take a switch and switch them. I did not like such talk from any man, so I told him that I was the worst American in camp. There were many who could thrash him but for the fact that they were afraid, and that if he used such expressions any more, I would rip his guts.

He said nothing but started for his rifle, mounted his horse, and made his appearance in front of the camp. As soon as I saw this, I mounted my horse also, seized the first weapon I could get hold of, which was a pistol, and galloped up to him and demanded if I was the one he intended to shoot. Our horses were touching. He said no, drawing his gun at the same time so he could have a fair shot at me. I was prepared and allowed him time to draw his gun. We both fired at the same time, and all present said that but one report was heard. I shot him through the arm and his ball passed my head, cutting my hair and the powder burning my eye, the muzzle of his gun being near my head when he fired. During the remainder of our stay in camp we had no more bother with this French bully.

 NOTES

1. The Uinta River.

2. At Ham's Fork on the Green River.

3. In *Run, River, Run*, Ann Zwinger notes that at the same time in St. Louis, wholesale prices for sugar and coffee were ten to fifteen cents a pound.

4. At Fort Bonneville, in the Green River Valley between Horse Creek and the New Fork River.

5. An agent for the American Fur Company.

An 1839 Wagon Train Journal

Thomas J. Farnham

THOMAS J. FARNHAM WAS ONE OF THE EARLIEST JOURNALISTS TO
RECORD THE AMERICAN WEST. UNDER THE AUSPICES OF HORACE
GREELEY, HE JOINED A WAGON TRAIN IN 1839 TO FOLLOW THE ORE-
GON TRAIL WESTWARD FROM INDEPENDENCE, MISSOURI, AND TO
REPORT ON THE EXPERIENCE. IN THE SECTIONS REPRODUCED HERE,
FARNHAM DESCRIBES CROSSING THE GRAND AND GREEN RIVERS
AND ARRIVING AT FORT DAVY CROCKETT IN BROWN'S HOLE. HIS
REPORTING COMBINES FACTUAL OBSERVATION, VAGUE GEOGRAPHI-
CAL DESCRIPTION, AND A SUBSTANTIAL PROPORTION OF THE LEG-
ENDARY AND FANTASTIC.

[J ULY] 29th. We forded Grand River, and encamped in the willows on the northern shore. The mountains in the west, on
which the snow was lying, were still in sight. The view to the
east and south was shut in by the neighboring hills; to the north and
northeast, it was open, and in the distance appeared the Wind River
and other mountains, in the vicinity of the "Great Gap." During the
evening, while the men were angling for trout, Kelly gave me some
account of Grand River and the Colorado of the West. Grand River,
he said, is a branch of the Colorado. It rises far in the east among the
precipitous hights [*sic*] of the eastern range of the Rocky Mountains,
about midway from the Great Gap and the Kenyon of the South Fork
of the Platte. It interlocks the distance of 60 miles with the waters of
the Great Platte; its course to the point where we crossed, is nearly
due west. From thence it continues in a west by north course 160
miles, where it breaks through the Anahuac Ridge. The cliffs of this
Kenyon are said to be many hundred feet high, and overhanging; within them is a series of cascades, which roar like Niagara when the river
is swollen by the freshets in June. After passing this Kenyon, it is said
to move with a dashing, foaming current in a westerly direction 50
miles, where it unites with Green River, or Sheetskadee, and forms the
Colorado of the West. From the junction of these branches the Colo-

rado has a general course from the north-east to the south-west, of 700 miles to the head of the Gulf of California. Four hundred of this 700 miles is an almost unbroken chasm of kenyon—with perpendicular sides hundreds of feet in hight, at the bottom of which the waters rush over continuous cascades. This kenyon terminates 30 miles above the Gulf. To this point the river is navigable. The country on each side of its whole course is a rolling desert of brown loose earth, on which the rains and dews never fall.

A few years since, two Catholic Missionaries and their servants, on their way from the mountains to California, attempted to descend the Colorado. They have never been seen since the morning they commenced their fatal undertaking. A party of trappers and others made a strong boat and manned it well, with the determination of floating down the river to take the beaver that they supposed lived along its banks. But they found themselves in such danger after entering the kenyon, that with might and main they thrust their trembling boat ashore and succeeded in leaping upon the crags and lightening it before it was swallowed up by the dashing torrent. But the death which they had escaped in the stream, still threatened them on the crags. Perpendicular and overhanging rocks frowned above them; these they could not ascent [sic]; they could not cross the river; they could not ascend the river, and the foaming cascades below forbade the thought of committing themselves again to their boat. Night came on, and the difficulty of keeping their boat from being broken to pieces on the rocks, increased the anxieties of their situation. They must have passed a horrible night,—so full of fearful expectations, of the certainty of starvation on the crags, or drowning in the stream. In the morning, however, they examined the rocks again, and found a small projecting crag, some 20 feet above them, over which, after many efforts, they threw their small boat-rope and drew the noose taught [sic]. One of the number then climbed to explore. He found a platform above the crag, of sufficient size to contain his six companions, and a narrow chasm in the over-hanging wall, through which it appeared possible to pass to the upper surface. Having all reached the platform, they unloosed their lassoo, and, bracing themselves as well as they could, with their rifles in the moving, dry earth beneath their feet, they undertook the ascent. It was so steep that they were often in danger of being plunged together in the abyss below. But by digging steps in the rocks, where they could be dug with their rifle-barrels, and by making use of their lassoo where it could be used, they reached the upper surface near sunset, and made their way back to the place of departure. The above is a mountain-legend, interesting indeed, but

> I cannot tell how the truth may be,
>
> I tell the tale as t'was told to me.

At day-light, on the 30th, our cavalcade was moving across the woody ridges and verdant valleys between the crossings of Grand River and its great north fork.[1] We struck that stream about 10 o'clock. Its water was beautifully clear,—average depth 2 feet, and current 4 miles the hour. It is said to take its rise in the mountains, near the south side of the "Great Gap," and to flow, in a south-westerly course, through a country of broken and barren plains, into Grand River, 20 miles below the crossings. We ascended rapidly all the day. There was no trail to guide us; but our worthy guide knew every mountain-top in sight. Bee lines through immense fields of wild sage and worm-wood, and over gravelly plains—a short halt for a short breakfast—a constant spurring, and trotting, and driving, deposited us at sunset at the foot of a lofty mountain, clothed with heavy timber. It was the dividing ridge between the waters of Grand and Green Rivers. We must cross it. We therefore turned out the animals to feed—ate a scanty morsel of dried meat, and went to our couches, for the strength requisite for the task. About the middle of the night the panthers on the mountain gave us a specimen of their growling capacities. It was a hideous noice [sic]: deep and broken by the most unearthly screams! They were gathering for prey; for our horses and ourselves. We drove up the animals, however, tied them near the camp, built a large and bright fire, and slept till daylight.

[August] 21th [sic] At about 11 o'clock, we came to a stream of good water and halted to slake our thirst, and cook the remainder of our dog mutton. Our animals' sufferings had nearly equalled our own. And while we ate and rested under the shade of a tree, it added much to our enjoyment to see the famished beasts regale themselves upon a plat of short wiry grass beside the stream. Some marks of dragging lodge poles along the now well defined trail, indicated to us that a portion of the Shoshonie or Snake tribe had lately left Brown's Hole. From this circumstance we began to fear what afterwards proved true, that our hopes of finding the Snakes at that post and of getting meat from them would prove fallacious. Our filthy meal being finished, we gathered up our little caravan and moved forward at a round pace for three hours, when the bluffs opened before us the beautiful plain of Brown's Hole. As we entered we crossed two cool streams that tumbled down from the stratified cliffs near at hand on the right; and a few rods beyond, the whole area became visible. The Fort, as it is called, peered up in the centre, upon the winding bank of the Sheetskadee. The dark mountains rose around it sublimely, and the green fields swept away into the deep precipitous gorges more beautifully than I can describe.

How glad is man to see his home again after a weary absence! Every step becomes quicker as he approaches its sacred portals; and kind smiles greet him; and leaping hearts beat upon his, and warm lips press his own. It is the holy sacrament of friendship. Yet there is another class of these emotions that appears to be not less holy. They arise when, after having been long cut off from every habit and sympathy of civilized life, long wandering among the deep and silent temples of the eternal mountains, long and hourly exposed to the scalping knife of savages and agonies of starvation, one beholds the dwelling of civilized men—kindred of the old Patriot blood, rearing their hospitable roofs among those hights, inviting the houseless, wayworn wanderer to rest; to relax eyes, and repose the heart awhile among generour [sic] spirits of his own race. Is not the hand that grasps your's [sic] then, an honest hand? And does it not distil by its sacred warmth and hearty embrace, some of the dearest emotions of which the soul is capable; friendship unalloyed, warm, holy and heavenly? Thus it seemed to me, at all events, as we rode into the hollow square and received from St. Clair, the person in charge, the hearty welcome of an old hunter to "Fort David Crockett." A room was appropriated immediately for our reception, our horses were given to the care of his horse guard, and every other arrangement within his means, was made, to make us feel, that within that little nest of fertility, amid the barrenness of the great Stony Rangs [sic]; far from the institutions of law and religion; far from the sweet ties of the family relations, and all those nameless endearing influences that shed their rich fragrance over human nature in its cultivated abiding places—that there even could be given us the fruits of the sincerest friendship. Such kindness, can be appreciated fully by those only, who have starved and thirsted in these deserts and been welcomed, and made thrice welcome, after months of weary wandering, to "Fort David Crockett."

After partaking of the hospitality of Mr. St. Clair, I strolled out to examine more minutely this wonderful little valley. It is situated in or about latitude 42 degrees north; 100 miles south of Wind River mountains, on the Sheetskadee (Prairie Cock) River. Its elevation is something more than 8,000 feet above the level of the sea. It appeared to be about six miles in diameter; shut in, in all directions, by dark frowning mountains, rising 1,500 feet above the plain. The Sheetskadee, or Green River runs through it, sweeping in a beautiful curve from the north-west to the south-west part of it, where it breaks its way through the encircling mountains, between cliffs 1,000 feet in hight, broken and hanging as if poised on the air. The area of the plain is thickly set with the rich mountain grasses, and dotted with little copses of cottonwood and willow trees. The soil is alluvial and capable of producing abundantly all kinds of small grains, vegetable, &c. that are raised in the northern States. Its climate is very remarkable. Although in all the country within 100 miles of it, the winter months bring snows and the severe cold that we should expect in such a latitude, and at such an elevation above the level of the sea, yet in this little nook, the grass grows all winter. So that, while the storm rages on the mountains in sight, and the drifting snows mingle in the blasts of December, the old hunters here, heed it not. Their horses are cropping the green grass on the banks of the Sheetskadee, while they, themselves, are roasting the fat loins of the mountain sheep, and laughing at the merry tale and song.

The Fort is a hollow square of one story log cabins, with roofs and floors of mud, constructed in the same manner as those of Fort William. Around these we found the conical skin lodges of the Squaws of the white trappers who were away on their "fall hunt," and also the lodges of a few Snake Indians, who had proceeded their tribe to this, their winter haunt. Here also were the lodges of Mr. Robinson, a trader, who usually stations himself here to traffic with the Indians and white trappers. His skin lodge was his warehouse; and buffalo robes spread upon the ground, his counter, on which he displayed his butcher knives, hatchets, powder, lead, fish-hooks and whiskey. In exchange for these articles he receives beaver skins from trappers, money from travelers, and horses from the Indians. Thus, as one would believe, Mr. Robinson drives a very snug little business. And indeed when all the "independent trappers" are driven by approaching winter into this delightful retreat; and the whole Snake village, 2 or 3,000 strong, impelled by the same necessity, pitch their lodges around the Fort, and the dances and merry makings of a long winter are thoroughly commenced, there is no want of customers.

A trader is living here with a young Eutaw squaw, for whose charms he has forsaken friends, wealth and ease, and civilization, for an Indian lodge among all the dangers and wants of a wilderness. This gentleman is said to have a standing offer of $700 for his dear one, whenever, in the course of a limited time, he will sell her graces. But it is believed that his heart has so much to do with his estimation of her value, that no consideration could induce him voluntarily to deprive himself of her society.

The above anecdotes, &c. were related to me during the first evening I spent at Fort David Crockett. It was a bright etherial [*sic*] night. The Fort stood in the shade of the wild and dark cliffs, while the light of the moon shone on the western peaks, and cast a deeper darkness into the inaccessible gorges on the face of the mountains. The Sheetskadee flowed silently among the alders—the fires in the Indian lodges were smouldering; sleep had gathered every animate thing in its embrace. It was a night of awful solitude—the grandeur of the immensity of silence! I enjoyed the lovely scene till near midnight in company with Mr. St. Clair; and when at last its excitements and the thrilling pleasure of being relieved from the prospect of death from hunger allowed me to slumber, that gentleman conducted me to his own room and bed, and bade me occupy both while I should remain with him. He expressed regret that he had so little provisions in the Fort;—a small quantity of old jerked meat; a little tea and sugar. "But," said he, "share it with me as long as it lasts; I have hunters out; they will be here in ten or twelve days; you have been starving; eat while there is anything left—and when all is gone we'll have a mountain sheep, or a dog to keep off starvation till the hunters come in." My companions and guide were less fortunate. We purchased all the meat that either money or goods could induce the Indians to sell. It amounted to one day's supply for the company. And as there was supposed to be no game within a circuit of 100 miles, it became matter of serious inquiry whether we should seek it in the direction of Fort Hall, or on the head waters of Little Snake River, 100 miles off our proper route to Oregon. In the latter place there were plenty of fine, fat buffalo; but on the way to the other point there was nothing but antelope, difficult to kill, and poor. A collateral circumstance turned the scale of our deliberations. That circumstance was dog meat. We could get a supply of these delectable animals from the Indians; they would keep life in us till we could reach Fort Hall; and by aid thereof we could immediately proceed on our journey, cross the Blue Mountains before the snow should render them impassable, and reach Vancouver on the lower Columbia during the autumn. On the contrary, if we sought meat on the waters of Little Snake River, it would be so late before we should be prepared to resume our journey, that we could not pass those mountains until May or June of the following spring.—The dogs, therefore, were purchased; and preparations were made for our departure for Fort Hall, as soon as ourselves and our animals were sufficiently recruited for the undertaking. Meanwhile my companions ate upon our stock of barking mutton. And thus we spent 7 days—delightful days. For although our fare was humble and scanty, yet the flesh began to creep upon our skeletons, our minds to resume their usual vivacity, and our hearts to warm again with the ordinary emotions of human existence.

The trials of a journey in the western wilderness can never be detailed in words. To be understood, they must be endured. Their effects upon the physical and mental system are equally prostrating. The desolation of one kind and another which meets the eye every where; the sense of vastness associated with dearth and barrenness, and of sublimity connected with eternal, killing frosts; and of loneliness coupled with a thousand natural causes of one's destruction; perpetual journeyings over endless declivities—among tempests—through freezing torrents; on half the time on foot, with nothing but moccasins to protect the feet from the flinty gravel and thorns of the prickly pear along the unbeaten way; and the starvings and the thirstings wilt the muscles, send preternatural activity into the nervous system, and through the whole animal and mental economy and feebleness and irritability altogether indescribable. But at Fort David Crockett there were rest, and food, and safety; and old Father Time, as he mowed away the passing moments and gathered them into a great garner of the Past, cast upon the Future a few blossoms of hope, and sweetened the hours now and then with a bit of information about this portion of his ancient dominion. I heard from various persons, more or less acquainted with the Colorado of the West, a confirmation of the account of that river given in the journals of previous days; and also that there resides at the lower end of its great kenyon a band of the Club Indians—very many of whom are seven feet in hight, and well proportioned; that these Indians raise large quantities of black beans upon the sandy intervals on the stream; that the oval-leaf prickly-pear grows there from fifteen to twenty feet in hight; that these Indians make molasses from its fruit; that their principal weapon of warfare is the club, which they wield with amazing dexterity and force; that they inhabit a wide extent of country north-west and south east of the lower part of this river; that they have never been subdued by the Spaniards, and are inimical to all white people. Subsequent inquiry in California satisfied me that this river is navigable only 30 or 40 miles from its mouth, and that the Indians who live upon its barren banks near the Gulf of [*sic*] such as I have described.

≋ NOTES

1. The Green River.

Report of the Exploring Expedition to the Rocky Mountains

John C. Frémont

WHILE SERVING WITH THE CORPS OF TOPOGRAPHICAL ENGINEERS,
FRÉMONT MADE NUMEROUS EXPEDITIONS TO COLLECT INFORMA-
TION ON THE STILL LARGELY UNKNOWN COUNTRY WEST OF THE
MISSOURI. IN THIS EXCERPT FROM HIS REPORT ON THE 1843–44
EXPEDITION, FRÉMONT NOTES HOW THE UPPER GREEN RIVER HAS
BEEN AFFECTED BY TRAFFIC ON THE OREGON TRAIL AND SPECU-
LATES ABOUT THE ORIGINS OF THE RIVER'S NAME AND THE COURSE
OF ITS LOWER SECTION.

[AUGUST 6, 1843]—Here passes the road to Oregon; and the broad smooth highway, where the numerous heavy wagons of the emigrants had entirely beaten and crushed the artemisia, was a happy exchange of our poor animals for the sharp rocks and tough shrubs among which they had been toiling so long; and we moved up the valley rapidly and pleasantly. With very little deviation from our route of the preceding year, we continued up the valley; and on the evening of the 12th, encamped on the Sweet Water, at a point where the road turns off to cross to the plains of Green river. The increased coolness of the weather indicated that we had attained a great elevation, which the barometer here placed at 7,220 feet; and during the night water froze in the lodge.

The morning of the 13th was clear and cold, there being a white frost; and the thermometer, a little before sunrise, standing at 26.5°. Leaving this encampment (our last on the waters which flow towards the rising sun,) we took our way along the upland, towards the dividing ridge which separates the Atlantic from the Pacific waters, and crossed it by a road some miles further south than the one we had followed on our return in 1842. We crossed very near the Table mountain, at the southern extremity of the South Pass, which is near twenty

miles in width, and already traversed by several different roads. Selecting as well as we could, in the scarcely distinguishable ascent, what
might be considered the dividing ridge in this remarkable depression
in the mountain, I took a barometrical observation, which gave 7,490
feet for the elevation above the Gulf of Mexico. You will remember
that, in my report of 1842, I estimated the elevation of this pass at
about 7,000 feet; a correct observation with a good barometer enables
me now to give it with more precision. Its importance, as the great
gate through which commerce and travelling may hereafter pass
between the valley of the Mississippi and the north Pacific, justifies a
precise notice of its locality and distance from leading points, in addition to this statement of elevation. As stated in the report of 1842, its
latitude at the point where we crossed is 42° 24' 32"; its longitude 109°
26' 00"; its distance from the mouth of the Kansas, by the common
travelling route, 962 miles; from the mouth of the Great Platte, along
the valley of that river, according to our survey of 1842, 882 miles; and
its distance from St. Louis about 400 miles more by the Kansas, and
about 700 by the Great Platte route: these additions being by steamboat conveyance in both instances. From this pass to the mouth of the
Oregon is about 1,600 by the common travelling route; so that, under
a general point of view, it may be assumed to be about half way between the Mississippi and the Pacific ocean, on the common travelling
route. Following a hollow of slight and easy descent, in which was
very soon formed a little tributary to the Gulf of California, (for the
waters which flow west from the South Pass go to this gulf,) we made
our usual halt four miles from the pass, in latitude by observation
42° 19' 53". Entering here the valley of the Green river—the Colorado
of the West—and inclining very much to the southward along the
streams which form the Sandy river, the road led for several days over
dry and level uninteresting plains; to which a low, scrubby growth of
artemisia gave a uniform dull grayish color; and on the evening of the
15th we encamped in the Mexican territory, on the left bank of the
Green river, 69 miles from the South Pass, in longitude 110° 05' 05"
and latitude 41° 53' 54", distant 1,031 miles from the mouth of the
Kansas. This is the emigrant road to Oregon, which bears much to the
southward, to avoid the mountains about the western heads of Green
river—the *Rio Verde* of the Spaniards.

AUGUST 16.—Crossing the river, here about 400 feet wide, by a very good ford, we continued to descend for seven or eight miles on a pleasant road along the right bank of the stream, of which the islands and shores are handsomely timbered with cottonwood. The refreshing appearance of the broad river, with its timbered shores and green wooded islands, in contrast to its dry sandy plains, probably obtained for it the name Green river, which was bestowed on it by the Spaniards, who first came into this country to trade some 25 years ago. It was then familiarly known as the Seeds-ke-dée-agie, or Prairie Hen (*tetrao urophasianus*) river; a name which it received from the Crows, to whom its upper waters belong, and on which this bird is still very abundant. By the Shoshonee and Utah Indians, to whom belongs, for a considerable distance below, the country where we were now travelling, it was called the Bitter-root river, from the great abundance in the valley of a plant which affords them one of their favorite roots. Lower down, from Brown's hole to the southward, the river runs through lofty chasms, walled in by precipices of *red* rock; and even among the wilder tribes who inhabit that portion of its course, I have heard it called by Indian refugees from the Californian settlements the Rio *Colorado*. We halted to noon at the upper end of a large bottom, near some old houses, which had been a trading post, in latitude 41° 46' 54". At this place the elevation of the river above the sea is 6,230 feet. That of Lewis's fork on the Columbia at Fort Hall is, according to our subsequent observations, 4,500 feet. The descent of each stream is rapid, but that of the Colorado is but little known, and that little derived from vague report. Three hundred miles of its lower part, as it approaches the gulf of California, is reported to be smooth and tranquil; but its upper part is manifestly broken into many falls and rapids. From many descriptions of trappers, it is probable that in its foaming course among its lofty precipices, it presents many scenes of wild grandeur; and though offering many temptations, and often discussed, no trappers have been found bold enough to undertake a voyage which has so certain a prospect of a fatal termination. The Indians have strange stories of beautiful valleys abounding with beaver, shut up among inaccessible walls of rock in the lower course of the river; and to which the neighboring Indians, in their occasional wars with the Spaniards, and among themselves, drive their herds of cattle and flocks of sheep, leaving them to pasture in perfect security.

The road here leaves the river, which bends considerably to the east; and in the afternoon we resumed our westerly course, passing over a somewhat high and broken country; and about sunset, after a day's travel of 26 miles; reached Black's fork of the Green river—a shallow stream, with a somewhat sluggish current, about 120 feet wide, timbered principally with willow, and here and there an occasional large tree. At 3 in the morning I obtained an observation of an emersion of the first satellite of Jupiter, with other observations. The heavy wagons have so completely pulverized the soil, that clouds of fine light dust are raised by the slightest wind, making the road sometimes very disagreeable.

Death Valley in '49

William Lewis Manly

MANLY'S AUTOBIOGRAPHY TAKES HIM "FROM A HUMBLE HOME IN
THE GREEN MOUNTAINS TO THE GOLD MINES OF CALIFORNIA."
THE CHAPTER EXCERPTED HERE, "ON TO SALT LAKE," RECOUNTS
THE ATTEMPT OF MANLY'S PARTY TO FLOAT THE GREEN RIVER TO
CALIFORNIA USING A RESURRECTED FERRYBOAT AND MAKESHIFT
CANOES, AN IDEA FROM WHICH THEY WERE EVENTUALLY DISSUADED
BY THE WISE ADVICE OF UTE CHIEF WAKARA.

About the first thing we did was to organize and select a captain, and, very much against my wishes, I was chosen to this important position. Six of us had guns of some sort; Richard Field, Dallas's cook, was not armed at all. We had one regular axe and a large camp hatchet, which was about the same as an axe, and several very small hatchets owned by the men. All our worldly goods were piled up on the bank, and we were alone.

An examination of the old ferryboat showed it to be in pretty good condition, the sand with which it had been filled keeping it very perfectly. We found two oars in the sand under the boat, and looked up some poles to assist us in navigation. Our cordage was rather scant but the best we could get and all we could muster. The boat was about twelve feet long and six or seven feet wide, not a very well proportioned craft, but having the ability to carry a pretty good load. We swung it up to the bank and loaded up our goods and then ourselves. It was not a heavy load for the craft, and it looked as if we were taking the most sensible way to get to the Pacific, and we almost wondered that everybody was so blind as not to see it as we did.

This party was composed of W. L. Manly, M. S. McMahon, Charles and Joseph Hazeirig, Richard Field, Alfred Walton and John Rogers. We untied the ropes, gave the boat a push and commenced to move down the river with ease and comfort, feeling much happier than we would had we been going toward Salt Lake with the prospect of wintering there.

At the mouth of Ham's Fork we passed a camp of Indians, but we kept close to the opposite shore to avoid being boarded by them. They beckoned very urgently for us to come ashore but I acted as if I did not understand them, and gave them the go-by.

As we were floating down the rapid stream it became more and more a rapid, roaring river, and the bed contained many dangerous rocks that were difficult to shun. Each of us had a setting-pole, and we ranged ourselves along the sides of the boat and tried to keep ourselves clear from the rocks and dangers. The water was not very deep and made such a dashing noise as the current rushed among the rocks that one had to talk pretty loud to be heard. As we were gliding along quite swiftly, I set my pole on the bottom and gave the boat a sudden push to avoid a boulder, when the pole stuck in the crevice between two rocks, and instead of losing the pole by the sudden jerk I gave, I was the one who was very suddenly yanked from the boat by the spring of the pole, and landed in the middle of the river. I struck pretty squarely on my back, and so got thoroughly wet, but swam for shore amid the shouts of the boys, who waved their hats and hurrahed for the captain when they saw he was not hurt. I told them that was nothing, as we were on our way to California by water anyway, and such things must be expected.

The next day after this I went on shore and sighted a couple of antelope, one of which I shot, which gave us good grub, and good appetites we already had. As near as we could estimate we floated about thirty miles a day, which beat the pace of tired oxen considerably. In one place there was a fringe of thick willows along the bank, and a little farther back a perpendicular bluff, while between the two was a strip of fine green grass. As we were passing this we scared up a band of elk in this grass meadow, and they all took a run down the river like a band of horses. One of them turned up a small ravine with walls so steep he could not get out, so we posted a guard at the entrance, and three of us went up the cañon after him, and after the others had each fired a shot, I fired the third and brought him down. This was about the finest piece of Rocky Mountain beef that one could see. We took the carcass on board and floated on again.

Thus far we had a very pleasant time, each taking his turn in working the boat while the others rested or slept. About the fifth day when we were floating along in very gently running water, I had lain down to take a rest and a little sleep. The mountains here on both sides of the river were not very steep, but ran gradually for a mile or so. While I was sleeping the boat came around a small angle in the stream, and all at once there seemed to be a higher, steeper range of mountains right across the valley. The boys thought the river was coming to a rather sudden end and hastily awoke me, and for the life of me I could not say they were not right, for there was no way in sight for it to go to. I remembered while looking over a map the military men had I found a place named Brown's Hole, and I told the boys I guessed we were elected to go on foot to California after all, for 1 did not propose to follow the river down any sort of a hole into any mountain. We were floating directly toward a perpendicular cliff, and I could not see any hole anywhere, nor any other place where it could go. Just as we were within a stone's throw of the cliff, the river turned sharply to the right and went behind a high point of the mountain that seemed to stand squarely on edge. This was really an immense crack or crevice, certainly two thousand feet deep and perhaps much more, and seemed much wider at the bottom that it did at the top, two thousand feet or more above our heads. Each wall seemed to lean in toward the water as it rose.[1]

We were now for some time between two rocky walls between which the river ran very rapidly, and we often had to get out and work our boat over the rocks, some times lifting it off when it caught. Fortunately we had a good tow line, and one would take this and follow along the edge when it was so he could walk. The mountains seemed to get higher and higher on both sides as we advanced, and in places we could see quite a number of trees overhanging the river, and away up on the rocks we could see the wild mountain sheep looking down at us. They were so high that they seemed a mile away, and consequently safe enough. This was their home, and they seemed very independent, as if they dared us fellows to come and see them. There was an old cottonwood tree on the bank with marks of an axe on it, but this was all the sign we saw that any one had ever been here before us. We got no game while passing through this deep cañon and began to feel the need of some fresh provisions very sorely.

We passed many deep, dark cañons coming into the main stream, and at one place, where the rock hung a little over the river and had a smooth wall, I climbed up above the high water mark which we could clearly see, and with a mixture of gunpowder and grease for paint, and a bit of cloth tied to a stick for a brush, I painted in fair sized letters on the rock, CAPT. W. L. MANLY, U.S.A.[2] We did not know whether we were within the bounds of the United States or not, and we put on all the majesty we could under the circumstances. I don't think the sun ever shone down to the bottom of the cañon, for the sides were literally sky high, for the sky, and a very small portion of that, was all we could see.

Just before night we came to a place where some huge rocks as large as cabins had fallen down from the mountain, completely filling up the river bed, and making it completely impassable for our boat. We unloaded it and while the boys held the stern line, I took off my clothes and pushed the boat out into the torrent which ran around the rocks, letting them pay the line out slowly till it was just right. Then I sang out to "let go," and away it dashed. I grasped the bow line, and at the first chance jumped overboard and got to shore, when I held the boat and brought it in below the obstructions. There was some deep water below the rocks; and we went into camp. While some loaded the boat, others with a hook and line caught some good fish, which resembled mackerel.

While I was looking up toward the mountain top, and along down the rocky wall, I saw a smooth place about fifty feet above where the great rocks had broken out, and there, painted in large black letters, were the words, "ASHLEY, 1824." This was the first real evidence we had of the presence of a white man in this wild place, and from this record it seems that twenty-five years before some venturesome man had here inscribed his name. I have since heard there were many persons in St. Louis of this name, and of some circumstances which may link them with this early traveler.

When we came to look around we found that another big rock blocked the channel three hundred yards below, the water rushing around it with a terrible swirl. We unloaded the boat again and made the attempt to get around it as we did the other rocks. We tried to get across the river but failed. We now, all but one, got on the great rock with our poles, and the one man was to ease the boat down with the rope as far as he could, then let go and we would stop it with our poles and push it out into the stream and let it go over, but the current was so strong that when the boat struck the rock we could not stop it, and the gunwale next to us rose, and the other went down, so that in a second the boat stood edgewise in the water and the bottom tight against the big rock, and the strong current pinned it there so tight that we could no more move it than we could move the rock itself.

This seemed a very sudden ending to our voyage and there were some very rapid thoughts as to whether we would not be safer among the Mormons than out in this wild country, afoot and alone. Our boat was surely lost beyond hope, and something must be done. I saw two pine trees, about two feet through, growing on a level place just below, and I said to them that we must decide between going afoot and making some canoes out of these pine trees. Canoes were decided on, and we never let the axes rest, night or day, till we had them completed. While my working shift was off, I took an hour or two, for a little hunting, and on a low divide partly grown over with small pines and juniper I found signs, old and new, of many elk, and so concluded the country was well stocked with noble game. The two canoes, when completed, were about fifteen feet long and two feet wide, and we lashed them together for greater security. When we tried them we found they were too small to carry our load for us, and we landed half a mile below, where there were two other pine trees—white pine— about two feet through, and much taller than the ones we had used. We set at work making a large canoe of these. I had to direct the work for I was the only one who had ever done such work. We worked night and day at these canoes, keeping a big fire at night and changing off to keep the axes busy. This canoe we made twenty-five or thirty feet long, and when completed they made me captain of it and into it loaded the most valuable things, such as provisions, ammunition, and cooking utensils. I had to take the lead for I was the only skillful canoeist in the party. We agreed upon signals to give when danger was seen, or game in sight, and leading off with my big canoe we set sail again, and went flying down stream.

This rapid rate soon brought us out of the high mountains and into a narrow valley when the stream became more moderate in its speed and we floated along easily enough.[3]

It took us two or three days to pass this beautiful valley, and then we began to get into a rougher country again, the cañon deeper and the water more tumultuous.[4] McMahon and I had the lead always, in the big canoe. The mountains seemed to change into bare rocks and get higher and higher as we floated along. After the first day of this the river became so full of boulders that many times the only way we could do was to unload the canoes and haul them over, load up and go ahead, only to repeat the same tactics in a very short time again. At one place where the river was more than usually obstructed we found a deserted camp, a skiff and some heavy cooking utensils, with a notice posted up on an alder tree saying that they had found the river route impracticable, and being satisfied that the river was so full of rocks and boulders that it could not be safely navigated, they had abandoned the undertaking and were about to start overland to make their way to Salt Lake. I took down the names of the parties at the time in my diary, which has since been burned, but have now forgotten them entirely. They were all strangers to me. They had left such heavy articles as could not be carried on foot. This notice rather disconcerted us, but we thought we had better keep on and see for ourselves, so we did not follow them, but kept on down the rocky river. We found generally more boulders than water, and the down grade of the river bed was heavy.

Some alders and willows grew upon the bank and up quite high on the mountains we could see a little timber. Some days we did not go more than four or five miles, and that was serious work, loading and unloading our Canoes, and packing them over the boulders, with only small streams of water curling around between them. We went barefoot most of the time, for we were more than half of the time in the water, which roared and dashed so loud that we could hardly hear each other speak. We kept getting more and more venturesome and skillful, and managed to run some very dangerous rapids in safety.

On the high peaks above our heads we could see the Rocky Mountain sheep looking defiantly at us from their mountain fastnesses, so far away they looked no larger than jack rabbits. They were too far off to try to shoot at, and we had not time to try to steal up any nearer for at the rate we were making, food would be the one thing needful, for we were consuming it very fast. Sometimes we could ride a little ways, and then would come the rough-and-tumble with the rocks again.

One afternoon we came to a sudden turn in the river, more than a right angle, and, just below, a fall of two feet or more.[5] This I ran in safety, as did the rest who followed and we cheered at our pluck and skill. Just after this the river swung back the other way at a right angle or more, and I quickly saw there was danger below and signaled them to go on shore at once, and lead the canoes over the dangerous rapids. I ran my own canoe near shore and got by the rapid safely, waiting for the others to come also. They did not obey my signals but thought to run the rapid the same as I did. The channel here was straight for two hundred yards, without a boulder in it, but the stream was so swift that it caused great, rolling waves in the center, of a kind I have never seen anywhere else. The boys were not skillful enough to navigate this stream and the suction drew them to the center, where the great waves rolled them over and over, bottom side up and every way. The occupants of our canoe let go and swam to shore. Field had always been afraid of water and had worn a life preserver every day since we left the wagons. He threw up his hands and splashed and kicked at a terrible rate, for he could not swim, and at last made solid ground. One of the canoes came down into the eddy below, where it lodged Close [*sic*] to the shore, bottom up. Alfred Walton in the other canoe could not swim, but held on the gunwale with a death grip, and it went on down through the rapids. Some times we could see the man and sometimes not, and he and the canoe took turns in disappearing. Walton had very black hair, and as he clung fast to his canoe his black head looked like a crow on the end of a log. Sometimes he would be under so long that we thought he must be lost, when up he would come again still clinging manfully.

McMahon and I threw everything out of the big canoe and pushed out after him. I told Mac to kneel down so I could see over him to keep the craft off the rocks, and by changing his paddle from side to side as ordered, he enabled me to make quick moves and avoid being dashed to pieces. We fairly flew, the boys said, but I stood up in the stern and kept it clear of danger till we ran into a clear piece of river and overtook Walton clinging to the over turned boat; McMahon seized the boat and I paddled all to shore, but Walton was nearly dead and could hardly keep his grasp on the canoe. We took him to a sandy place and worked over him and warmed him in the sun till he came to life again, then built a fire and laid him up near to it to get dry and warm. If the canoe had gone on twenty yards farther with him before we caught it, he would have gone into another long rapid and been drowned. We left Walton by the fire and, crossing the river in the slack water, went up to where the other boys were standing, wet and sorry-looking, saying all was gone and lost. Rogers put his hand in his pocket and pulled out three half dollars and said sadly, "Boys, this is all I am worth in the world." All the clothes he had were a pair of overalls and a shirt. If he had been possessed of a thousand in gold he would have been no richer, for there was no one to buy from and nothing to buy. I said to them: "Boys, we can't help what has happened, we'll do the best we can. Right your canoe, get the water out, and we'll go down and see how Walton is." They did as I told them, and lo and behold when the canoe rolled right side up, there were their clothes and blankets safe and sound. These light things had floated in the canoe and were safe. We now tried by joining hands to reach out far enough to recover some of the guns, but by feeling with their feet they found the bottom smooth as glass and the property all swept on below, no one knew where. The current so powerful that no one could stand in it where it came above his knees. The eddy which enabled us to save the first canoe with the bedding and clothes was caused by a great boulder as large as a house which had fallen from above and partly blocked the stream. Everything that would sink was lost.

We all got into the two canoes and went down to Walton, where we camped and stayed all night for Walton's benefit. While we were waiting I took my gun and tried to climb up high enough to see how much longer this horrible cañon was going to last, but after many attempts, I could not get high enough to see in any direction. The mountain was all bare rocks in terraces, but it was impossible to climb from one to the other, and the benches were all filled with broken rocks that had fallen from above.

After a day or two we began to get out of the cañons, but the mountains and hills on each side were barren and of a pale yellow cast, with no chance for us to climb up and take a look to see if there were any chances for us further along. We had now been obliged to follow the cañons for many miles, for the only way to get out was to get out endwise, climbing the banks being utterly out of the question. But these mountains soon came to an end, and there were some cottonwood and willows on the bank of the river, which was now so smooth we could ride along without the continual loading and unloading we had been forced to practice for so long. We had begun to get a little desperate at the lack of game, but the new valley, which grew wider all the time, gave us hope again, if it was quite barren everywhere except back of the willow trees.[6]

We were floating along very silently one day, for none of us felt very much in the mood for talking, when we heard a distant sound which we thought was very much like the firing of a gun. We kept still, and in a short time a similar sound was heard, plainer and evidently some ways down the stream. Again and again we heard it, and decided that it must be a gunshot, and yet we were puzzled to know how it could be. We were pretty sure there were not white people ahead of us, and we did not suppose the Indians in this far-off land had any fire arms. It might be barely possible that we were coming now to some wagon train taking a southern course, for we had never heard that there were any settlements in this direction and the barren country would preclude any such thing, as we viewed it now. If it was a hostile band we could not do much with a rifle and shotgun toward defending ourselves or taking the aggressive. Some of the boys spoke of our scalps ornamenting a spear handle, and indulged in such like cheerful talk which comforted us wonderfully.

Finally we concluded we did not come out into that wild country to be afraid of a few gunshots, and determined to put on a bold front, fight if we had to, run away if we could not do any better, and take our chances on getting scalped or roasted. Just then we came in sight of three Indian lodges just a little back from the river, and now we knew for certain who had the guns. McMahon and I were in the lead as usual, and it was only a moment before one of the Indians appeared, gun in hand, and made motions for us to come on shore. A cottonwood tree lay nearly across the river, and I had gone so far that I had to go around it and land below, but the other boys behind were afraid to do otherwise than to land right there as the Indian kept his gun lying across his arm. I ran our canoe below to a patch of willows, where we landed and crawled through the brush till we came in sight of the other boys where we stood and waited a moment to see how they fared, and whether our red-men were friends or enemies. There were no suspicious movements on their part so we came out and walked right up to them. There was some little talk, but I am sure we did not understand one another's language, and so we made motions and they made motions, and we got along better. We went with them down to the tepee, and there we heard the first word that was at all like English and that was "Mormonee," with a sort of questioning tone. Pretty soon one said "buffalo," and then we concluded they were on a big hunt of some sort. They took us into their lodges and showed us blankets, knives and guns, and then, with a suggestive motion, said all was "Mormonee," by which we understood they had got them from the Mormons. The Indian in the back part of the lodge looked very pleasant and his countenance showed a good deal of intelligence for a man of the mountains. I now told the boys that we were in a position where we were dependent on some one, and that I had seen enough to convince me that these Indians were perfectly friendly with the Mormons, and for our own benefit we had better pass ourselves off for Mormons, also. So we put our right hand to our breast and said "Mormonee," with a cheerful countenance, and that act conveyed to them the belief that we were chosen disciples of the great and only Brigham and we became friends at once, as all acknowledged. The fine-looking Indian who sat as king in the lodge now, by motions and a word or two, made himself known as Chief Walker, and when I knew this I took great pains to cultivate his acquaintance.

I was quite familiar with the sign language used by all the Indians, and found I could get along pretty well in making him understand and knowing what he said. I asked him first how many "sleeps" or days it was from there to "Mormonee." In answer he put out his left hand and then put two fingers of his right astride of it, making both go up and down with the same motion of a man riding a horse. Then he shut his eyes and laid his head on his hand three times, by which I understood that a man could ride to the Mormon settlement in three sleeps or four days. He then wanted to know where we were going, and I made signs that we were wishing to go toward the setting sun and to the big water, and I said "California." The country far off to the west of us now seemed an open, barren plain, which grew wider as it extended west. The mountains on the north side seemed to get lower and smaller as they extended west, but on the south or east side they were all high and rough. It seemed as if we could see one hundred miles down the river, and up to the time we met the Indians we thought we had got through all our troublesome navigation and could now sail on, quietly and safely to the great Pacific Ocean and land of gold.

When I told Chief Walker this he seemed very much astonished, as if wondering why we were going down the river when we wanted to get west across the country. I asked him how many sleeps it was to the big water, and he shook his head, pointed out across the country and then to the river and shook his head again; by which I understood that water was scarce, out the way he pointed, he then led me down to a smooth sand bar on the river and then, with a crooked stick, began to make a map in the sand. First he made a long crooked mark, ten feet long or so, and pointing to the river to let me know that the mark in the sand was made to represent it. He then made a straight mark across near the north end of the stream, and showed the other streams which came into the Green River which I saw at once was exactly correct. Then he laid some small stones on each side of the cross mark, and making a small hoop of a willow twig, he rolled it in the mark he had made across the river, then flourished his stick as if he were driving oxen. Thus he represented the emigrant road. He traced the branches off to the north where the soldiers had gone, and the road to California, which the emigrants took, all of which we could see was correct. Then he began to describe the river down which we had come. A short distance below the road he put some small stones on each side of the river to represent mountains. He then put down his hands, one on each side of the crooked mark and then raised them up again saying "e-e-e-e-e-e" as he raised them, to say that the mountains were very high. Then he traced down the stream to a place below where we made our canoes; then he placed the stone back from the river farther, to show that there was a valley there; then he drew them in close again farther down, and piled them up again two or three tiers high, then placing both fists on them he raised them higher than the top of his head, saying "e-e-e-e-e-e" and looking still higher and shaking his head as if to say, "Awful bad cañon," and thus he went on describing the river till we understood that we were near the place where we now were, and then I pointed to his tepee, showing that I understood him all right. It was all correct which assured me that he knew all about the country.

I became much interested in my new found friend, and had him continue his map down the river. He showed two streams coming in on the east side and then he began piling up stones on each side of the river and then got longer ones and piled them higher and higher yet.

Then he stood with one foot on each side of his river and put his hands on the stones and then raised them as high as he could, making a continued "e-e-e-e-e" as long as his breath would last, pointed to the canoe and made signs with his hands how it would roll and pitch in the rapids and finally capsize and throw us all out. He then made signs of death to show us that this was a fatal place. I understood very plainly from this that below the valley where we now were was a terrible cañon, much higher than any we had passed, and the rapids were not navigable with safety. Then Walker shook his head more than once and looked very sober, and said "Indiano" and, reaching for his bow and arrows, he drew the bow back to its utmost length and put the arrow close to my breast, showing how I would get shot. Then he would draw his hand across his throat and shut his eyes as if in death to make us understand that this was a hostile country before us, as well as rough and dangerous.

I now had a description of the country ahead and believed it to be reliable. As soon as I could conveniently after this, I had a council with the boys, who had looked on in silence while I was holding the silent confab with the chief. I told them where we were and what chances there were of getting to California by this route, that for my part I would as soon be killed by Mormons as by savage Indians, and that I believed the best way for us to do was to make the best of our way to Salt Lake. "Now," I said, "those of you who agree with me can follow—and I hope at will."

McMahon said that we could not understand a word the old Indian said, and as to following his trails I don't believe a word of it, and it don't seem right.

McMahon and Field still persisted they would not go with us and so we divided our little stock of flour and dried meat with them as fairly as possible and decided we would try the trail. When our plans were settled we felt in pretty good spirits again, and one of the boys got up a sort of corn-stalk fiddle which made a squeaking noise and in a little while there was a sort of mixed American and Indian dance going on in which the squaws joined in and we had a pretty jolly time till quite late at night. We were well pleased that these wild folks had proved themselves to be true friends to us.

The morning we were to start I told the boys a dream I had in which I had seen that the course we had decided on was the correct one, but McMahon and Field thought we were foolish and said they had rather take the chances of going with the Indians, or going on down the river. He seemed to place great stress on the fact that he could not understand the Indians.

Said he: "This Indian may be all right, and maybe he will lead us all into a dreadful trap. They are treacherous and revengeful, and for some merely fancied wrong done by us, or by some one else of whom we have no control or knowledge, they may take our scalps, wipe us out of existence and no one will ever know what became of us. Now this map of mine don't show any bad places on this river, and I believe we can get down easily enough, and get to California sometime. Field and I cannot make up our minds so easily as you fellows. I believe your chances are very poor."[7]

Reading people of to-day, who know so well the geography of the American continent, may need to stop and think that in 1849 the whole region west of the Missouri River was very little known, the only men venturesome enough to dare to travel over it were hunters and trappers who by a wild life had been used to all the privations of such a journey, and were shrewd as the Indians themselves in the mysterious ways of the trail and the chase. Even these fellows had only investigated certain portions best suited to their purpose.

The Indians here have the reputation of being blood thirsty savages who took delight in murder and torture, but here, in the very midst of this wild and desolate country we found a chief and his tribe, Walker and his followers, who were as humane and kind to white people as could be expected of any one. I have often wondered at the knowledge of this man respecting the country, of which he was able to make us a good map in the sand, point out to us the impassable cañon, locate the hostile Indians, and many points which were not accurately known by our own explorers for many years afterward. He undoubtedly saved our little band from a watery grave, for without his advice we had gone on and on, far into the great Colorado cañon, from which escape would have been impossible and securing food another impossibility, while destruction by hostile Indians was among the strong probabilities of the case. So in a threefold way I have for these more than forty years credited the lives of myself and comrades to the thoughtful interest and humane consideration of Chief Walker.

≋ NOTES

1. Flaming Gorge.

2. Manly's graphics, like Ashley's mentioned below, now lie beneath the waters of Flaming Gorge Reservoir.

3. Brown's Park.

4. Lodore Canyon.

5. This section of Lodore Canyon contains many treacherous rapids, some of which the Powell expedition would later give such names as Disaster Falls and Hell's Half Mile.

6. Wonsits (Antelope) Valley in the Uinta Basin.

7. McMahon and Field continued down the river on their own, but eventually abandoned the idea, probably somewhere in Desolation Canyon, and ended up traveling overland to Salt Lake as well.

Report of the Exploring Expedition from Santa Fe, New Mexico, to the Junction of the Grand and Green Rivers of the Great Colorado of the West

John Strong Newberry

Captain J. N. Macomb's 1859 expedition was one of many commissioned by the U.S. government in the mid-nineteenth century to explore and gather scientific data on the unknown West. In this excerpt from the official report, expedition geologist John Strong Newberry evokes the combination of wonder and dismay that accompanied the first, and ultimately unsuccessful, overland attempt to reach the confluence of the Green and Grand rivers.

August 23, Camp 29 to Grand River—Leaving servants and packs in camp, we today descended the Cañon of Labyrinth Creek, to its junction with Grand River.[1] Until within a mile of the junction, the character of the cañon remains the same; a narrow gorge, with vertical sides, from 150 to 300 feet in height, its bottom thickly grown with bushes and obstructed with fallen rocks and timber, passable but with infinite difficulty. At the place mentioned above, however, our progress was arrested by a perpendicular fall, some 200 feet in height, occupying the whole breadth of the canyon, and to reach Grand River it was necessary to scale the walls which shut us in. This we accomplished with some difficulty on the south side, to find ourselves upon the level of the rocky plain into which we sunk when entering the cañon. The view we here obtained was most interesting, yet too limited to satisfy us. Looking down into the cañon we had been following, we could see it deepening by successive falls until, a mile below, it opened into the greater Cañon of Grand River, a dark yawning chasm, with vertical sides, in which we caught glimpses of the river 1,500 feet below where we stood. On every side we were surrounded by columns, pinnacles, and castles of fantastic shapes, which limited our view, and by impassable cañons, which restricted our movements. South of us, about a mile distant, rose one of the castle-like buttes, which I have already mentioned, and to which, though with difficulty, we made our way. This butte was composed of alternate layers of chocolate-colored sandstone and shale, about 1,000 feet in height; its sides nearly perpendicular, but most curiously ornamented with columns and pilasters, porticos and colonnades, cornices and battlements, flanked here and there with tall outstanding towers, and crowned with spires so slender that it seemed as though a breath of air would suffice to topple them from their foundations. To accomplish the object for which we had come so far, it seemed necessary that we should ascend this butte. The day was perfectly clear and intensely hot; the mercury standing at 92° in the shade, and the red sandstone, out of which the landscape was carved, glowed in the heat of the burning sunshine. Stripping off nearly all our clothing, we made the attempt, and after two hours of most arduous labor succeeded in reaching the summit. The view which there burst upon us was such as amply repaid us for all our toil. It baffles description, however, and I can only hope that our sketches will give some faint idea of its strange and unearthly character.

The great cañon of the Lower Colorado, with its cliffs a mile in height, affords grander and more impressive scenes, but those having far less variety and beauty of detail than this. From the pinnacle on which we stood the eye swept over an area some fifty miles in diameter, everywhere marked by features of more than ordinary interest; lofty lines of massive mesas rising in successive steps to form the frame of the picture; the interval between them more than 2,000 feet below their summits. A great basin or sunken plain lay stretched out before us as on a map. Not a particle of vegetation was anywhere discernable; nothing but bare and barren rocks of rich and varied colors shimmering in the sunlight. Scattered over the plain were thousands of the fantastically formed buttes to which I have so often referred in my notes; pyramids, domes, towers, columns, spires, of every conceivable form and size. Among these by far the most remarkable was the forest of Gothic spires, first and imperfectly seen as we issued from the mouth of the Cañon Colorado. Nothing I can say will give an adequate idea of the singular and surprising appearance which they presented from this new and advantageous point of view. Singly, or in groups, they extend like a belt of timber for a distance of several miles. Nothing in nature or in art offers a parallel to these singular objects, but some idea of their appearance may be gained by imagining the island of New York thickly set with spires like that of Trinity church, but many of them full twice its height. Scarcely less striking features in the landscape were the innumerable cañons by which the plain is cut. In every direction they ran and ramified deep, dark, and ragged, impassable to everything but the winged bird. Of these the most stupendous was the Grand River, which washes two sides of the base of the pinnacle on which we stood, a narrow chasm, as we estimated, full 1,500 feet in depth, into which the sun scarcely seemed to penetrate. At the bottom the whole breadth of this cañon is occupied by the turbid waters of Grand River, here a sluggish stream, at least with no current visible to us who were more than 2,000 feet above it. In this great artery a thousand lateral tributaries terminate, flowing through channels precisely like that of Labyrinth Creek; underground passages by which intermittent floods from the distant highlands are conducted through this country, producing upon it no other effect than constantly to deepen their own beds. Toward the south the cañon of the Grand was easily traced. Perhaps four miles below our position it is joined by another great chasm coming from the northwest, said by the Indians to be that of Green River. From the point where we were it was inaccessible, but we had every reason to credit their report in reference to it.

After reaching the elevated point from which we obtained the view, I neglected to take the rest I so much needed, but spent the little time at my command in endeavoring to put on paper some of the more striking features of the scene before us. Standing on the highest point, I made a hasty panoramic sketch of the entire landscape. The effort had, however, nearly cost me dear; for before I had completed the circle of the horizon I was seized with dreadful headache, giddiness, and nausea, and alone as I then was, had the greatest difficulty rejoining my companions.

≋ NOTES

1. This Labyrinth Creek is probably what is now called Indian Creek, emptying into the Colorado near the Needles District in Canyonlands National Park.

Uinta Not What Was Represented

Deseret News

On August 25, 1861, Mormon leader Brigham Young, having heard reports of lush pastures in the Uinta Basin, formed two scouting parties to travel to the area and assess its potential for Mormon settlement. The parties set out within two weeks and returned shortly thereafter with a decidedly negative report, which was summarized in the September 25 issue of the *Deseret News*.

The exploring and surveying party that started for Uinta Valley on the 2d, and also the road makers who followed after them on the 9TH inst., have returned with a very unfavorable report in relation to that part of the Territory. The fertile vales, extensive meadows, and wide pasture ranges so often reported to exist in that region, were not to be found; and the country according to the statements of those sent thither to select a location for a settlement, is entirely unsuitable for farming purposes, and the amount of land at all suitable for cultivation extremely limited.

The explorers having, on their arrival there, found things so very different from what had been anticipated, after searching up and down the streams flowing eastward from the Wasatch range to the Colorado without finding an oasis, sent back two of their number with a report of what discoveries they had made up to that time; which report was read from the stand at the Bowery on Sunday week. The balance of the party continued their exploration several days longer, but without discovering the land of the "walnut and the vine."

After becoming thoroughly satisfied that all the section of country, lying between the Wasatch Mountains and the eastern boundary of the Territory, and south of Green River County, was one vast "contiguity of waste," and measurably valueless, excepting for nomadic purposes, hunting grounds for Indians and to hold the world together, the whole party returned home, by different routes, some arriving on

Wednesday, others on Thursday last, unanimously reporting that there is no such country there as had been described by hunters, trappers, and other wanderers, who have unreservedly asserted that it was a beautiful valley and more to be desired than any they had seen in the Great Basin, not excepting that of Great Salt Lake.

Why men who have lived for years in this country, have roamed over its mountains and sterile plains, and have witnessed the experiments that have been made in tilling the soil, where any exists, have not by observation learned what portions of the desolate wastes can, and cannot, be cultivated, we are unable to say, but such is the case as had been demonstrated more than once. The men who were sent out, in this instance, to view Uinta, and select a location for a settlement if one could be found, were persons of experience in such matters and in their report the most implicit confidence is placed, consequently all arrangements for establishing a settlement there have ceased.

Green River: The Gateway

Wallace Stegner

IN THIS EXCERPT FROM *Beyond the Hundredth Meridian,* STEGNER'S DEFINITIVE TREATMENT OF JOHN WESLEY POWELL AND HIS PIVOTAL ROLE IN "THE SECOND OPENING OF THE WEST," WE ARE INTRODUCED TO AN UNLIKELY COLLECTION OF MEN AS THEY PREPARE TO EMBARK INTO THE GREAT UNKNOWN.

They waited below the Green River bridge on the bank of the Green, the old Seedskeedee-agie of the mountain men, until Powell should come with the boats. While they waited they might have thought of the blankness of the map south of them, the half-known course of the river, the remote junction of Grand and Green to form the Colorado, the unlocated mouth of the San Juan and other tributaries, the unknown and unnamed creeks, the untouched country that stretched back away from the canyons on both sides. That country had been barely penetrated here and there. Coronado's men had reached the south rim of the Grand Canyon in 1540 and peered over into that awesome ditch. Father Garcés had visited the Supais in Havasu Canyon before the American Revolution. Escalante had crossed the Green in the Uinta Valley in 1776, and come back across the southwestern marches to ford the Colorado at the foot of a canyon that Powell would name Glen Canyon, where James Ohio Pattie may have trapped beaver in the eighteen-twenties. Frémont had crossed the northern edge of the region in 1844, the southern edge in 1853; he had all but died in its mountains in 1848. Ives in 1857 had come up the lower Colorado as far as Diamond Creek, within the lower Grand Canyon, and had traversed the plateaus south of the Grand Canyon to the Hopi towns and across the Painted Desert to Fort Defiance and the New Mexico settlements. Captain Gunnison had surveyed a railroad route, some of it impracticable, along the 35th parallel in 1853. Captain J. N. Macomb in 1859 had run an exploration out from Santa Fe in an unsuccessful attempt to reach the junction of

Grand and Green. Berthoud and Bridger in 1861 had gone from Golden, Colorado, across the western Wasatch to Provo, Utah. From the eighteen-twenties until the near-extermination of the beaver the mountain men had trapped eastern and northern Utah, southern Wyoming, and western Colorado. But these were traverses only, touches; this country had never been spread out and walked over and brought within the control of definite lines on paper. Large parts of it had only been circumnavigated, never really visited at all. The real unknown lay between the Uinta Valley and Gunnison's Crossing, now Greenriver, Utah; and between that crossing and the mouth of the Paria, now Lee's Ferry, Arizona; and below that to the foot of the Grand Wash Cliffs, south of present St. George, Utah. The crossings had been located; the hinterlands were a tantalizing blank marked, in a cartographer's neat lettering, "Unexplored."

They were a meager force with which to conduct a major exploration: five trappers, a war-psychotic ex-captain and a one-armed ex-major of artillery.[1] It was important, and would have serious consequences, that both Powells represented military discipline and the officer class, and that the men who were to accompany them represented frontier independence and a violent distaste for discipline of any kind. Sumner, Dunn, Seneca Howland, and Hawkins had all been Union soldiers, but all had served in the ranks, Hawkins so obstreperously that he was wanted by the law in Missouri. Oramel Howland, the oldest man of the party, was a printer, an outdoorsman by preference rather than by calling.

In purpose, as in background, the party split. Powell himself was intense, ambitious, intellectually curious, wanting to know, committed to the abstract cause of Science. But of the mountain men, only Oramel Howland and perhaps Sumner had any notion what science was about, or any understanding of Powell's motives. Their view of all his activities was likely to be tinged by that contemptuous amusement with which they had watched Keplinger try to find a lost wilderness trail by squinting at a star through a sextant.[2] But action they understood, hardihood they all had. And there were the possible gravel bars. Green and Grand together drained a vast semicircle of mountains from the Wind Rivers in Wyoming through all the ranges of western Colorado and on down to the San Francisco peaks in northern Arizona. Where water ran and rock disintegrated, gold would wash down; where a river cut through thousands of feet of rock, veins would be exposed. Gilpin had said it for them.[3] These were things the trappers understood well enough, and they appreciated Powell's gift of being able to tell one rock from another, however cold his other scientific achievements might leave them.

Four trappers in buckskin pants, a printer, two ex-officers. And for backing, financial support? That was the principal reason, aside from the boats, for Powell's trip east.

Leaving the specifications for the four boats with a Chicago boatbuilder, he went on to Washington, one more among the throng of office-seekers, carpet baggers, pork-barrelers, men with schemes, thronging those muddy streets. He was not quite the unbacked unknown Illinois school teacher who had wangled a meager bone from Congress the year before, but he had little better luck. His hope was for a Congressional appropriation like that enjoyed by other government explorers and scientific investigators, Clarence King and Ferdinand V. Hayden among them. That hope failed him; an acquaintance with Grant, with Professor Henry of the Smithsonian, with Senator Trumbull and a few others, was not enough, and he had little time. When he came away he had exactly the same kind of governmental help that he had had the previous season. A joint resolution of Congress implemented with an order from the office of the Adjutant General allowed him to draw rations for 12 men from any western army post; to draw other supplies in lieu of the regular army rations if they were available; and (what actually gave him the bare minimum of cash he needed to proceed) to commute certain unneeded parts of the ration into money.

As Powell took pains to explain later in a letter to the Chicago *Tribune* from Green River, just before he shoved off, the party was not a government exploration at all. It was under the auspices of the Illinois Natural History Society, of which he was secretary. The funds available from the Society totaled less than a thousand dollars annually, and additional funds donated by the Illinois Industrial University amounted to only $1100 in all. Certain favors had been extended, principally in the form of instruments, by the Chicago Academy of Sciences and the Smithsonian Institution.

And that was all. Powell apparently arranged some sort of wages for the hunters by taking cash in lieu of part of the bacon ration, on the theory that fresh meat was a legitimate part of the ration if it could be provided. The hunters would help manage the boats, as they had for the past year managed the pack train. Sumner later asserted, without proof, that he was in on a partnership basis, providing part of the outfit and some of the supplies for the winter of 1868. Powell provided the rations and the boats, and obtained free transportation for men and supplies from several railroads as well as from Wells, Fargo and Adams and the American Express.

So except for the wages provided the hunters, it was entirely a volunteer party. Before it started down the swollen current of the Green three more volunteers would join it, and one comic-valentine volunteer would try.

Two of the three actual volunteers simply happened by at Green River. One, Frank Goodman, a red-faced Englishman rattling around the West in search of adventure, wanted so badly to go that he even offered Powell money to take him. There is no record of whether Powell took his money or not, but he took Goodman. Another, Andy Hall, was a cheerful, husky, eighteen-year-old bullwhacker and vagabond whom Powell saw resting on the oars of a homemade boat and enlisted on the spot. The third, George Bradley, Powell went to some trouble to get. He had met Bradley the autumn before, sadly sitting out an army enlistment at Fort Bridger and whiling away his time in melancholia and amateur fossil hunting. Bradley was a New Englander, and he knew boats, and he would do anything to get out of the army. Powell's one real success in Washington in May, 1869, was a War Department order authorizing Bradley's discharge to allow him to go on the river expedition. On May 14 the hypochondriac sergeant was mustered out and came down from Fort Bridger in time to teach the mountain men how to calk and paint the boats.

Of those boats a good deal has been written, and Colorado boatmen ever since have argued their virtues and their faults. It is not even clear who was responsible for their design, since Jack Sumner, in his later years of bitter grudge holding, claimed to have drawn them on the White River. The fact remains that Powell, who had taken solitary collecting trips by towboat on the Ohio, Mississippi, Illinois, and Des Moines, undoubtedly knew more about river travel than Sumner or any other member of his crew. Whatever the boats' qualities, they were probably Powell's design.

Rivermen since have designed boats much better adapted for the running of rapids. In particular the variety of "cataract boat" perfected by Nate Galloway has been used by most of the expeditions since 1909 except the Clyde Eddy Expedition of 1927, which returned to Powell's heavy and clumsy craft. But Galloway, Norman Nevills, and the later boatmen have not had the double problem of constructing a boat that would both ride bad water and carry tons of supplies. And they were not facing an unknown river. Powell intended to stay in the canyons a full ten months. Because there was no sure way of getting out once he plunged in, he thought he had to take everything he needed, and prepare against every imaginable emergency, including the possibility of ice in the canyons. His boats, in consequence, even the light sixteen-foot pine pilot boat, were unwieldy, hard to handle, backbreaking on a portage, sluggish in rapids. But they were stoutly built, with airtight compartments at both ends. The three large boats, designed to carry forty-five hundred pounds apiece, were of oak, twenty-one feet long, with a long stern sweep for steering—as it turned out, an awkward and ineffective arrangement in the rock-choked rapids they would meet.

The boats came off the cars at Green River with Major Powell on May 11, 1869, one day after Governor Stanford, General Dodge, and an extraordinary collection of celebrities, frontiersmen, saloonkeepers, Indians, Irish workmen, Chinese coolies, and plain spectators had ceremoniously put the transcontinental rails together between the cowcatchers of two facing locomotives at Promontory, a few hundred miles west. While the Powell party was still camped amid its stacked duffle below the Green River bridge, the first transcontinental train crossed the bridge above them and by its mere passing drew a line between periods of history.

Green River, which a little while before had a population of 2000, and was now a diminished shacktown of a hundred or so, came to the riverbank to watch the party calk and paint and load. It speculated and spit and laid bets, and according to its constitution joked or looked solemn. In the river the four boats rode like a little navy, with the flag snapping at the jackstaff of the pilot boat, the *Emma Dean*, named for Mrs. Powell, now back in Detroit with her family awaiting the outcome. Under the bridge and past the camp the river went, swollen by the runoff from Horse Creek, the Pineys, Fontanelle Creek, and on the east the creeks from the Wind Rivers and the high bare divide along South Pass. In autumn almost pistachio green, the water now was thick with grayish mud. It moved fast, straining the flooded willows, hurrying with nervous whirlpools.

There is something ominous about a swift river, and something thrilling about a river of any kind. The nearest upstream bend is a gate out of mystery, the nearest downstream bend a door to further mystery. Even at Green River the waters of the Green in flood move swiftly. Powell's men watched the river pour by, and felt with their hands the powerful push of the current, and reflected that this was quiet water, perhaps as quiet as any they would have all the way except in Brown's Hole and at the mouth of the White. They looked southward at the badlands that hid the river's course, and sometimes climbed to the bluffs and looked across the broken, yellow ocher and brown barrens, across an expanse of sage that in August would be purple with bloom, but was now faintly green with spring. Beyond the broken land and the tortuous, disguised cut of the river came up the blue roll of the Uintas, whose east end they had skirted on their trip from the White River, and into whose flaming canyons, threaded by the thin green line of the stream, they had peered from high cliffs. They would soon be looking up at those cliffs; they would be shooting on the river's back through the split mountains. Briefly, they would recognize the country where they had touched it in their explorations of the previous fall: in one or two of the Uinta canyons, at Brown's Hole, at the junction of White and Green in the broad Wonsits Valley. Then there would be the unknown again, a mystery clothed in rumor, secret water trails where perhaps not even Indians had passed.

It was a thing to hurry the pulse. Even in 1869, with the railroad demonstrably transcontinental at their backs, the northern and southern plains split in two, the Indians doomed along with the buffalo by whom they had lived, Omaha only four days by palace car from San Francisco and elegant passengers leaning from the windows to stare down on the little fleet, there was still this opportunity to look upon something, as Sam Garman had said on Long's Peak, just as God made it.

What they record in their journals and letters as they wait for the preparations to be finished and listen for the signal to start is not doubt, not fear, not any legitimate foreboding about a journey from which none of them might return. What they record is impatience and eagerness. The grumbling of the fall and winter, the cabin fever and distrust between dudes and mountain men, are gone and forgotten. They are tugged at as strongly as their four boats, pulling in the swollen current of the Green.

≋ NOTES

1. Walter and John Wesley Powell, respectively.

2. L. W. Keplinger, a college student who accompanied Powell on his Rocky Mountain Scientific Exploring Expedition in 1868.

3. William Gilpin, wilderness explorer and author of a popular book exaggerating the abundance of gold in the West.

The Lost Journal

John Colton Sumner

JOHN COLTON (JACK) SUMNER WAS THE HEAD BOATMAN ON POW-
ELL'S 1869 EXPEDITION. POWELL REQUESTED THAT HE KEEP A JOUR-
NAL, PARTS OF WHICH WERE PUBLISHED IN THE *Missouri Democrat*
ON AUGUST 24 AND 25, 1869. THE EXCERPTS REPRINTED HERE DE-
SCRIBE THE EXPEDITION FROM GREEN RIVER, WYOMING, THROUGH
FLAMING GORGE, RED CANYON, AND ASHLEY FALLS.

MAY 24, 1869.—After many weeks of weary waiting, today
sees us all ready for the adventures of an unknown country.
Heretofore all attempts in exploring the Colorado of the
West, throughout its entire course, have been miserable failures. Whether our attempt will turn out the same time alone can show. If we fail
it will not be for the want of a complete outfit of material and men
used to hardships. After much blowing off of gas and the fumes of
bad whiskey, we were all ready by two o'clock and pulled out into the
swift stream. The Emma Dean, a light four-oared shell, lightly loaded
carrying as crew Professor J. W. Powell, W. H. Dunn, and a trapper,
designed as a scouting party, taking the lead. The "Maid of the Canon"
followed close in her wake, manned by Walter H. Powell and George
Y. Bradley, carrying two thousand pounds of freight. Next on the way
was "Kitty Clyde's Sister," manned by as jolly a brace of boys as ever
swung a whip over a lazy ox, W. H. Rhodes, of Missouri, and Andrew
Hall, of Fort Laramie, carrying the same amount of freight. The last
to leave the miserable adobe village was the "No Name" (piratic craft)
manned by O. G. Howland, Seneca Howland, and Frank Goodman.
We make a pretty show as we float down the swift, glossy river. As
Kitty's crew have been using the whip more of late years than the
oars, she ran on a sand-bar in the middle of the river, got off of that,
and ran ashore on the east side, near the mouth of Bitter creek, but
finally got off and came down to the rest of the fleet in gallant style,
her crew swearing she would not "gee" or "haw" a "cuss." We moved

down about seven miles and camped for the night on the eastern shore where there is a large quantity of cord wood. As it was a cold, raw night, we stole a lot of it to cook with. Proff., Walter, and Bradley spent a couple of hours geologising on the east side. Howland and Dunn went hunting down the river: returned at dark with a small sized rabbit. Rather slim rations for ten hungry men. The balance of the party stopped in camp, and exchanged tough stories at a fearful rate. We turned in early, as most of the men had been up for several proceding [sic] nights, taking leave of their many friends, "a la Muscovite." The natural consequence were fog[g]y ideas and snarly hair.

How strange it is that adopting foreign ways will so change us in many respects. If there is any meanness in a man, get him drunk and you soon see the Devil's claws, if not the whole of the traditional "Auld Cootie." If he is a goodhearted man when sober, he will be willing to sell his only shirt to help his friend. When I see how drink shows the true colors so plainly, I sometimes wish the whole world could be drunk for a short time, that the scoundrels might be all killed off through their own meanness.

MAY 26TH—All afloat early; went about three miles when we came to our first rapid.[1] It cannot be navigated by any boat with safety, in the main channel, but the river being pretty high, it made a narrow channel, under the overhanging willows on the west shore, so that we were not delayed more than twenty minutes, all the boats but Kitty's Sister getting through easily. She getting on a rock, compelled Rhodes to get overboard and pry her off. About 4 o'clock, came to a meadow of about a thousand acres, lying between Green River and Henry's Fork. Camped for the night on the east shore, about a mile above the mouth of Henry's Fork. Passed the mouth of Black's Fork of the Green River today; it is but a little wider at the mouth than at Fort Bridger, but deep. Henry's Fork is a stream about thirty feet wide, and is fed by the snows of the Uinta Mountains, about seventy-five miles northwest of this camp; it has some good pasturage on it, but no farming land, as it is at too great an altitude. At the mouth is a good place for one or two ranches. There are about three hundred acres of good land, but is inundated nearly every spring by freshets. There is a large stack of hay standing in the meadow, that has been left over from last year's crop.

Horseshoe Canyon, from Powell, *Exploration of the Colorado River and Its Canyons.*

MAY 27TH—Raised a cache that we made two months since, and found everything safe; moved down to the head of a canyon and camped on the east side, under a grove of cottonwood trees. Proff., Walter, and Bradley went geologising. Tramped around most of the day in the mud and rain to get a few fossils. Distance from Green River City to mouth of Henry's Fork sixty miles, general course 30 degrees E. of S; estimated land distance forty miles. Country worthless. Grease wood and alkali on the river bottom; on the hills sparse bunch grass, Artemissia, and a few stunted cedars. At intervals of four or five miles on the river there are a few scrubby cottonwoods, but none large enough for anything but fuel. Rained most of the day.

MAY 28TH—Still in camp. Proff. and "The Trapper" repaired a broken barometer. Walter and Bradley went geologising on the west side. Bradley did not get into camp until night, having lost his way, and had a long, weary tramp through the mud and rain.

MAY 29TH—Proff climbed the hill on the east side of the canyon and measured it with a barometer; h[e]ight above the river 1140 feet, not perpendicular. There is a cliff on the west side that is fifty feet higher, and perpendicular. The rock is hard, fiery-red sandstone. It has been named Flaming Gorge.

MAY 30—Professor, Bradley, Senica, and Hall went up the river five miles, measuring a geological section. All in camp by three o'clock, when we loaded up and pulled on again into a channel as crooked as a street in Boston. Passed out of Flaming Gorge into Horseshoe Canon, out of Horseshoe Canon into Kingfisher Canon.[2] While rounding a bend, we came on a herd of mountain sheep, that scampered up a steep rocky side of the canon at astonishing rate. The crews of the freight boats opened a volley on them that made the wilderness ring, reminding us all of other scenes and times, when we were the scampering party. Passed the mouth of a small stream coming in from the west, which we named King Fisher Creek, as there was a bird of that species perched on the branch of a dead willow, watching the finny tribe with the determination of purpose that we often see exhibited by politicians while watching for the spoils of office. Killed two geese, and saw a great number of beavers today, but failed to get any of them. No sooner would we get within gun-shot, than down they would go with a plumping noise like dropping a heavy stone into the water. Made seven miles today, and camped for the night on the west bank opposite a huge grayish white sandstone that loomed up a thousand feet from the water's edge, very much the shape of an old-fashioned straw beehive, and we named it "Beehive Point." Saw the tracks of elk, deer and sheep on the sand. Near our camp, Goodman saw one elk, but missed it.

MAY 31ST.—This morning Professor, Bradley, and Dunn went up the river two miles to examine some rocks and look for a lost blank book. Howland and Goodman climbed a high mountain on the west side to get a good view of the country at large, and so draw a good map. All ready by ten o'clock when we pull out and are off like the wind; ran about two miles through a rapid and into still water for half an hour, then to a bad rapid through which no boat can run; full of sunken rocks, and having a fall of about ten feet in two hundred yards. We were compelled to let our boats down along the west side with ropes from men holding the line, two men with oars keeping them off the rocks; made the passage in about two hours, and ran a large number of them in ten miles travel.

About 5 o'clock we came to the worst place we had seen yet; a narrow gorge full of sunken rock, for 300 yards, through which the water run with a speed that threatened to smash everything to pieces that would get into it. All the boats were landed as quick as possible on the east side of the river, when we got out to examine the best point to get through, found ourselves on the wrong side of the river, and how to cross was the next question. We all plainly saw that it would be no child's play. Dunn and the trapper finally decided to take the small boat across or smash her to pieces; made the passage safe, unloaded and returned to relieve the freight boats, they taking out half their loads by making two trips with the freight boats and five with the small; we got everything safely across where we wanted it by sunset. Had supper; turned in, and in two minutes all were in dreamland.

JUNE 1ST.—After an early breakfast, all hands went to work letting the boats down with ropes, made the passage in three hours, when we jumped aboard again, and off we go like a shot; ran through about a dozen rapids in the course of ten miles, when we came to some signs of the country opening out. The walls were getting lower, and not so rough, and the current gradually slackens till it almost ceases. As the roaring of the rapids dies away above us, a new cause of alarm breaks in upon us from below. We ran along on the still water, with a vague feeling of trouble ahead, for about two miles, when, turning an abrupt corner, we came in sight of the first fall, about three hundred yards below us.[3] Signaled the freight boats to land, when the Emma was run down within a rod of the fall, and landed on the east side. Her crew then got out to reconnoitre; found a fall of about ten feet in twenty-five. There is a nearly square rock in the middle of the stream about twenty-five by thirty feet, the top fifteen above the water. There are many smaller ones all the way across, placed in such a manner that the fall is broken into steps, two on the east side, three on the west. We all saw that a portage would have to be made here. Without any loss of time the Emma Dean was unloaded and pushed into the stream, four men holding the line, the remainder of the party stationed on the rocks, each with oar, to keep her from being driven on some sharp corners and smashed to pieces. Got her under the fall in fifteen minutes, when we returned, unloaded Kitty's Sister, had supper and went to sleep on the sand. There is not much of a canyon at the falls. Three hundred yards from the east side there is a cliff about 450 feet high, from whence the rocks have fallen to make the dam.

JUNE 2D—All out early to breakfast; dispatched it, and let Kitty's Sister over the falls as we did the small boat. Then came the real hard work, carrying the freight a hundred yards or more over a mass of loose rocks, tumbled together like the ruins of some old fortress. Not a very good road to pack seven thousand pounds of freight. Got the loads of the two boats over, loaded them, and moved down three hundred yards to still water; tied up and returned to the other boats, to serve them the same; got everything around in still water by 11 o'clock; had dinner and smoked all round; distance from Bee-hive point unknown; course east of south, continuous canyon of red sand-stone; estimated height of one thousand feet; three highest perpendicular walls estimated at two thousand two hundred feet; named Red Canyon; on a rock the east side there is the name and date—"Ashley,

1825"—scratched on evidently by some trapper's knife; all aboard, and off we go down the river; beautiful river, that increases speed as leave the fall, till it gets a perfect rapid all the way, but clear of sunken rocks; so we run through the waves at express speed; made seventeen miles through Red Stone Canyon in less than an hour running time, the boats bounding through the waves like a school of porpoise. The Emma being very light is tossed about in a way that threatens to shake her to pieces, and is nearly as hard to ride as a Mexican pony. We plunge along singing, yelling like drunken sailors, all feeling that such rides do not come every day. It was like sparking a black-eyed girl— just dangerous enough to be exciting. About three o'clock we came suddenly out to a beautiful valley about two by five miles in extent. Camped in the middle of it, on the west side, under two large pine trees;[4] spread our bedding out to dry, while we rested in the shade. Two of the party came in at sunset, empty handed except the Professor, he being fortunate enough to get a brace of grouse. Spread our blankets on the clear, green grass, with no roof but the old pines above us, through which we could see the sentinel stars shining from the deep blue pure sky, like happy spirits looking out through the blue eyes of a pure hearted woman.

As we are guided on this voyage by the star in the blue; so may it be on the next, by the *spirit* in the blue.

≈≈≈ NOTES

1. Unidentified; Powell says the first rapid they came to was in Horseshoe Canyon, now beneath Flaming Gorge Reservoir.

2. All these canyons were inundated by the reservoir that today fills Flaming Gorge.

3. Ashley Falls.

4. These pine trees are still standing, at what is now called Little Hole, seven miles below Flaming Gorge Dam.

The Exploration of the Colorado River and Its Canyons

John Wesley Powell

POWELL'S BOOK *The Exploration of the Colorado River and Its Canyons* CONFLATES HIS 1869 AND 1871 EXPEDITIONS. THE EXCERPTS FROM CHAPTERS 6 AND 7 REPRODUCED HERE RECOUNT THE TEAM'S PASSAGE THROUGH FLAMING GORGE AND THE CANYON OF LODORE, INCLUDING THE DISASTROUS WRECK OF THE NO-NAME AND THE CONSEQUENT LOSS OF A SUBSTANTIAL PORTION OF THE EXPEDITION'S FOOD SUPPLIES AND SCIENTIFIC INSTRUMENTS.

One must not think of a mountain range as a line of peaks standing on a plain, but as a broad platform many miles wide from which mountains have been carved by the waters. One must conceive too, that this plateau is cut by gulches and canyons in many directions and that beautiful valleys are scattered about at different altitudes. The first series of canyons we are about to explore constitutes a river channel through such a range of mountains. The canyon is cut nearly halfway through the range, then turns to the east and is cut along the central line, or axis, gradually crossing it to the south. Keeping this direction for more than 50 miles, it then turns abruptly to a southwest course, and goes diagonally through the southern slope of the range.

This much we know before entering, as we made a partial exploration of the region last fall, climbing many of its peaks, and in a few places reaching the brink of the canyon walls and looking over precipices many hundreds of feet high to the water below.

Here and there the walls are broken by lateral canyons, the channels of little streams entering the river. Through two or three of these we found our way down to the Green in early winter and walked along the low water-beach at the foot of the cliffs for several miles. Where the river has this general easterly direction the western part only has cut for itself a canyon, while the eastern has formed a broad valley, called, in honor of an old-time trapper, Brown's Park, and long known as a favorite winter resort for mountain men and Indians.

MAY 30—This morning we are ready to enter the mysterious canyon, and start with some anxiety. The old mountaineers tell us that it cannot be run; the Indians say, "Water heap catch 'em"; but all are eager for the trial, and off we go.

Entering Flaming Gorge, we quickly run through it on a swift current and emerge into a little park. Half a mile below, the river wheels sharply to the left and enters another canyon cut into the mountain. We enter the narrow passage. On either side the walls rapidly increase in altitude. On the left are overhanging ledges and cliffs,— 500, 1,000, 1,500 feet high.

On the right the rocks are broken and ragged, and the water fills the channel from cliff to cliff. Now the river turns abruptly around a point to the right, and the waters plunge swiftly down among great rocks; and here we have our first experience with canyon rapids. I stand up on the deck of my boat to seek a way among the wave-beaten rocks. All untried as we are with such waters, the moments are filled with intense anxiety. Soon our boats reach the swift current; a stroke or two, now on this side, now on that, and we thread the narrow passage with exhilarating velocity, mounting the high waves, whose foaming crests dash over us, and plunging into the troughs, until we reach the quiet water below. Then comes a feeling of great relief. Our first rapid is run. Another mile, and we come into the valley again.

Let me explain this canyon. Where the river turns to the left above, it takes a course directly into the mountain, penetrating to its very heart, then wheels back upon itself, and runs out into the valley from which it started only half a mile below the point at which it entered; so the canyon is in the form of an elongated letter U, with the apex in the center of the mountain. We name it Horseshoe Canyon.

Soon we leave the valley and enter another short canyon, very narrow at first, but widening below as the canyon walls increase in height. Here we discover the mouth of a beautiful little creek coming down through its narrow water-worn cleft. Just at its entrance there is a park of two or three hundred acres, walled on every side by almost vertical cliffs hundreds of feet in altitude, with three gateways through the walls—one up the river, another down, and a third through which the creek comes in. The river is broad, deep, and quiet, and its waters mirror towering rocks.

Kingfishers are playing about the streams, and so we adopt as names Kingfisher Creek, Kingfisher Park, and Kingfisher Canyon. At night we camp at the foot of this canyon.

Our general course this day has been south, but here the river turns to the east around a point which is rounded to the shape of a dome. On its sides little cells have been carved by the action of the water, and in these pits, which cover the face of the dome, hundreds of swallows have built their nests. As they flit about the cliffs, they look like swarms of bees, giving to the whole the appearance of a colossal beehive of the old-time form, and so we name it Beehive Point.

The opposite wall is a vast amphitheater, rising in succession of terraces to a height of 1,200 or 1,500 feet. Each step is built of red sandstone, with a face of naked red rock and a glacis clothed with verdure. So the amphitheater seems banded red and green, and the evening sun is playing with roseate flashes on the rocks, with shimmering green on the cedars' spray, and with iridescent gleams on the dancing waves. The landscape revels in the sunshine.

MAY 31.—We start down another canyon and reach rapids made dangerous by high rocks lying in the channel; so we run ashore and let our boats down with lines. In the afternoon we come to more dangerous rapids and stop to examine them. I find we must do the same work again, but, being on the wrong side of the river to obtain a foothold, must first cross over—no very easy matter in such a current, with rapids and rocks below. We take the pioneer boat, "Emma Dean," over, and unload her on the bank; then she returns and takes another load. Running back and forth, she soon has half our cargo over. Then one of the larger boats is manned and taken across, but is carried down almost to the rocks in spite of hard rowing. The other boats follow and make the landing, and we go into camp for the night.

At the foot of the cliff on this side there is a long slope covered with pines; under these we make our beds, and soon after sunset are seeking rest and sleep. The cliffs on either side are of red sandstone and stretch toward the heavens 2,500 feet. On this side the long, pine-clad slope is surmounted by perpendicular cliffs, with pines on their summits. The wall on the other side is bare rock from the water's edge up 2,000 feet, then slopes back, giving footing to pines and cedars.

As the twilight deepens, the rocks grow dark and somber; the threatening roar of the water is loud and constant, and I lie awake with thoughts of the morrow and the canyons to come, interrupted now and then by characteristics of the scenery that attract my attention. And here I make a discovery. On looking at the mountain directly in front, the steepness of the slope is greatly exaggerated, while the distance to its summit and its true altitude are correspondingly diminished. I have heretofore found that to judge properly of the slope of a mountain side, one must see it in profile. In coming down the river this afternoon, I observed the slope of a particular part of the wall and made an estimate of its altitude. While at supper, I noticed the same cliff from a position facing it, and it seemed steeper, but not half so high. Now lying on my side and looking at it, the true proportions appear. This seems a wonder, and I rise to take a view of it standing. It is the same cliff as at supper time. Lying down again, it is the cliff as seen in profile, with a long slope and distant summit. Musing on this, I forget "the morrow and the canyons to come"; I have found a way to estimate the altitude and slope of an inclination, in like manner as I can judge of distance along the horizon. The reason is simple. A reference to the stereoscope will suggest it. The distance between the eyes forms a base line for optical triangulation.

June 1.—To-day we have an exciting ride. The river rolls down the canyon at a wonderful rate, and, with no rocks in the way, we make almost railroad speed. Here and there the water rushes into a narrow gorge; the rocks on the side roll it into the center in great waves, and the boats go leaping and bounding over these like things of life, reminding me of scenes witnessed in Middle Park—herds of startled deer bounding through forests beset with fallen timber. I mention the resemblance to some of the hunters, and so striking is it that the expression, "See the blacktails jumping the logs," comes to be a common one. At times the waves break and roll over the boats, which necessitates much bailing and obliges us to stop occasionally for that purpose. At one time we run twelve miles in an hour, stoppages included.

Last spring I had a conversation with an old Indian named Páriats, who told me about one of his tribe attempting to run this canyon. "The rocks," he said, holding his hands above his head, his arms vertical, and looking between them to the heaven, "the rocks h-e-a-p, h-e-a-p high; the water go h-oo-woogh, h-oo-woogh; water pony h-e-a-p buck; water catch 'em; no see 'em Injun any more! No see 'em squaw any more! No see 'em papoose any more!"

Those who have seen these wild Indian ponies rearing alternately before and behind, or "bucking," as it is called in the vernacular, will appreciate his description.

At last we come to calm water, and a threatening roar is heard in the distance. Slowly approaching the point whence the sound issues, we come near to falls, and tie up just above them on the left. Here we shall be compelled to make a portage; so we unload the boats, and fasten a long line to the bow of the smaller one, and another to the stern, and moor her close to the brink of the fall. Then the bowline is taken below and made fast; the stern line is held by five or six men, and the boat let down as long as they can hold her against the rushing waters; then, letting go one end of the line, it runs through the ring; the boat leaps over the fall and is caught by the lower rope.

Now we rest for the night.

JUNE 2.—This morning we make a trail among the rocks, transport the cargoes to a point below the fall, let the remaining boats over, and are ready to start before noon.

On a high rock by which the trail passes we find the inscription: "Ashley 18-5." The third figure is obscure—some of the party reading it 1835, some 1855. James Baker, an old-time mountaineer, once told me about a party of men starting down the river, and Ashley was named as one. The story runs that the boat was swamped, and some of the party drowned in one of the canyons below. The word "Ashley" is a warning to us, and we resolve on great caution. Ashley Falls is the name we give to the cataract.

The river is very narrow, the right wall vertical for 200 or 300 feet, the left towering to a great height, with a vast pile of broken rocks lying between the foot of the cliff and the water. Some of the rocks broken down from the ledge above have tumbled into the channel and caused this fall. One great cubical block, thirty or forty feet high, stands in the middle of the stream, and the waters, parting to either side, plunge down about twelve feet, and are broken again by the smaller rocks into a rapid below. Immediately below the falls the water occupies the entire channel, there being no talus at the foot of the cliffs.

We embark and run down a short distance, where we find a landing place for dinner.

On the waves again all the afternoon. Near the lower end of this canyon, to which we have given the name of Red Canyon, is a little park, where streams come down from distant mountain summits and enter the river on either side; and here we camp for the night under two stately pines.

JUNE 3.—This morning we spread our rations, clothes, etc., on the ground to dry, and several of the party go out for a hunt. I take a walk of five or six miles up to a pine-grove park, its grassy carpet bedecked with crimson velvet flowers, set in groups on the stems of pear-shaped cactus plants; patches of painted cups are seen here and there, with yellow blossoms protruding through scarlet bracts; little blue-eyed flowers are peeping through the grass; and the air is filled with fragrance from the white blossoms of the *Spiraea*. A mountain brook runs through the midst, ponded below by beaver dams. It is a quiet place for retirement from the raging waters of the canyon.

It will be remembered that the course of the river from Flaming Gorge to Beehive Point is in a southerly direction and at right angles to the Uinta Mountains, and cuts into the range until it reaches a point within five miles of the crest, where it turns to the east and pursues the axis slowly in a direction a little south of east. Thus there is a triangular tract between the river and the axis of the mountain with its acute angle extending eastward. I climb the mountain overlooking this country. To the east the peaks are not very high, and already most of the snow has melted, but little patches lie here and there under the lee of ledges of rock. To the west the peaks grow higher and the snow fields larger. Between the brink of the canyon and the foot of these peaks, there is a high bench. A number of creeks have their sources in the snowbanks to the south and run north into the canyon, tumbling down from 3,000 to 5,000 feet in a distance of five or six miles. Along their upper courses they run through grassy valleys, but as they

approach Red Canyon they rapidly disappear under the general surface of the country, and emerge into the canyon below in deep, dark
gorges of their own. Each of these short lateral canyons is marked by
a succession of cascades and a wild confusion of rocks and trees and
fallen timber and thick undergrowth.

The little valleys above are beautiful parks; between the parks are
stately pine forests, half hiding ledges of red sandstone. Mule deer and
elk abound; grizzly bears, too, are abundant; and here wild cats, wol-
verines, and mountain lions are at home. The forest aisles are filled
with the music of birds, and the parks are decked with flowers. Noisy
brooks meander through them; ledges of moss covered rocks are seen;
and gleaming in the distance are the snow fields, and the mountain
tops are away in the clouds.

JUNE 4.—We start early and run through to Brown's Park. Halfway
down the valley, a spur of a red mountain stretches across the river,
which cuts a canyon through it. Here the walls are comparatively low,
but vertical. A vast number of swallows have built their *adobe* houses
on the face of the cliffs, on either side of the river. The waters are deep
and quiet, but the swallows are swift and noisy enough, sweeping by
in their curved paths through the air or chattering from the rocks,
while the young ones stretch their little heads on naked necks through
the doorways of their mud houses and clamor for food. They are a
noisy people. We call this Swallow Canyon.

Still down the river we glide until an early hour in the afternoon,
when we go into camp under a giant cottonwood standing on the
right bank a little way back from the stream. The party has succeeded
in killing a fine lot of wild ducks, and during the afternoon a mess of
fish is taken.

JUNE 5.—With one of the men I climb a mountain, off on the right.
A long spur, with broken ledges of rock, puts down to the river, and
along its course, or up the "hogback," as it is called, I make the ascent.
Dunn, who is climbing to the same point is coming up the gulch. Two
hours' hard work has brought us to the summit. These mountains are
all verdure-clad; pine and cedar forests are set on green terraces; snow-
clad mountains are seen in the distance, to the west; the plains of the
upper Green stretch out before us to the north until they are lost in

the blue heavens; but half of the river-cleft range intervenes, and the river itself is at our feet.

This half range, beyond the river, is composed of long ridges nearly parallel with the valley. On the farther ridge, to the north, four creeks have their sources. These cut through the intervening ridges, one of which is much higher than that on which they head, by canyon gorges; then they run with gentle curves across the valley, their banks set with willows, box-elders, and cottonwood groves. To the east we look up the valley of the Vermillion, through which Fremont found his path on his way to the great parks of Colorado.

The reading of the barometer taken, we start down in company, and reach camp tired and hungry, which does not abate one bit our enthusiasm as we tell of the day's work with its glory of landscape.

JUNE 6.—At daybreak I am awakened by a chorus of birds. It seems as if all the feathered songsters of the region have come to the old tree. Several species of warblers, woodpeckers, and flickers above, meadow larks in the grass, and wild geese in the river. I recline on my elbow and watch a lark near by, and then awaken my bedfellow, to listen to my Jenny Lind. A real morning concert for *me;* none of your *"matinées"!*

Our cook has been an ox-driver, or "bull-whacker," on the plains, in one of those long trains now no longer seen, and he hasn't forgotten his old ways. In the midst of the concert, his voice breaks in: "Roll out! roll out! bulls in the corral! chain up the gaps! Roll out! roll out! roll out!" And this is our breakfast bell. To-day we pass through the park, and camp at the head of another canyon.

JUNE 7.—To-day two or three of us climb to the summit of the cliff on the left, and find its altitude above camp to be 2,086 feet. The rocks are split with fissures, deep and narrow, some times a hundred feet or more to the bottom, and these fissures are filled with loose earth and decayed vegetation in which lofty pines find root. On a rock we find a pool of clear, cold water, caught from yesterday evening's shower. After a good drink we walk out to the brink of the canyon and look down to the water below. I can do this now, but it has taken several years of mountain climbing to cool my nerves so that I can sit with my feet over the edge and calmly look down a precipice 2,000 feet. And yet I cannot look on and see another do the same. I must either bid him come away or turn my head. The canyon walls are buttressed on a grand scale, with deep alcoves intervening; columned crags crown the cliffs, and the river is rolling below.

When we return to camp at noon the sun shines in splendor on vermilion walls, shaded into green and gray where the rocks are lichened over; the river fills the channel from wall to wall, and the canyon opens, like a beautiful portal, to a region of glory. This evening, as I write, the sun is going down and the shadows are settling in the canyon. The vermilion gleams and roseate hues, blending with the green and gray tints, are slowing changing to somber brown above, and black shadows are creeping over them below; and now it is a dark portal to a region of gloom—the gateway through which we are to enter on our voyage of exploration tomorrow. What shall we find?

The distance from Flaming Gorge to Beehive Point is 9 2/3 miles. Besides passing through the gorge, the river runs through Horseshoe and Kingfisher canyons, separated by short valleys. The highest point on the walls at Flaming Gorge is 1,300 feet above the river. The east wall at the apex of Horseshoe Canyon is about 1,600 feet above the water's edge, and from this point the walls slope both to the head and foot of the canyon.

Kingfisher Canyon, starting at the water's edge above, steadily increases in altitude to 1,200 feet at the foot.

Red Canyon is 25 2/3 miles long, and the highest walls are about 2,500 feet.

Brown's Park is a valley, bounded on either side by a mountain range, really an expansion of the canyon. The river, through the park, is 35 1/2 miles long, but passes through two short canyons on its way, where spurs from the mountains on the south are thrust across its course.

JUNE 8.—We enter the canyon, and until noon find a succession of rapids, over which our boats have to be taken.

Here I must explain our method of proceeding at such places. The "Emma Dean" goes in advance; the other boats follow, in obedience to signals. When we approach a rapid, or what on other rivers would often be called a fall, I stand on deck to examine it, while the oarsmen back water, and we drift on as slowly as possible. If I can see a clear chute between the rocks, away we go; but if the channel is beset entirely across, we signal the other boats, pull to land, and I walk along the shore for closer examination. If this reveals no clear channel, hard work begins. We drop the boats to the very head of the danger-ous place and let them over by lines or make a portage, frequently carrying both boats and cargoes over the rocks.

The waves caused by such falls in a river differ much from the waves of the sea. The water of an ocean wave merely rises and falls; the form only passes on, and form chases form unceasingly. A body floating on such waves merely rises and sinks—does not progress unless impelled by wind or some other power. But here the water of the wave passes on while the form remains. The waters plunge down ten or twenty feet to the foot of a fall, spring up again in a great wave, then down and up in a series of billows that gradually disappear in the more quiet waters below; but these waves are always there and one can stand above and count them.

A boat riding such billows leaps and plunges along with great velocity. Now, the difficulty in riding over these falls, when no rocks are in the way, is with the first wave at the foot. This will sometimes gather for a moment, heap up higher and higher, and then break back. If the boat strikes it the instant after it breaks, she cuts through, and the mad breaker dashes its spray over the boat and washes overboard all who do not cling tightly. If the boat, in going over the falls, chances to get caught in some side current and is turned from its course, so as to strike the wave "broadside on," and the wave breaks at the same instant, the boat is capsized; then we must cling to her, for the water-tight compartments act as buoys and she cannot sink; and so we go; dragged through the waves, until still waters are reached, when we right the boat and climb aboard. We have several such experiences to-day.

At night we camp on the right bank, on a little shelving rock be-tween the river and the foot of the cliff; and with night comes gloom into these great depths. After supper we sit by our camp fire, made of driftwood caught by the rocks, and tell stories of wild life; for the men have seen such in the mountains or on the plains, and on the battlefields of the South. It is late before we spread our blankets on the beach.

Lying down, we look up through the canyon and see that only a little of the blue heaven appears overhead--a crescent of blue sky, with two or three constellations peering down upon us. I do not sleep for some time, as the excitement of the day has not worn off. Soon I see a bright star that appears to the rest on the very verge of the cliff over-head to the east. Slowly it seems to float from its resting place on the rock over the canyon. At first it appears like a jewel set on the brink of the cliff, but as it moves out from the rock I almost wonder that it does not fall. In fact, it does seem to descend in a gentle curve, as though the bright sky in which the stars are set were spread across the canyon, resting on either wall, and swayed down by its own weight. The stars appear to be in the canyon. I soon discover that it is the bright star Vega; so it occurs to me to designate this part of the wall as the "Cliff of the Harp."

JUNE 9.—One of the party suggests that we call this the Canyon of Lodore, and the name is adopted. Very slowly we make our way, often climbing on the rocks at the edge of the water for a few hundred yards to examine the channel before running it. During the afternoon we come to a place where it is necessary to make a portage. The little boat is landed and the others are signaled to come up.

When these rapids or broken falls occur usually the channel is suddenly narrowed by rocks which have been tumbled from the cliffs or have been washed in by lateral streams. Immediately above the nar-row, rocky channel, on one or both sides, there is often a bay of quiet water, in which a landing can be made with ease. Sometimes the water descends with a smooth, unruffled surface from the broad, quiet spread above into the narrow, angry channel below by a semi-circular sag. Great care must be taken not to pass over the brink into this deceptive pit, but above it we can row with safety. I walk along the bank to examine the ground, leaving one of my men with a flag to guide the other boats to the landing-place. I soon see one of the boats make shore all right, and feel no more concern; but a minute after, I hear a shout, and, looking around, see one of the boats shooting down the center of the sag. It is the "No Name," with Captain Howland, his brother, and Goodman. I feel that its going over is inevitable, and run to save the third boat. A minute more, and she turns the point and heads for the shore. Then I turn down stream again and scramble along to look for the boat that has gone over. The first fall is not great, only 10 or 12 feet, and we often run such; but below, the river tumbles

Gate of Lodore, from Powell, *Exploration of
the Colorado River and Its Canyons.*

down again for 40 or 50 feet, in a channel filled with dangerous rocks
that break the waves into whirlpools and beat them into foam. I pass
around a great crag just in time to see the boat strike a rock and, re-
bounding from the shock, careen and fill its open compartment with
water. Two of the men lose their oars; she swings around and is

Wreck at Disaster Falls, from Powell, *Exploration of
the Colorado River and Its Canyons.*

carried down at a rapid rate, broadside on for a few yards, when, striking amidships on another rock with great force, she is broken quite in
two and the men are thrown into the river. But the larger part of the
boat floats buoyantly, and they soon seize it, and down the river they
drift, past the rocks for a few hundred yards, to a second rapid filled
with huge boulders, where the boat strikes again and is dashed to

pieces, and the men and fragments are soon carried beyond my sight. Running along, I turn a bend and see a man's head above water, washed about in a whirlpool below a great rock. It is Frank Goodman, clinging to the rock with a grip upon which life depends. Coming opposite, I see Howland trying to get to his aid from an island on which he has been washed. Soon he comes near enough to reach Frank with a pole, which he extends toward him. The latter lets go the rock, grasps the pole, and is pulled ashore. Seneca Howland is washed farther down the island and is caught by some rocks, and, though somewhat bruised, manages to get ashore in safety. This seems a long time as I tell it, but it is quickly done.

And now the three men are on an island, with a swift dangerous river on either side and a fall below. The "Emma Dean" is soon brought down, and Sumner, starting above as far as possible, pushes out. Right skillfully he plies the oars, and a few strokes set him on the island at the proper point. Then they all pull the boat up stream as far as they are able, until they stand in water up to their necks. One sits on a rock and holds the boat until the others are ready to pull, then gives the boat a push, clings to it with his hands, and climbs in as they pull for mainland, which they reach in safety. We are as glad to shake hands with them as though they had been on a voyage around the world and wrecked on a distant coast.

George Y. Bradley's Journal

George Y. Bradley

WHEN INVITED BY POWELL TO JOIN HIS EXPEDITION THROUGH
GRAND CANYON, CIVIL WAR VETERAN GEORGE BRADLEY, BORED
WITH HIS ASSIGNMENT AT FORT BRIDGER, WYOMING, JUMPED AT
THE CHANCE, WRITING IN HIS DIARY THAT HE "WOULD BE WILLING
TO EXPLORE THE RIVER STYX." THIS SECTION OF HIS JOURNAL PICKS
UP THE STORY WITH THE WRECK OF THE *No-Name* AND CONTINUES
THROUGH THE PARTY'S ARRIVAL AT THE CONFLUENCE OF THE
GREEN AND BEAR (YAMPA) RIVERS.

JUNE 8, '69. Started quite early this morning and find that what
seemed comparatively easy rapids from the top of the mountains
are quite bad ones, and as we advanced they grew worse until we
came to the wildest rapid yet seen. I succeeded in making a landing in
an eddy just above where the dangerous part began. So did one other
of the heavy boats, but one (the "No Name") with three men in it
with one-third of our provisions, half our mess-kit and all three of
our barometers went over the rapid and though the men escaped with
their lives yet they lost all of their clothing, bedding and everything
except shirt and drawers, the uniform in which we all pass rapids. It is
a serious loss to us and we are rather low spirited [*sic*] tonight for we
must camp right at the head of a roaring rapid more than a mile in
length and in which we have already lost one of our boats and nearly
lost three of our number. Yet I trust the sun of another day will bring
better cheer. "All's well that ends well," but the end is not yet.

JUNE 9, '69. Have lowered our boats and brought part of the baggage
down with great labor, having first to clear an imperfect road through
the broken rocks and stunted mountain cedars and have had better
luck with the wrecked boat than we anticipated, for two of the men
(Jack and Andy) with great risk have succeeded in getting a boat out

to an island on which they found a small part of the boat and the barometers. They are what we cared the most about after the men's outfit, for without them we should have to make the trip and never know the height of the mountains which we pass through. We have plenty of rations left, much more than we care to carry around the rappids [*sic*], especially when they are more than a mile long. The scenery at this point is sublime. The red sand-stone rises on either side more than 2000 ft., shutting out the sun for much of the day while at our feet the river, lashed to foam, rushes on with indescribable fury. O how great is He who holds it in the hollow of His hand, and what pygmies we who strive against it. It will take us nearly or quite another day before we can start in again. Major and brother are gone ahead to *see what comes next.* Hope for a favorable report but can't rely on anything but actual tryal [*sic*] with the boats, for a man can't travel so far in a whole day in these cañons as we go in a single hour.

JUNE 10, '69. Brought down the rest of the stores and having loaded the boats we lowered them about a mile with ropes and crossed the river and camped for the night. The river in this cañon is not a succession of rappids as we have found before but a *continuous* rapid.

JUNE 11, '69. Have been working like galley-slaves all day. Have lowered the boats all the way with ropes and once unloaded and carried the goods around one very bad place. The rapid is still continuous and not improving. Where we are tonight it roars and foams like a wild beast. The Major as usual has chosen the worst camping-ground possible. If I had a dog that would lie where my bed is made tonight I would kill him and burn his collar and swear I never owned him. Have been wet all day and the water flies into the boats so badly that it is impossible to keep anything dry. The clothes in my valise are all wet and I have nothing dry to put on, but fortunately it is not cold for though I have only one shirt and drawers on and they are only half dry, yet I am not cold though the sun does not reach us more than 5 or 6 hours in the [day]. I fell today while trying to save my boat from a rock and have a bad cut over the left eye which I fear will make an ugly scar. But what odds, it can't disfigure my ugly mug and it may improve it, who knows?

June 12, '69. Today has been the repetition of yesterday only more of it. We have carried the goods around two bad places and run several others. One run of nearly or quite a mile is the largest for 4 days. We camp tonight in a fine spot on the east side of the cañon, but below us about a stone's throw is another furious rapid near a mile long, past which we must take the goods tomorrow and if possible get our boats over, though the prospects of success are not bright. Still there is no retreat if we desired it. We must go on and shall—and shall no doubt be successful. I am fishing while I write but the fish in this cañon are scarce for the water is too swift for whitefish and too muddy for trout. The sun shone on us until nearly 5 o'clock this p.m., for we being on the east side and a notch on the bluff on the west affoarded [sic] clear space for it and it was very fortunate for me as we landed here about 3 o'clock. I put out all my clothing, papers, etc., and have got 2 hour's good sun on them which in this pure air will dry almost anything. My eye is very black today and if it is not very *useful* it is very ornamental.

June 13, '69. We remain in camp today for we are tired out from the effects of constant hard labor and constant wetting. It is Sunday and the first one we have paid any attention to and whether this is accident or design I can't tell, but I am inclined to think it accidental for don't think anyone in this party except myself keeps any record of time or events. The sun reached our camp at 10 a.m., and will afford us another excellent opportunity to dry clothing etc. Our rations are getting very sour from constant wetting and exposure to a hot sun. I imagine we shall be sorry before the trip is up that we took no better care of them. It is none of my business, yet if we fail it will be want of judgment that will defeat it and if we succeed it will be *dumb luck,* not good judgment that will do it. The men have all come in from hunting, as ever without game. We frequently see mountain sheep as we pass along, and if we kept *still* we might kill them but as soon as we land the men begin to shoot and make a great noise and the game for miles around is allarmed [sic] and takes back from the river. This makes one think that these are not *hunters* and I believe that if left to maintain themselves with their rifles they would fare worse than Job's turkey. They seem more like school-boys on a holiday than like men accustomed to live by the chase, but as I am no hunter myself I must not criticize others. Still as usual I have my opinion.

June 14, '69. Up to this hour (1 o'clock p.m.) we remain in camp. Have landed the provisions on the rocks above the rapid and spread them to dry. The weather is clear and while the sun reaches us very warm, our camp is finely shaded by box-elder trees (a variety of the ash) that make it delightfully cool where our beds are made. Some of the men are making moccasins, some playing cards or reading, others mending clothing or sleeping, while I am lying flat on my back with a geology for a desk, writing. Major's brother lies beside me singing "John Anderson, My Jo." The Major and Howland are fixing up as well as possible the map of the river over which we have passed, for all was lost in the lost boat and must be made again as correct as possible from memory. I have been fixing my boat and calking the cubfins to keep my clothing dry while in the waves. Below each rapid there is a heavy sea and one would actually fancy himself in a gale at sea if he could not see the land so near him. Our boats being heavily loaded ride the sea badly and that is the way we get so wet and get our clothing wet, for sometimes the boats will be nearly full before we can get through to smooth water again. We estimate that we have already come 15 miles in this cañon and it cannot be much longer unless it is longer than any we have seen. The longest before this was 25 miles. We are getting near the mouth of Bear River and hope for some favorable change after we reach it. If I knew I could keep them dry I would write a lot of letters but it is so uncertain that I must wait until we get into smoother water before I write, for I think there be no chance to send them for another month or more at this rate. Remained in camp all day.

JUNE 15, '69. Another day finds us past that rapid and at another five times as bad as the last.[1] We have made a trail along the mountainside and think that from that point we can run it. We encamped for the night after making the trail. My boat was sunk while being lowered over the rapid this morning and all my books and papers soaked with water, and I fear both my albums and most of my photographs and tintypes [are] spoiled. Some of them I value very highly for I can never replace them. My notes were soaked but I have dried them and since that have carried them in my *hat*. My clothing is of course all wet again but aside from the trouble of drying it, it is no matter for I need only shirt and drawers in this warm weather and lately have seldom worn anything else.

JUNE 16, '69. We labored hard all day and got all down. We shortened the distance somewhat by loading the boats and hauling them through a large eddy and then carrying the goods again across a point. We sank one boat today and another got away from us but we recovered both without serious damage. We camp tonight on the top of a small rapid which we can run and we hope and expect that the worst of this cañon is over, for the softer rock is getting near the water and the softer the rock the better the river generally. This cañon is mostly dark red sandstone containing much iron. What is coming is white sand-stone containing lime and most of it is shaley so we have the "testimony of the rocks" that the future is favorable.

JUNE 17, '69. Have had a little better running today. Have made over 5 miles. Ran many little rappids. Several times let down with ropes and once made a short portage. Have passed 5 or 6 whirlpools today, one so bad we had to take the boats around it with ropes. It whirled them around so fast we couldn't row them through it. One rapid we ran today was full of rocks and we all struck our boats and tonight they are leaking badly, but we can repair them with pitch from the mountain pine. We camped for this night on a little point where the mountain pine and sage-brush was very thick and the cook built his fire and had supper on the way when the fire spread to the pines. At first we took little notice of it but soon a whirlwind swept through the cañon and in a moment the whole point was one sheet of flames. We seized whatever we could and rushed for the boats and amid the rush of wind and flames we pushed out and dropped down the river a few rods. My handkerchief was burned that I had tied around my neck, and my ears and face badly scorched. We had hardly landed before the fire was again upon us and we were forced to run a bad rapid to escape it. We got through safe, however, and are all right tonight except that we lost most of our mess-kit.

JUNE 18, '69. After a run of almost railroad speed for 5 miles we came to Bear River which comes into the Green from the east, and at this season of the year has almost or quite as much water. What its effect on the future stream will be is uncertain. I predict that the river will improve from this point, for the more water there is the wider channel it will make for itself and the less liability will there be of its falling in and blocking up clear across, and if there is one side clear we can run it or at least have one good side to let down the boats with ropes. I commenced fishing soon after we arrived but the fish were so large they broke four hooks and three lines for me; in a few moments I could haul them to the top of the water, great fellows some of them quite a yard long, but the moment they saw me they were off and the hook or line must break. At last by twisting four silk lines together and putting on a hook two inches long I managed to secure one that weighed 10 lbs., and will make a fine breakfast for all hands. We intend to stay here several days and take a set of observations. Have named the cañon above this point "Lodore Cañon," for as the banks here are not over 400 ft. high the Major thinks we had better commence a new cañon at this point, but the cañon is really continuous and has now reached 25 miles. It has been the worst by far and I predict *the worst we shall ever meet.*

≈ NOTES

1. Triplet Falls and Hell's Half Mile.

A Canyon Voyage: The Narrative of the Second Powell Expedition

Frederick S. Dellenbaugh

AT AGE SEVENTEEN, FREDERICK DELLENBAUGH JOINED POWELL'S 1871 EXPEDITION, UNDERTAKEN TO REPLACE THE SCIENTIFIC DATA LOST DURING THE MISHAPS OF THE 1869 TRIP, AS THE OFFICIAL ARTIST, ALTHOUGH FEW OF HIS SKETCHES SURVIVED THE VOYAGE. THESE EXCERPTS FROM CHAPTERS 6 AND 7 OF DELLENBAUGH'S ACCOUNT DESCRIBE THE PASSAGE THROUGH THE UINTA BASIN, ENCOUNTERS WITH THE WHITE RIVER UTES, AND THE ENTRY TO DESOLATION CANYON.

Our thoughts now were mainly directed to pushing on to the mouth of the Uinta River and picking up our advance party,[1] which by this time must have gotten in touch with the Uinta Agency. We felt gratified that another of the long line of canyons was a thing of the past and that for a brief time we would have easy water, so far as rapids were concerned. We were reminded that this was Indian country by discovering on a smooth face of rock wall not far from camp a lot of drawings pecked into the stone. They represented figures of natives, bison, elk, deer, mountain sheep, grizzly tracks, etc., and as they were the first pictographs I had ever seen I was particularly interested. The bison pictures indicated the former presence here in this valley of that fine animal. Numbers indeed once ranged these hills and valleys, but they had all disappeared many years before our voyage. We were on the lookout for Indians. As long as we were encompassed by the mighty walls of the canyons there was little probability of our meeting with any of the original people of this soil, but the valley now opening wide before us was their favourite haunt. Two divisions of Utes roamed the surrounding region. On the west it was the Uinta Utes who, we knew, were peaceable, and on the east it was the White River Utes, whose status as to peace and war was at that period somewhat vague and uncertain. We expected no trouble with any of them, yet the possibility of running at any moment on a band gave added interest and colour to the voyage. This was intensified by the feeling that we had suddenly been thrown out of doors, unprotected, as the huge, dominating precipices broke so suddenly back on both sides, leaving us hardly a rock with which, in case of necessity, to emulate the example of Roderick Dhu.[2] Probably if we had traveled here on horseback in the open there would not have been this sense of having left our fortification behind.

July 12TH the boats proceeded down a river so sluggish that the term "down" seemed a misnomer, and we actually had to row; had to work at the oars to make the boats go; these same boats which so recently had behaved like wild horses. This was not to our taste at all, the weather being extremely hot. But there was no help for it. The boats fairly went to sleep and we tugged away at their dull, heavy weight, putting the miles behind and recalling the express-train manner of their recent action. On each side of us there were occasional groves of cottonwoods and wide bottoms bounded by low hills. After about ten miles of steady pulling we discovered that we were only 2 1/2 miles from our starting place in a straight line. Here there was a superb cottonwood grove, massive trees with huge trunks like oak, on the left. We found the remains of a camp-fire and decided that our advance party had come this far from Island Park the first day. They had accomplished a phenomenal run, but it showed what might be done with light boats and a full crew. As Steward desired to make some geological examinations at this point, Prof. announced that we would stay till morning.[3] Another cause for stopping was a gale which blew with great force, making rowing exceedingly hard work and it was hard enough anyhow with no good current to help.

Steward wished to go across the river, and I went with him. We tramped with our Winchesters on our shoulders for several hours, examining rocks and fossils. On our return we found that Andy was occupied in boiling a goose which Prof.'s sure aim had bestowed on the larder, and we had the bird for supper. If it was not one of the fossils it certainly was one of the "oldest inhabitants," which are found in every locality, and though a steady diet of bacon enthused us with an ambition to masticate this noble morsel, it had to be relegated to the impossibilities. We had a good deal of entertainment out of it, and while so engaged every ear caught the sound of a faint, distant gunshot. This was proof that we were no longer alone, and the question was, "How many Indians are there?" We simply waited developments. Night came and on and the fierce wind died away completely as the sun went down. We gave no more thought to the shot, but all went to bed without even leaving a watch, so confident was Prof. that there was no enemy, and no danger of a surprise. He was always "levelheaded" and never went off on a tangent doing wild or unwarranted things. He was a man of unusually sound judgment.

In the absence of Cap.[4] the duty of reading barometer had fallen to me, and sometimes, when waiting for the hour to arrive, I had to sit alone for a time when the others already had turned in. It was that way on this night, and I waited with some impatience for nine o'clock to come. For the purpose of reading the scale we used a small bull's-eye lantern belonging to a transit instrument, and it threw out a long beam of light. I entertained myself by flashing this beam in various directions to the distress of one member lying near not asleep, who was somewhat nervous as to the character of the Indians responsible for the shot.

"Confound it," he growled, "you'll have the whole Ute tribe down on us! You know they are not far off!"

Of course I desisted in my "signaling," but Prof., not yet asleep, spoke up saying he did not believe any Indians would bother us. Finishing the observations I put out the lantern, and settled in my blankets. At that instant there was the flash of a light through the trees and then it glowed steadily for a moment and went out. My nervous neighbour saw it too. "There," he cried, "an answer to your confounded signal!" Several saw it. "The evening star setting beyond the hill," they declared, derisively, but we two maintained that it was nothing less than a light near by. Then sleep ruled the camp. In the middle of the night there was a sudden terrific cracking, rending, and crashing, starting all to their feet except Clem,[5] who was not wakened by it. What had happened? We perceived in a second. One of the enormous limbs, weakened by the wind, had broken off and dropped to the ground in the middle of the camp. Luckily no one was under it and no harm was done, but for a moment, in connection with the light episode and the gunshot, it gave us a shock. Every one laughed, and soon the camp was still again. The sun was well up before we awoke. Immediately the discussion of the strange light came up, and it formed a lively and amusing topic, not only then, but ever after for months. Breakfast became a stirring debating scene, when plump into the midst of our hilarity, as if to emphasise the declarations of the nervous member, there came a sharp call from beyond a line of bushes. Almost on the instant appeared an Indian mounted on a dark bay horse trotting towards us exclaiming, "How, how!" and holding out his hands in token of friendship. His long black hair hung behind in two tails braided with red and black cotton cloth. The scalp at the part was painted vermilion, and around each eye was a ring of the same bright colour. His shirt was of the kind called hickory, and his leggings were of red woolen stuff. Altogether he was a good looking specimen of his race, and about twenty-five years old. How many more might be behind we could not tell.

He dismounted and Clem grasped him warmly by the hand, exclaiming with his most cordial smile, "Well, how are all the folks at home?" to which the visitor of course made no answer. Not one of our party understood Ute, and I had never seen a "wild" Indian at such close quarters before. The man motioned for something to eat, so Andy gave him a plate of breakfast, but there was a twinkle in Andy's blue eye, for the breakfast consisted largely of the rejected goose. When the red man's vision rested on the goose he gave a grunt of disgust and made no effort to even taste it, though he relished the other things and a cup of hot coffee. I have noticed that all Indians are very fond of coffee. We gleaned that he was alone with his squaw, and had a wickiup down the river a short distance. Doubtless he had examined our camp the previous night. The barometer hanging to a tree-branch caught his eye, and I tried by signs to explain it to him with no success except to convulse the whole crew. At length with the exclamation "Squaw," he rode away and came back with his fair partner riding behind. By this time we were packed up and we pushed off, the pair watching us with deep interest. About a mile and a half below the river, we came on them again at their camp, they having easily beaten us by a short cut. Here was his wickiup made of a few cottonwood boughs, and in front of it the ashes of a fire. Our side immediately claimed this was the light we had seen, and the discussion of this point continued until another night put an end to it. In the bough

Warrior and Bride, from Powell, *Exploration of
the Colorado River and Its Canyons.*

shelter sat the blooming bride of "Douglas Boy," as he called himself,
Douglas being the chief of the White River Utes. She was dressed well
in a neat suit of navy-blue flannel and was lavishly adorned with orna-
ments. Her dress was bound at the waist by a heavy belt of leather,
four inches wide, profusely decorated with brass discs and fastened by
a brass buckle. She was young and quite pretty, and they were a handsome couple. He intimated that he would be grateful to be ferried
across the river, here almost half a mile wide, so his blankets, saddles,
and whole paraphernalia were piled on the boats, while the two horses
were driven into the water and pelted with stones till they made up
their minds that the farther shore offered greater hospitality, and
swam for it. Then the squaw and the brave were taken on separate
boats. She hesitated long before finally trusting herself, and was exceedingly coy about it. She had probably never seen a boat before. At

last, overcoming her fear she stepped tremblingly on board and in a few minutes we had them landed on the other side, where we said farewell and went on.

In the afternoon we discovered a number of natives on the right bank and landed to see what they were. Nothing more terrible than several badly frightened squaws and children occupied the place, the men being away. We thought this call on the ladies would suffice, and presenting them with a quantity of tobacco for their absent lords, we pulled away, leaving them still almost paralysed with fright and astonishment at our sudden and unexpected appearance and disappearance. The valley was now very wide, and the river spread to a great width also, giving conditions totally different from any we had found above. Rowing was real labour here, but Prof. was eager to arrive at the mouth of the Uinta the next day so it was row, row, with a strong, steady, monotonous stroke, hour after hour till we had put twenty miles behind when we stopped for the night. Next morning the same programme was continued from seven o'clock on, with a brief halt for dinner. About four a storm came up, compelling us to wait an hour, when on we pulled, with a temperature something like 100° F., in the shade, till sunset, when about forty miles from our starting point, we arrived at the mouth of a river on the right, which we thought must be the Uinta. But finally as there was no sign of our advance party we concluded there must be a mistake. There was so little current in the tributary we thought it might be something besides a river, the mouth of a lake perhaps, and that the Uinta was farther on. About a mile down in the dim light there appeared to be a river mouth, but on reaching the place there was nothing of the kind. Several signal shots were fired. They fell dead on the dull stillness of the night which was dropping fast upon us. We took to the oars once more and pulled down nearly another mile till the dark grew so thick it was not prudent to proceed, and Prof. ordered a landing on the left where we made a hasty cup of coffee to refresh the inner man, and turned in, much puzzled and troubled by the absence of any kind of a signal from the advance party. Some one suggested that they had all been killed, but Prof. met this with scornful ridicule and went to sleep. When daylight came a river was discovered less than half a mile below our camp coming in from the east. Prof. knew this to be White River from the map, the mouths of White and Uinta rivers having long been quite accurately established. The mouth of the Uinta must therefore be where we had been the night before and Prof. walked back till he came opposite to it. We then got the boats back by rowing and towing, and landed on the right or west bank about a quarter mile above the mouth of the Uinta, where the old time crossing had been, and which we had passed unnoticed in the evening light. Here were the ashes of a camp-fire, and after much searching a tin can was found with a note in it from the major, saying they had all gone out to the Agency, and that we were to wait here.

A large cottonwood tree stood on the low bank where travelers before had camped, not in going up and down the river, but on their way across country. It was a very old tree and its bark presented many marks, names and dates, and I regret now that I did not copy them for reference. This was one of the known crossings for a long period, in fact, it was through this valley that Escalante, the first white man to cross Green River, traveled in 1776, and it is possible that he may have camped under this very tree. We settled there to wait, harassed by multitudes of voracious mosquitoes. All day we remained, expecting the absentees, but the sun went down and still there was no word. About seven o'clock while we were eating supper, some shots and yells from the west took us to the top of the bank, and we saw two horsemen galloping towards our position. We soon made them out to be Cap. and Jones. They brought a large mail, a portion of it the same we had tried to stop at Salt Lake, and have returned to us at the Gate of Lodore, and they reported that the Major had gone out to Salt Lake. We built up a good fire, and by its light every one was quickly lost in letters from home.

By 7:30 in the morning of August 7TH we were again on our way towards the depths ahead, between walls of rapidly increasing altitude showing that we were cutting into some great rock structure. Here and there we came to shoals that compelled us to get overboard and wade alongside lifting the boats at times. As these shoals had the peculiarity of beginning gradually and ending very abruptly we got some unexpected plunge baths during this kind of progression. But the air was hot, the thermometer being about 90° F., and being soaked through was not uncomfortable. At one place Prof. succeeded in shooting a beaver which was near the bank and it was secured before it could get to its hole, being badly wounded. Steward caught it around the middle from behind and threw it into the boat—he had jumped into the water—and there it was finished with an oar. It measured three feet from tip to tip. We had heard a good deal about a beaver as food would now have a chance to try it. About eleven o'clock, we stopped for examinations and for dinner on the right but, of course, could not yet cook the beaver. Prof., Steward, and Cap. climbed to the top of a butte 1050 feet above the river upon which they found a small monument left there by the major on the former trip. Though this butte was so high the average of the walls was only about five hundred feet. We made seventeen miles this day.

That night our camp (No. 35) was again on an island. There Cap skinned and dressed the beaver and turned over the edible portions to Andy who cooked some steak for breakfast the next morning. It tasted something like beef, but we were not enthusiastic for I fear this beaver belonged to the same geological epoch as the goose we had cooked at the upper end of the valley. Fortified by the beaver steak we pushed off and ran about a mile on a smooth river when a stop was made for pictures and geologising. This consumed the whole morning, a fact Andy took advantage of to make some beaver soup for dinner. This concoction was voted not a success and we turned to bacon and beans as preferable thereafter. Opposite this dinner place was a rough lateral canyon full of turrets and minarets which had the remarkable property of twice distinctly repeating a shout as loud as the original, and multiplying a rifle shot to peals of thunder. There had been people here before any white men, for Steward found an artificial wall across an indentation of the cliff, the first work of the ancient builders we had encountered. It was mysterious at the time, the South-western ruins having then not been discovered with one or two exceptions. We ascribed this wall, however, to the ancestors of the Moki (Hopi).

In the afternoon as we pulled along we came to a small rapid and the walls by this time being closer together and growing constantly higher, we knew that we were now fairly within the Canyon of Desolation and for about one hundred miles would have a rough river. Not more than two miles below our dinner camp we reached a locality where the stream doubled back on itself forming a vast and beautiful amphitheatre. We could not pass this by without taking a picture of it

Light-House Rock in the Canyon of Desolation,
from Powell, *Exploration of the Colorado River
and Its Canyons.*

and Beaman was soon at work with his apparatus while I got out my
pencils. The photograph did not turn out well, and Prof. determined
to remain till the next day. Our camp was on the left in a thick grove
of cottonwoods, and box-elders or ash-leaved maples, at the end of the
point. As the sun sank away bats flew about and an insect orchestra
began a demoniacal concert that shrilled through the night and made
us feel like slaughtering the myriads if we could. The noises ceased
with the day, or most of them, though some seemed to intensify with
the light. We helped Beaman get his dark box and other paraphernalia
up to the summit of the ridge back of camp, which was easy so far as
climbing was concerned, the rocks rising by a series of shelves or

steps. I made several pencil sketches there, which I have never seen since the close of the expedition. The crest of the promontory was about forty yards wide at its maximum and three yards at the minimum, with a length of three-fourths of a mile. From the middle ridge one could look down into the river on both sides, and it seemed as if a stone could almost be thrown into each from one standpoint. The opposite amphitheatre was perhaps one thousand feet high, beautifully carved by the rains and winds. It was named Sumner's Amphitheatre after Jack Sumner of the first expedition. Several of our men climbed in different directions, but all did not succeed in getting out. The day turned out very cloudy with sprinkles of rain and Prof. decided to wait still longer to see if Beaman could get a good photograph, and we had another night of insect opera. The next day by noon the photographer had caught the scene and we continued our descending way. The river was perfectly smooth, except a small rapid late in the day, with walls on both sides steadily increasing their altitude. Desolation in its beginning is exactly the reverse of Lodore and Split Mountain. In the latter the entrance could hardly be more sudden, whereas the Canyon of Desolation pushes its rock walls around one so diplomatically that it is some little time before the traveler realizes that he is caught. The walls were ragged, barren, and dreary, yet majestic. We missed the numerous trees which in the upper canyons had been so ornamental wherever they could find a footing on the rocks. Here there were only low shrubs as a rule and these mainly along the immediate edge of the water, though high up on north slopes pines began to appear. Altitude, latitude, and aridity combine to modify vegetation so that in an arid region one notices extraordinary changes often in a single locality. The walls still had the tendency to break into turrets and towers, and opposite our next camp a pinnacle stood detached from the wall on a shelf high above the water suggesting a beacon and it was named Lighthouse Rock. Prof. with Steward and Cap. in the morning, August 11TH, climbed out to study the contiguous region which was found to be not a mountain range but a bleak and desolate plateau through which we were cutting along Green River toward a still higher portion. This was afterwards named the Tavaputs Plateau, East and West divisions, the river being the line of separation.

≋≋ NOTES

1. Powell had gone ahead of the rest in the *Emma Dean* and had arranged to meet them at the Uinta River, where the Uinta Indian Agency was located.

2. A character in Sir Walter Scott's *The Lady of the Lake*.

3. John F. Steward, a Civil War veteran and amateur geologist; Prof. Almon Harris Thompson, Powell's brother-in-law and second in command of the expedition.

4. Captain Francis M. Bishop, a former teacher at Illinois Normal School.

5. Clements Powell, the major's cousin.

"Queen Ann" of Brown's Park

Ann Bassett Willis

THE BASSETT FAMILY WERE AMONG THE EARLIEST PERMANENT SET-
TLERS IN BROWN'S PARK, ARRIVING IN 1877. ANN AND HER SISTER,
JOSIE, GREW UP TO BE TOUGH, INDEPENDENT-MINDED WOMEN, AND
BOTH WERE RUMORED TO HAVE BEEN INVOLVED WITH FREQUENT
BROWN'S PARK VISITOR BUTCH CASSIDY. IN THE FOLLOWING EX-
CERPTS FROM A FOUR-PART ARTICLE PUBLISHED IN THE *Colorado
Magazine* IN 1952–53, ANN REMINISCES ABOUT THE UTE INDIANS
WHO HELPED RAISE HER AND THE OUTLAWS KNOWN TO LOCALS AS
"THAT WILD BUNCH FROM BROWN'S HOLE."

It was before our house was built, while my parents were living
with Uncle Sam Bassett, that I was born, in Brown's Park, Routt
County, Colorado, in the year 1878. Dr. Parsons attended my
mother. By all reports it looked pretty tough for me. There was no
mother's milk and some source of food had immediately to be provided.

A tribe of Ute Indians were camped about two hundred yards
from the cabin, among these was an Indian mother, See-a-baka, who
had a new-born papoose. Buffalo Jack Rife, good old "Buff," spoke
their language like a Ute, so after consultation with Dr. Parsons, he
held a pow-wow with Chief Marcisco and Medicine Man Mucha-qua-
gant, "Star." After making considerable medicine and sign talk, it was
decided to permit the squaw to become my wet nurse and me to
become a foster twin to her papoose, a boy named Kab-a-weep, meaning Sunrise.

Indians do not coddle newborn infants by covering the head. I've
been told it was storming when they carried me to the Indian wickiup, and I can imagine how I must have blinked and grimaced as the
snow settled on my little face.

It was the custom of the Indians to move from the river bottoms
where they wintered, to cooler summer camp grounds on the moun-

tain tops. For that reason my Uncle Sam built the "double cabins" for
mother at the head of Willow Creek, so she could be near my foster
mother. To this cabin See-a-baka came at regular intervals to feed me.
I nursed her for six months, until cow's milk could be provided. It was
Judge Conway who rounded up a milk cow and presented her to me,
so I got into the cow business at a decidedly early age.

I've often wondered if more than milk was not imparted through
those months of feeding. Certainly during all my remembered life I
have cherished for Indians a definite friendliness, a sympathy and understanding of them which I do not believe is common. I also have
learned that they are superior to many whites in both behavior and
standard of morals.

My father, Herbert Bassett, was born at Bridgewater, Herkmer
County, New York. From there he moved to Springfield, Illinois,
where he taught school prior to the Civil War. At the breaking out of
war, he joined what were known as "Lincoln's Own Volunteers" in
1861. Father had a decided musical bent and could play various instruments. He became a leader of the company band and served continu-
ously until 1865. After the war he was appointed Collector of Internal
Revenue for the United States Government at Norfolk, Virginia.
There he met Mary Elizabeth Chamberlain, a grand-daughter of Judge
Crawford Miller. They were married in 1868 and moved to Little
Rock, Arkansas. In 1871 they started on the final stage of their jour-
ney westward, looking to California as their goal. Coming by train to
Rock Springs, Wyoming, they stopped there to meet and visit my
father's brother, Samuel Clark Bassett. He had been employed by the
United States Government since the early 1850s as a scout along the
Overland Trail through Wyoming to Salt Lake City, Utah. And he is
one of the first pioneers my memory can introduce into the history of
Brown's Park.

In 1847 Joseph Herrara, a political refugee from Santa Fe, New
Mexico, obtained maps and records of early expeditions and with his
brother Pablo, and other Spaniards, went in search of the valley of the
Green River. The camp site of earlier explorers was located east of
Vermillion Creek in the Escalante Hills. And among relics picked up
there was an old musket, which was taken to Herrara's headquarters
at Joe Springs, now the Bassett Ranch.

When Joseph Herrara arrived at Green River, he met other white men, among them Jim and John Baker and Jimmie Reed. All were trappers who wintered in the mild climate where the great herds of roaming wild game furnished ample food. There also was available a plentiful supply of the valuable white swan skins. "Bible-back Brown," a French trapper, had strongly recommended the sheltered valley as being a good place to "hole up" for the winter. From this the name "Brown's Hole" became fixed.

Samuel Clark Bassett's Diary for 1852 and 1854 contains some notations of interest. For instance:

"Brown's Hole." November, the month of Thanksgiving. 1852 Louie[1] and I down in. Packs off. Mules in lush meadows. Spanish Joe's trail for travel could not be likened to an "up state" high land, suitable for coach and four.

Mountains to right of us, not in formation but highly mineralized. To the south a range of uncontested beauty of contour. Its great stone mouth drinking a river.

Called on our neighbors, lest we jeopardize our social standing, "Chief Catump" and his tribe of Utes. "Male and Female created He them" and Solomon in all his glory was not arrayed so fine. Beads, bones, quills and feathers of artistic design. Buckskin tanned in exquisite coloring of amazing hues, resembling velvet of finest texture. Bows and arrows. "Let there be no strife between thee and me."

SAMUEL CLARK BASSETT

A later entry in the diary reads:

"Brown's Hole," June 22, 1854

Warren D. Parsons and his wife Annie have arrived. And our first white squaw, "Snapping Annie," is expertly driving her slick oxen, Turk and Lion. "Whoa, Turk!" and "Gee, Lion!" Commanded by a female bullwhacker. "Houri" tells me that "Man's freedom in this Paradise is doomed."

SAMUEL CLARK BASSETT

(Bassett was a confirmed bachelor)

Some writers have conveyed the impression that white women were in the Park at an earlier date, at Fort Davy Crockett (Camp Misery), the old fort on Dummy Bottom. But Joseph Herrara, Jim Baker and others definitely reported "No white women in the Hole until Snapping Annie Parsons came."

From a country to the northward and far on towards the sunset, flows the mighty Green River. In northwestern Colorado and northeastern Utah lies Brown's Park, along both sides of the river, and comprising an area approximately sixty miles long and from five to twenty miles in width. This is Colorado's western extremity of the vast cattle and sheep range which extends eastward one hundred and fifty miles, to the slopes of the Continental Divide.

To the east and north of the Park is Cold Spring Mountain, where sarvis berries grow in moist, shady nooks beneath the tall quaking aspens, and pine trees dot the mountain meadows with emerald islands. Westward is the forbidding wall of Diamond Mountain, with Wild Mountain alongside. Douglas Mountain on the south is bounded by the great canyon on the Green River, the entrance to which reminds one of Southey's poem, "How the water comes down at Lodore." Major John Wesley Powell, the intrepid adventurer who first navigated the Green and Colorado Rivers from source to outlet, gave this canyon the name Lodore.

During the summer of 1869, two wealthy English noblemen, Sir Griffeth W. Edwards and his brother John G., with Judge Asbury B. Conway, of Boston, drove the first domestic cattle into Brown's Park. As a cowboy with this herd, came the unforgettable character, Buffalo Jack Rife. These men established headquarters with the Herrara brothers at Pablo and Joe Springs, at the foot of the Awaikuts Mountain, locally known by the name of Cold Springs Mountain. Twenty miles to the south a summer place was built at Douglas Springs, from which Buffalo Jack gave the name Douglas to the range of mountains from the Snake and Yampa Rivers to the Green.

In that same year the Edwards cattle were followed by those of Frank ("Granny") Hoy. He located on the abundant natural meadows along the Green River. Hoy's nephews, Valentine, Harry and Ade Hoy, later bought the business started thus by their Uncle Frank. The Griff Edwards and Frank Hoy herds were the beginning of the cattle in Brown's Park. Judge Conway engaged in the raising of fine horses, using imported stock. The result was an extensive and lucrative business.

While the Bassetts were in Rock Springs, Wyoming, which was the typical railroad distributing point for north, south, east, and west, they met other adventurous families on their way to what they regarded as the promised land. From this group composed of New England farmers, people from the eastern part of the United States, Herbert Bassett heard rumors of a lovely valley, a mysterious spot beyond the mountains. Winters there were mild, it was said, and wild game fleeing before the storms found refuge there. It was a place where cottonwoods grew to immense size, shading parks that spread like lawns from the river to the sandy hills at the base of the mountains. And this tempting Eden was known as "Brown's Hole."

Later when my mother glimpsed the richly green, natural meadows, and the groves of stately, wide-branched cottonwoods, she was reminded of a beautiful park in the eastern land where she was born. At once she re-christened the lovely valley, "Brown's Park."[2]

We are told and we read extensively of the sufferings and struggles of the pioneers who first occupied the various parts of our West. Sometimes I wonder if some of this is not the product of sentimentalists and sobsters, who encourage their imaginations to embroider all pioneering experience with the dark colorings applicable to some. Certainly this band of first settlers enjoyed their journeying into Brown's Park. There was green grass and thickly blooming wild flowers. They traveled on full stomachs, for there were buffalo, deer, antelope, and elk always to be had for the cost of a shot. Other good things filled their supply store. They were not poverty stricken nor were they obliged to push handcarts.[3] They rode all the way in their Peter Shutler wagons.

I had the privilege of living in a bronco West, and began life as a cow hand at the mature age of six. In a roomy out doors where cow critters spread themselves over the grass valleys and sage brush hills of southern Wyoming and northwestern Colorado as far as the eyes could see. I attended the great round-ups held on open terrain, when the vast expanse of milling, bellowing cattle were worked, cut out and branded. They were handled without confusion by men trained to work, to make instant decisions, and who had the individualism to act in any emergency.

The cattle business joined me in interest with the Texas cowboys of the early eighties. Men with clean minds, and able bodies disciplined by physical exercise to do any job well. Putting in time and a half, and over time, was an essential feature of their training. For them, there was no such limitation as an eight hour day.

Cowboys held womenkind in high esteem. Conversational passes and barbed jokes aimed at the opposite sex, were decidedly out of range dictum. Good horses and the best equipment were a cowboy's pride. They stuck to their chosen profession, they would not flank hay or grub sage brush. The charm of their picturesque lives has gone on in song and story, exciting and appealing to the human emotion as no other profession has ever done. I am deeply grateful to those who captured the spell and have kept alive the profound meaning of a cowboy's life on the range.

This country, itself undergoing the processes of birth, developed a new generation radically different from their New England ancestors, and presenting a problem that kept the parents in a state of mental agitation. We were completely western by birth and environment, actively disliking anything that resembled a pattern.

I turned a deaf ear to mother's long-winded lectures upon the conduct of, and correct clothing for, "little ladies," and early adopted buckskin breeches for my personal use. Capering about on a skittish bronc, plastered to a lopsided contraption called a side-saddle, while swathed in yard-long riding togs was not my idea of frolic. I cared not a whit for social customs, and could not understand a world designed especially for privileged little boys to romp in, to enjoy sports and play, sternly denied to "little ladies." With spirit and determination I wore my befringed, buckskin breeches. My point was difficult to prove in a puritanical sphere where girl's legs were strictly hush-hush, and anything resembling trousers for women or girls taboo.

Imagine my mother's disturbance of mind! Her own outfit consisted of a beautifully fitted "habit" of rich, dark blue material, long skirted and draped with grace. For trimming there was a number of gleaming brass buttons. She was a blonde, five feet, six-and-a-half inches tall. Mounted on her thoroughbred saddle horse, "Calky," she was a picture to remember.

There can be no question that pants were more suitable riding gear, but the grown-up's agony over such "disgraceful" apparel was pathetic. However—the buckskins won out. The result was an unbridle-wised revolter from custom, riding straddle-back in a no-woman's sphere, amidst dust or mud, and steers. I was not a romantic, inspirational number but a perfect "burr in a saddle blanket" to cowpunchers. But I brushed off ridicule. My ambitions were centered upon ability to flank a calf or stick a wild cow's head through a loop, as neatly as any of them.

When haying time drew near, the summer of 1884, father sent a wagon to Rock Springs for hands. With the crew of haymakers that came to the ranch was Elza Lay, a well bred appearing young fellow with a winning smile and perfect manners. He was a capable workman, strong and active, with a gentle good-nature that won the hearts of old and young alike. Elza remained on the ranch for a year and he was the only young easterner who was never bitten by the "cowboy bug."

Young men by the score came to the western ranches. At one time father had for adjustment a Clark and a Converse, sons of the well known railroad magnates, boys that had gotten out from under parental control by having too much money to spend. They were all good boys, but none were as generally liked as Elza Lay. When the year was up he went back to Rock Springs. Not long afterward rumor circulated that he had joined forces with Butch Cassidy, and that they were carrying on a series of bank and train robberies.

Elza and Butch returned to Brown's Park at times, but we did not pry into affairs concerning their private lives, for we were not the instigators of the short cut to riches Elza was taking, and we did not channel the course he had set.

Friendly relations between the Brown's Parkers and the bank robbers caused a great deal of comment. The question has frequently been asked "How could a people permit themselves to harbor committers of crime without becoming involved in the deals." The answer is simple. We were in a constant struggle to protect our own interests on the range where our living was at stake. Bank robbers were not a menace to personal interests, and we had no reason to carry the ball for the banks and trains. We had a fair sized job to do in itself. Law officers were elected and paid by the taxpayers to assume jurisdiction over legal matters in the country.

We had accepted Elza Lay as our friend. And friendship among those pioneers was no light bond. Because he had with youthful fool-hardiness stepped into the limelight of crime, seemed insufficient reason to desert him. That breaking of the law could not contaminate us, unless we permitted it to do so. And we believed that possibly, given time, true friendship might become a substitute for the excitement of robbery. This was not a futile gesture. In the end, its purpose was accomplished.

Dishonest financiers had robbed Elza Lay's widowed mother of an inheritance. His lust for vengeance started Elza on his career of crime. This neither remedied the evil nor worked any change in conditions, outside of altering his own life into one of shame and misery. He lost incalculable time from his best years and brought untold sorrow and anxiety to his family before he made a fresh beginning. When that change was accomplished, he held a good position in Southern California and proved himself to be the possessor of sterling qualities. He educated his children, who became successful and respected citizens.

Butch Cassidy's name was associated with Elza Lay's and Cassidy also is concerned with these old Brown's Park memories, though the story I can relate of him differs, particularly in its ending, from that of Elza.

During the year 1886, Charley Crouse of the Park, and Ken Hatch of Vernal, Utah, matched a race between Hatch's black mare and a sorrel gelding belonging to Crouse. This race was run on an old Indian track on one of the Valentine Hoy ranches. Racing fans may assemble in greater numbers at Churchill Downs, but never could they have gathered at spur of keener interest and excitement than did those who then assembled in Brown's Park. Betting ran high and the atmosphere was taut.

When the thoroughbred gelding appeared on the track, he was ridden by a slender, brown-haired young fellow of about nineteen years. Small for his age he was a quiet, unobtrusive chap. Hearing rumors of this projected horse race, he had come to Crouse's ranch a few days previously. Crouse had sized him up with favor and hired him as jockey. And he rode the Brown's Park horse to a glorious victory. We were tremendously proud of that racer, he not only could run, but he was a handsome animal. His rider was hailed with enthusiastic acclaim. He modestly told us his name was Ed Cassidy. Later he became widely known as "Butch" Cassidy, outlaw.

A dancing party was given at the Charles Allen Ranch to celebrate the winning of the race. The youthful jockey stabled the horse, joined us at supper, then went quietly to bed, without sharing in the jubilant merrymaking that went on until dawn streaked the sky.

He continued to work for Charley Crouse for a year, then went away. He was always well mannered. I never saw Butch Cassidy drunk nor wearing a gun—in sight. I have no personal knowledge of any of his deeds of outlawry, but I do know that he never lived in the Park after he was "wanted" by the law. Occasionally he came that way, stopping for a meal, or over night at different ranches. But he took no part in the social life, nor ever attended a party after that which followed the race. Within a few years tales came back to us of his train and bank robberies.

Cassidy had not harmed nor otherwise bothered the people of our neighborhood. If the law officers wanted him, it was their place to take him, not ours. But if the Law wished to come into our country and make such an arrest not one hand would have been raise to protect an outlaw.

Everyone knew there was a large reward offered for the capture of Butch, dead or alive. I AM PROUD TO SAY NOT ONE OF US WANTED THAT KIND OF MONEY! We had no commendation nor excuse for his "profession," but we knew that his life was an unfortunate one, a hard, unhappy existence.

That is what I personally know of the notorious Butch Cassidy—whose exploits are a favorite topic of all the old liars, young liars and damn liars in the northwest, southwest, and as far away as South America, some of whom claimed either to have killed him or to have seen him die. If anyone knows how Butch Cassidy met death, be sure they have never told.

He never robbed anybody in the Park, he appeared there only when of necessity, passing from Utah to Wyoming. He was often seen in Baggs and other Wyoming towns, and in Vernal, Utah, according to fairly well authenticated reports. Why was he not taken into custody by the law, in any of these places? And why were those towns not censured for sheltering him?

If an outlaw is at some time in a certain community, is that sound reason for widespread condemnation of all the inhabitants of that section?

Brown's Park, because of its location geographically, was a natural stopping place for regular travelers of the country and for strangers. We had no padlocks on our doors and the latch string hung outside. To place money value on a meal was never done. If anyone arrived at mealtime, he was naturally supposed to eat, just as any one of us would do, if we came to a ranch at such an hour; it was not expected that travelers should furnish their genealogy and past history when they appeared at the Park. People of all types came and went in the ordinary transaction of their business. On the whole, we kept our noses out of the affairs of other people as well as most frontier communities did.

I knew several of the so-called "Badmen." Some of them were bad. That is, they were criminals, wanted to be tough and were tough. They were not welcome in our neighborhood, yet they were treated with courtesy and fed, as we would any other human being who came there. Men like Cassidy and Elza Lay were decidedly not of this type. It is my firm belief, which I know is shared by many others, that the utmost bad taste and ingratitude—to state it mildly—were shown by certain men who came later to Brown's Park. These men were sheltered in our homes, treated in friendly manner, were fed and cared for, and went away as they came, unquestioned. They sailed under false colors, disguised their purpose, and misrepresented their motives in coming there, later writing and publishing what purported to be an authentic and general history of the Park. This supposedly true description of people and events was compiled without regard for truth, correct dates or historical accuracy on any point. Certainly more respect is due men of the type of Butch Cassidy and Elza Lay, who were frankly what they were and carried on no underhand schemes, than those bearers of false tales. These self-elected chroniclers of events, with self-authorized judgment, acquitted a hired assassin who was legally convicted and hanged for the proven murder of an innocent boy. And those writers place a character of that type on a pedestal and shout "Glory, glory," while they class hospitable, law-abiding citizens as criminals, people whose food they have eaten.

Butch Cassidy and Elza Lay were known to have often made headquarters in Vernal, Utah, the home of the Super-Man Sheriff Pope. Elza married one of the girls of Pope's "home town." It is a well known fact that Pope never arrested either of these men, whom he knew personally. According to history which has been satisfactorily authenticated, Cassidy and Lay were notorious bank and train robbers, successful at obtaining large sums of money by that method. Is their success the answer to this failure to effect their capture? Is that the reason it was said that Butch had "just stepped out of the door," when Sheriff Pope was supposed to have attempted such an arrest? Nearly every locality in the west that I have seen or visited has characters about whom have been woven a tale that has been told and retold, added to with each telling until the character and his or her exploits exceed those of fiction thrillers in luridness. These characters, if by some strange freak of unknown Powers, were brought face to face with their fiction counterparts, would not know themselves. If the shades of Jesse James, Bill Hickok, Billy the Kid, or Butch Cassidy should emerge from the shadows, be able to see what I have seen, hear what I heard, and read what I have read, I am sure their comments would be interesting—possibly not printable!

In the 1870s Indians had not yet been put on reservations as "Subjugated People." They were still free to roam over meadows which had been their home for centuries. Utes, with a few of the Sioux Tribe, were living in Brown's Park when the white settlers came. Their rights were unquestioned by the colonists, who "tendered unto Indians the thinks [*sic*] that belonged to Indians," thus avoiding racial disagreement. When whites were being massacred sixty miles to the Eastward (a tragedy brought about largely by their bigotry and hypocritical fanaticism)[4] the Brown's Parkers felt no uneasiness. Chief Maracisco [*sic*] had assured them they would not be molested, and they were not. They did not practice intolerance, nor belittle the cleverness and knowledge of a people who had survived for generations while wresting their living from the natural resources of that country.

From our Indian friends we learned many helpful lessons. They taught us the use of medicinal herbs, the art of lying on game trails to select the fat, desirable meat. And, most important, how to make "jerkey." Another valuable lesson was in the use of marrow in tanning skins, to make them soft and unshrinkable. We learned how to insure comfort when sleeping on the ground, by making a slight depression in the earth and covering this with leaves and bits of bark.

One of the Utes said of mother: "Bassett's squaw all-time talk, maybe so Magpie." I am glad to remember that "Magpie" whom they regarded as their "Great White Squaw and heap good friend," never let them down. Never did she fail to respect their dignity and human rights.

How wonderful if one could wipe out the false recording of "clatter-boned, goose-quill wranglers," disguised as honest historians, who have too often taken over a subject wholly unfamiliar to them, settling in motion waves of misrepresentation regarding the American Indian.

How many of these tales depict the trials and tribulations endured by the Utes when subjected to the dominion of the Government Agent, Meeker? His plowing up of the race track which the Indians had made? This man, supposed to be representing a free government, where personal liberty is placed high, was determined to force these hunters of deer and tanners of buckskin to raise "tame" hay for their ponies, when the hills were covered with a rich growth of bluestem. The Indians well knew that was better feed for horses than any tame hay ever produced. Meeker's coercion appeared senseless.

In later years when agents were sent out from Washington to take charge of the wild game and police the Indians, they seemed like foreigners. Their ways were strange, not only to the Indians, but to the whites who were living in neighborly fashion with the red people. The restrictions that were imposed appeared totally uncalled for. Wild game was plentiful. We took only what we needed and used that without wastefulness. To the eastward, on the more accessible ranges, it is true that game was lavishly slaughtered by white-faced "market" hunters, to be sold in great quantities, without regard to the preservation of our game species. That was not true in the region of Brown's Park.

When the game wardens came to take the Indians from their hunting grounds, as they did on Little Snake River, about forty miles distant, word was sent among the Utes to "get rid of the meat" if they had any.

This message was carried by white folks, the friends of the Indians. And when the game-smellers came, there was no meat to be found. The wardens were disappointed and angered at the failure of their mission. They scattered the equipment and supplies belonging to the Indians. They were arrogant and overbearing. Many times have I wondered, would the wardens have been so bold had the Indian men been in camp?

But of course, they were brave men, these whites, backed by the strong arm of the Law, shaking a threatening fist instead of extending a hand from the Great White Father in Washington. A Ute squaw subjected to the rough treatment attempted to defend her family and personal property. When she protested a brutal attack on a young boy, these brave Americans shot and killed her. After shooting the woman, they hung the boy by his hands and emptied their guns into his body. Through such representatives was the Law sent to the Indians of Western Colorado.

The eloquent evidence of the manner through which this arm of the law operated, was not a true representation of our form of Government. It was the act of crackpots, moving in the shelter of misplaced power. Perhaps they had listened to the tales of other uninformed persons and were too stupid or too lazy to obtain factual information for themselves. They certainly had no comprehension of the words fairness and justice.

The Snake River slaughter of Indians was stopped by the timely arrival of Henry Templeton, a resident of that section, a man of understanding and decisive character. He courageously interfered with the perpetrators of law-protected villainy, and later played an active role in securing the dismissal from the Service of these misfit agents. Circumstances entirely disassociated from the game law enforcement put me on the scene during one of the resultant incidents. That summer Beth Brown was at the Bassett Ranch. She was a city girl who so loved ranch life that she spent her vacations cowgirling with our outfit. She became a good hand with stock, too. Father had sold Jim Norvel a bunch of cattle, and these were to be delivered at the Thompson Ranch on Little Snake River. When Sam Bassett set out with the herd, Beth and I accompanied him. Arrived at the Thompson's, Sam went on to Big Gulch with the cattle, but Beth and I remained to look after the extra saddle horses until he returned. And that was the time the Government game wardens had chosen to start the row with the Utes over the killing of deer out of season.

After their raid, these extraordinary government executives came to the Thompson Ranch. And never again do I want to witness such yellow cowardice as those men exhibited in their attempt to make a hasty getaway, leaving the ranch families to face the irate Indians alone. I was exceedingly keen to have the culprits turned over to the fighting braves, who got on their trail. A more levelheaded majority ruled otherwise. And Mrs. Thompson took charge of the rescue of the game wardens. Aunty Thompson took her everready shotgun, her two babies and her blind mother, and driving her swift team of mules, gave the cowering agents free-wheeling to safety in the little town of Maybell. They rode in the wagon box, concealed beneath a thick covering of hay.

They had argued unsuccessfully with Beth to induce her to go with them. She had insisted upon returning to the Bassett Ranch with me, though the mere sight of an Indian would give poor Beth the shivers. I knew that after the wardens had retreated to the Thompson Ranch for shelter, it was no place for See-a-baka's white papoose. Slapping on our saddles with all speed, we lit out for Brown's Park over the Boone Trail, thirty-three miles to go, through hills scattered thickly with Utes on the war path, sending up their alarming signal fires as they prepared for their scalp harvest. I hadn't much fear in passing near these fires, for I was confident the sharp trained eyes of the Indians would recognize the pinto horse and its girl rider. I had many friends among these redmen, but I was less sure of the safety of my companion.

As we rode, I instructed Beth what to do if by chance we were run down and her capture was attempted. If we saw any approaching Indians, she was to bolt for the cedars and hide herself. She was to remain perfectly still until the afternoon of the next day, then slip through broken country to the Bassett Ranch, with out trying to find me. Such an attempt would certainly lead smack into trouble.

It was growing dark when we reached the top of the divide, too dark to see any distance. We suddenly heard horses' hoofs running towards us down the slope of a hill. Beth instantly ducked into the timber, while I rode out to meet the clattering horses. They proved to be merely a bunch of range animals, running out to meet and look us over, then race off again, as such often did.

I rode back to the place where Beth had slid into hiding. I called and whistled and went round and round among the dark cedars receiving no reply. At last, I decided to tie up, and bed down until morning. My horse didn't take to that, for he had smelled out the hiding place of his pard, Beth's horse. I gave him his head and he found her. She had heard me calling, but had feared it was some trick of the Indians, so did not answer, but crept deeper into her hiding place, until convinced that it was really I, trying to find her. Also, that I was alone, without Indian companions.

We proceeded on toward home and had gone about five miles when we heard a horse coming behind us. From the regular hoof beats, without a stop, I knew that horse was being ridden. I got off and put my ear to the ground to be sure of it. That time we hid together. The horseman passed us without pausing, and when he was near, we could hear the squeaking of new leather.

He was going our way, so we followed for about a quarter of a mile. The horse fell into a tired lope, that lagged more and more. I was sure the unseen rider was not an Indian, for in those days they had no leather stock saddles. Turning aside into the shadow of a near cliff wall, we whistled to him.

When he replied to the signal and came close to us, we were considerably surprised to recognize Walt Nisbet, a grocery salesman from Denver, who had been in our country taking orders for a firm in that city. Walt and his companion had been traveling in a buggy on the Templeton Mesa, when they were overtaken by Aunty Thompson and her load of terrified government officials. When Nisbet learned of the dangerous trip Beth was making with me, he unhitched his team, saddled one of them and hied it to the Thompson Ranch as fast as he could go. He was without weapon, and the wardens refused to give him one of their guns. But that did not deter him.

He reached the ranch about dark, his horse spent from its ten-mile race. When he spied horses grazing near the corral he decided to secure a fresh mount. He selected one with saddle marks on its back, for somebody had told Walt that was an indication of a gentle animal. However, in that case, the marks were misleading. He got Bill Snort, an outlaw none of the cowboys could stay on. The horse had gotten his marks when he threw off a bronco buster and ran around on the range for a week, before the peeler caught him and could get the saddle off.

We kept him in the cavvy for a bed-horse because he was so easy to handle, if no one tried to ride him.[5] Just when Nisbet hit the saddle the Utes opened fire on him and Bill Snort let loose. He was a tough bucker. But with bullets flying around him Nisbet had to stick. He was lucky to be off balance, when one shot passed through the cantle of the saddle and landed in the fork, and another ripped off a part of his jacket while he was desperately clinging to some part of the gear. He took a terrific roughing, but he did not let fighting Indians nor a frantically bucking horse check him. He came in hot pursuit of Beth.

They had met several times that summer, and each was much impressed by the other. When they recognized each other, Walt sprang from the saddle and they went into a clinch, absolutely forgetting anything but themselves. While they stayed in an ecstatic daze, muttering what sounded to me like sticky nonsense, I walked over to inspect poor Bill Snort. As I did so, his wobbling legs relaxed, and he toppled over dead. His strong heart had given out.

I removed the saddle sadly and hung it on a cedar. I had known Bill Snort a long time, and had considerable respect for his cunning. It was really an impressive spectacle to watch him unseat self-confident bronc busters who took every advantage of him with ropes, bits and spurs. He won over every trick and contraption they could contrive, leaving them on the ground to wonder how they got off.

I felt no great elation over Nisbet and his narrow escape, although he was a daring young fellow who had exhibited a lump of real nerve in braving all odds against him to find Beth. Of course, I did admire him for that courage, even if he had used the poorest of judgment by running into an almost certain gunfight, minus a shooting iron.

Beth and I had eaten nothing since a five o'clock breakfast the morning before. Going at a fast jolt had got me edgy and I let out a frosty link of words to untangle the cooing pigeons. I advised them to hop on Beth's horse and be moving, if we wanted to beat the Utes to the Bassett Ranch in time for breakfast. It was eight miles to chuck, and quite evident that Beth and Walter intended to go double in future, so they just as well start right away.

Father enthused over Nisbet's bravery and his fortunate escape from Indian gunfire. Commonplace human affairs were exciting to father, when he approved. He was an incurable romantic, and did not care a whoop about the loss of Bill Snort, when there was a love-knot to be tied.

A couple of thick steaks and ten hours sleep transformed my flustered self to something like normal. Father wrote a report and sent our depositions to the Indian Department. Within a few weeks Beth and I were called to testify before the Indian Affairs Committee, at Washington, D.C., and again to repeat the same testimony before a committee representing the Indian Department in Denver.

Complete destruction of the Thompson ranch buildings and several casualties suffered by the settlers resulted from this unforgivable blundering of officials, who should have exercised judgment instead of giving free rein to their own self conceit and ignorance.

After the investigation was completed, which took several months, the Washington agents who committed the heinous crime against the Indians were dismissed from government service. The incident couldn't so readily be dismissed from memory. It marked a still further widening of the gulf between redmen and white.

≋ NOTES

1. The "Louie" referred to here was Louis Simmons, Kit Carson's son-in-law. (Willis's note.)

2. Actually Powell had already "rechristened" Brown's Hole—he refers to it as Brown's Park throughout chapter 6 of *The Exploration of the Colorado River and Its Canyons,* published two years before the Bassetts arrived.

3. A reference to the Mormon emigrants who traveled on foot from Illinois to Utah, many of whom died en route.

4. A reference to the Meeker massacre of 1879.

5. "Cavvy"—the horse herd. A "bed-horse" is presumably one that helps stabilize the herd.

Through the Grand Canyon from Wyoming to Mexico

Ellsworth Kolb

IN 1911 PHOTOGRAPHERS ELLSWORTH AND EMERY KOLB RAN THE
GREEN AND COLORADO RIVERS FROM GREEN RIVER, WYOMING,
TO NEEDLES, CALIFORNIA (THEY DID NOT ACTUALLY REACH MEX-
ICO) TO MAKE THE FIRST MOTION PICTURE RECORD OF THE TRIP.
THE FOLLOWING SELECTIONS FROM ELLSWORTH KOLB'S BOOK DE-
PICT THE DIFFICULTIES OF FILMING WHILE SHOOTING THE RAPIDS,
MEMORABLE INHABITANTS OF THE RANCHES IN BROWN'S PARK, AND
THE WONDERS OF THE LANDSCAPE SURROUNDING THE CONFLUENCE
OF THE GREEN AND COLORADO.

Camp routine was hurriedly disposed of the next morning, Saturday, September the 23d. Everything was made snug beneath the hatches, except the two guns, which were too long to go under the decks, and had to be carried in the open cockpits. "Camp No. 13, at the head of Lodore", as it is entered in my journal, was soon hidden by a bend in the river. The open, sun-lit country, with its pleasant ranches and grazing cattle, its rolling, gray, sage-covered hills and its wild grass and cottonwood-covered bottoms, was left behind, and we were back in the realm of the rock-walled canyon, and beetle-browed, frowning cliffs with pines and cedars clutching at the scanty ledges.

We paused long enough to make a picture or two, with the hope that the photographic record would give to others some idea of the geological and scenic wonder—said to be the greatest known example of its kind—which lay before us. Here is an obstructing mountain raised directly in the river's path. Yet with no deviation whatever the stream has cut through the very centre of the peak! The walls are almost sheer, especially at the bottom, and are quite close together at the top. A mile inside, the mountain on the left or east side of the gorge is 2700 feet high. Geologists say that the river was here first, and that the mountain was slowly raised in its pathway—so slowly that the river could saw away and maintain its old channel. The quicksand found below the present level would seem to indicate that the walls were once even higher than at present, and that a subsidence had taken place after the cutting.

The river at the entrance of this rock-walled canyon was nothing alarming, four small rapids being passed without event. Then a fifth was reached that looked worse. The *Edith* was lined down. This was hard work, and dangerous too, owing to the strength of the current and the many rocks; so I concluded that my own boat, the *Defiance,* must run the rapid. Jimmy went below, with a life-preserver on a rope. Emery stood beside the rapid with a camera and made a picture as I shot past him. Fortunately I got through without mishap. I refused to upset even to please my brother.

MONDAY, THE 25TH, found us at the same camp. Having concluded that Disaster Falls was an ideal place for a moving picture, we sent the balance of the material across on the pulley and wire, making a picture of the operation; stopping often because it continued to shower. Between showers we resumed our work and picture making.

The picture was to have been concluded with the operation of lining the boat across. E. C. [Emery] stood on the shore about sixty feet away, working the camera; Jimmy was on the island,[1] paying out the rope; while I waded in the water, holding the bow of the boat as I worked her between the rocks. Having reached the end of the rope, I coiled it up, advising Jimmy to go up to a safe crossing and join my brother while I proceeded with the boat. All was going well, and I was nearing the shore, when I found myself suddenly carried off my feet into water beyond my depth, and calling lustily to my brother to save me. At first he did not notice that anything was wrong, as he was looking intently through the finder. Then he suddenly awoke to the fact that something was amiss, and came running down the boulder-strewn shore, but he could not help me, as we had neglected to leave a rope with him. Things were beginning to look pretty serious, when the boat stopped against a rock and I found myself once more with solid footing under me. It was too good a picture to miss; and I found the operator at the machine, turning the crank as I climbed out.

We developed some films and plates that evening, securing some satisfactory results from these tests. It continued to rain all that night, with intermittent showers the next morning. The rain made little difference to us, for we were in the water much of the following day as the boats were taken along the edge of another unrunnable rapid, a good companion rapid for the one just passed.

We awoke bright and early the next morning, much refreshed by our day of rest and variety. With an early start we were soon pulling down the river, and noon found us several miles below the camp, having run eleven rapids with no particular difficulty. A reference in my notes reads: "Last one has a thousand rocks, and we could not miss them all. My rowing is improving, and we both got through fairly well." In the afternoon they continued to come—an endless succession of small rapids, with here and there a larger one. The canyon was similar to that at our camp above, dark red walls with occasional pines on the ledges,—a most charming combination of colour. At 2:30 p.m. we reached Ashley Falls, a rapid we had been expecting to see for some time. It was a place of singular beauty. A dozen immense rocks had fallen from the cliff on the left, almost completely blocking the channel—or so it seemed from one point of view. But there was a crooked channel, not more than twelve feet wide in places, through which the water shot like a stream from a nozzle.

We wanted a motion picture of our dash through the chute. But the location for the camera was hard to secure, for a sheer bank of rock or low wall prevented us from climbing out on the right side. We overcame this by landing on a little bank at the base of the wall and by dropping a boat down with a line to the head of the rapid, where a break occurred in the wall. Jimmy was left with the camera, the boat was pulled back, and we prepared to run the rapid.

We first had to pass between two square rocks rising eight feet above the water so close together that we could not use the oars; then, when past these, pull ten feet to the right in order to clear the large rock at the end of the main dam, or barrier, not more than twenty feet below. To pull down bow first and try to make the turn, would mean to smash broadside against this rock. It could only be done by dropping stern first, and pulling to the right under the protection of the first rocks; though it was doubtful if even this could be accomplished, the current was so swift. The *Defiance* was ready first, the *Edith* was to follow as closely as safety allowed.

Almost before I knew it I was in the narrow channel, so close to the right rock that I had to ship that oar, and pull altogether on the left one. As soon as I was through I made a few quick strokes, but the current was too strong for me; and a corner of the stern struck with a bang when I was almost clear. She paused as a wave rolled over the decks, then rose quickly; a side current caught the boat, whirling it around, and the bow struck. I was still pulling with all my might, but everything happened so quickly,—with the boat whirling first this way, then that,—that my efforts were almost useless. But after that second strike I did get in a few strokes, and pulled into the quiet pool below the line of boulders.

Emery held his boat in better position than I had done, and it looked for a while as if he would make it. But the *Edith* struck on the stern, much as mine had done. Then he pulled clear and joined me in the shelter of the large rock, as cool and smiling as if he had been rowing on a mill-pond. We were delighted to find that our boats had suffered no damage from the blows they had received. Striking on the ends as they did, the shock was distributed throughout the whole boat.

This completed our run for that day, and we went into camp just below the "Falls." Emery painted the name *Edith* on the bow of his boat, at this camp. The name was given in honour of his four-year-old daughter, waiting for us at the Grand Canyon. I remarked that as no one loved me, I would name my boat the *Defiance*. But I hesitated about putting this name on the bow. I would look rather foolish, I thought, if the *Defiance* should be wrecked in the first bad rapid. So the christening of my boat was left until such time as she should have earned the title, although she was constantly referred to as the *Defiance*.

We remained until noon of the following day at Ashley Falls, exploring, repairing, and photographing this picturesque spot. The canyon walls here dropped down to beautiful, rolling foot-hills eight or nine hundred feet high, tree covered as before but more open. The diversity of rocks and hills was alluring. There was work to be done and no pleasanter spot could be found in which to do it. Among other things that had to be looked after were some adjustments to the

motion-picture camera—usually referred to by us as the M. P. C.—
this delicate work always falling to Emery, for he alone could do it.

There was much to interest us here. Major Powell reported finding the name "Ashley" painted under an overhanging rock on the left
side of the river. Underneath was a date, rather indistinct, but found
to have been 1825, by Dellenbaugh, after carefully tracing the career
of Colonel Ashley who was responsible for the record. Accompanied
by a number of trappers, he made the passage though this canyon
at that early day. We found a trace of the record. There were three
letters—A-s-h—the first two quite distinct, and underneath were two
black spots. It must have been pretty good paint to leave a trace after
eighty-six years!

Resuming our journey we passed into deep canyon again,—the
deepest we had found up to this time,—with steeply sloping, verdure-
covered walls about 2700 feet high. The rapids still continued. At one
rapid the remark was made that "Two feet of water would cover two
hundred rocks so that our boats would pass over them." But we did
not have the two feet needed.

We had previously been informed that some of these mountains
were the hiding-places of men who were "wanted" in the three states
which bordered near here. Some escaping prisoners had also been
traced to the mountains in this direction; then all tracks had ceased.
The few peaceable ranchers who lived in these mountains were much
alarmed over these reports. We found one such rancher on the plateau
above the canyon, whom we will call Johnson for convenience,—
living in one of the upper canyons. He sold us some provisions. In
return he asked us to help him swim some of his horses across the
river. He said the high water had taken out his own boat. The horses
were rounded up in a mountain-hidden valley and driven into the
water ahead of the boat. After securing the horses, Johnson's welcome
seemed to turn to suspicion and he questioned our reasons for being
there, wanting to know what we could find in that wild country to
interest us. Johnson's sons, of whom there were several, seemed to put
in most of their time at hunting and trapping, never leaving the house
without a gun. The cabin home looked like an arsenal, revolvers and
guns hanging on all the walls—even his daughters being familiar with
their use. Although we had been very well treated after all, Mrs. Johnson especially having been very kind to us, we felt just a little relieved

when the Johnson ranch was left behind. We use, in fact, a fictitious name, not caring to visit on them the suspicions we ourselves felt in return.

Another morning passed in repairing the M. P. camera, and another afternoon's work was necessary to get us out of the walls and the rapids of Red Canyon. But on the evening of the 20th, we did get out, and pulled into an open country known as Brown's Park, one week after entering Flaming Gorge. It had not been very fast traveling; but we were through, and with no mishap more serious than a split board on the side of my boat. Under favourable conditions, and in experienced hands, this distance might have been covered in three days. But meanwhile, we were gaining a lot of experience.

About the lower end of Red Canyon the river turned directly east, paralleling the northern boundary of Utah, and continued to flow in this general direction until it crossed into Colorado.

On emerging from Red Canyon we spied a ranch house or log cabin close to the river. The doors were open and there were many tracks in the sand, so we thought some one must be about. On approaching the house, however, we found the place was deserted, but with furniture, books, and pictures piled on the floor in the utmost confusion, as if the occupants had left in a great hurry. This surmise afterward proved to be correct; for we learned that the rancher had been murdered for his money, his body having been found in a boat farther down the river.[2] Suspicion pointed to an old employee who had been seen lurking near the place. He was traced to the railroad, over a hundred miles to the north; but made his escape and was never caught.

We found Brown's Park, once known as Brown's Hole, to be a beautiful valley several miles in width, and thirty-five or forty miles in length. The upper end of the valley was rugged in places, with rocky hills two or three hundred feet high. To the south, a few miles away, were the mountains, a continuation of those we had come through. We saw many cattle scattered over some of these rocky hills, grazing on the bunch-grass. At one place our course led us through a little canyon about two miles long, and scarcely more than two hundred feet deep. This was Swallow Canyon—a name suggested by the many birds of that species which had covered the canyon's walls with their little clay nests. The openings of some of these nests were so small that it scarcely seemed possible for a bird to enter.

The water was deep and quiet in this short canyon, and a hard wind blowing up the stream made it difficult for us to gain any headway. In this case, too, the forms of the boat were against us. With the keel removed and with their high sides catching the wind, they were carried back and forth like small balloons. Well, we could put up with it for a while, for those very features would prove most valuable in the rough-water canyons which were to follow!

Emerging from the canyon at last, we saw a ferry loaded with sheep crossing the stream. On the left shore was a large corral, also filled with sheep which a half dozen men were driving back and forth into different compartments. Later these men told us there were 2400 sheep in the flock. We took their word for it, making no attempt to count them. The foreman of the ranch agreed to sell us some sugar and honey,—these two articles being a welcome addition to our list of supplies, which were beginning to show the effects of our voracious appetites.

We found many other log cabins and ranches as we proceeded. Some of them were deserted; at others men were busily engaged in cutting hay or the wild grass that grew in the bottoms. The fragrance of new-mown hay was in the air. Young boys and women were among these busy workers, some of the women being seated on large harvesters, handling the horses with as much dexterity as any of the men.

The entire trip though this pretty valley was full of interest. We were hailed from the shore by some of the hay ranchers, it being a novel sight to them to see a river expedition. At one or two of these places we asked the reason for the deserted ranches above, and were given evasive answers. Finally we were told that cattle rustlers from the mountains made it so hard for the ranchers in the valleys that there was nothing for them to do but get out. They told us, also, that we were fortunate to get away from Johnson's ranch with our valuables! Our former host, we were told, had committed many depredations and had served one term for cattle stealing. Officers, disguised as prospectors, had taken employment with him and helped him kill and skin some cattle; the skins, with their telltale brands, having been partially burned and buried. On this evidence he was afterwards convicted.

Our cool welcome by the Johnsons, their suspicions of us, the sinister arsenal of guns and pistols, all was explained! Quite likely some of these weapons had been trained against us by the trappers on the chance that we were either officers of the law, or competitors in the horse-stealing industry. For that matter we were actually guilty of the latter count, for come to think of it, we ourselves had helped them steal eight horses and a colt!

[Approximately one month later]

An hour or two at the oars the next morning sufficed to bring us to the junction of the Green and the Grand rivers. We tied up our boats, and prepared to climb out on top, as we had a desire to see the view from above. A mile back on the Green we had noticed a sort of canyon or slope breaking down on the west side, affording a chance to reach the top. Loading ourselves with a light lunch, a full canteen, and our smaller cameras, we returned to this point and proceeded to climb out. Powell's second expedition had climbed out at this same place; Wolverton had also mentioned the fact that he had been out; so we were quite sure of a successful attempt before we made the climb.

The walk close to the river, over rocks and along narrow ledges, was hard work; the climb out was even more so. The contour maps which we carried credited these walls with 1300 feet height. If we had any doubt concerning the accuracy of this, it disappeared before we finally reached the top. What we saw, however, was worth all the discomfort we had undergone. Close to the top, three branches of dry, rock-bottomed gullies, carved from a gritty, homogenous sandstone, spread out from the slope we had been climbing. These were less precipitous. Taking the extreme left-hand gully, we found the climb to the top much easier. At the very end we found an irregular hole a few feet in diameter, not a cave, but an opening left between some immense rocks, touching at the top, seemingly rolled together.

Gazing down through this opening, we were amazed to find that we were directly above the Colorado itself. It was so confusing at first that we had to climb to the very top to see which river it was, I contending that it was the Green, until satisfied that I was mistaken. The view from the top was overwhelming, and words can hardly describe what we saw, or how we were affected by it.

We found ourselves on top of an irregular plateau of solid rock, with no earth or vegetation save a few little brushes and some very small cedars in cracks in the rocks. Branching canyons, three or four hundred feet in depth, and great fissures ran down in this rock at intervals. Some were dark and crooked, and the bottom could not be seen. Between these cracks, the rock rounded like elephants' backs sloping steeply on either side. Some could be crossed, some could not. Others resembled a "maze," the puzzle being how to get from one point to another a few feet away. The rock was a sandstone and presented a rough surface affording a good hold, so there was little danger of slipping. We usually sat down and "inched" our way to the edge of the cracks, jumping across to little ledges when possible, always helping each other.

The rock at the very edge of the main canyon overhung in places 75 to 100 feet, and the great mass of gigantic boulders—sections of shattered cliffs—on the steep slope near the river gave evidence of a continual breaking away of these immense rocks.

To the north, across the canyon up which we had climbed, were a great number of smooth formations, from one hundred to four hundred feet high, rounded on top in domes, reminding one of Bagdad and tales from the Arabian Nights. "The Land of Standing Rocks," the Utes call it. The rock on which we stood was light gray or nearly white; the river walls at the base for a thousand feet above the river were dark red or chocolate brown; while the tops of the formations above this level were a beautiful light red tint.

But there were other wonders. On the south side of the Colorado's gorge, miles away, were great spires, pointing heavenward, singly and in groups, looking like a city of churches. Beyond the spires were the Blue Mountains, to the east the hazy LaSalle range, and nearest of all on the west just north of the Colorado lay the snow-covered peaks of the Henry Mountains. Directly below us was the Colorado River, muddy, swirling and forbidding. A mile away boomed a rapid, beyond that was another, then the river was lost to view.

Standing on the brink of all this desolation, it is small wonder if we recalled the accounts of the disasters which had overtaken so many others in the canyon below us. Many who had escaped the water had climbed out on to this death trap, as it had proven to be for them, some to perish of thirst and starvation, a few to stagger into the ranch below the canyon, a week or more after they had escaped from the water. Small wonder that some of these had lost their reason. We could only conjecture at the fate of the party whose wrecked boat had been

Bird's-eye View of the Land of Standing Rocks, from Powell,
Exploration of the Colorado River and Its Canyons.

found by the Stone expedition, a few miles below this place, with their tracks still fresh in the sand. No trace of them was ever found.

For the first time it began to dawn on us that we might have tackled a job beyond our power to complete. Most of the parties which had safely completed the trip were composed of several men, adding much to the safety of the expedition, as a whole. Others had boats much lighter than ours, a great help in many respects. Speaking for myself, I was just a little faint-hearted, and not a little overawed as we prepared to return to the boats.

While returning, we saw evidences of ancient Indians—some broken arrow-heads, and pottery also, and a small cliff ruin under a shelving rock.

What could an Indian find here to interest him! We had found neither bird, nor rabbit; not even a lizard in the Land of Standing Rocks. Perhaps they were sun worshippers, and wanted an unobstructed view of the eastern sky. That at least could be had, in unrivalled grandeur, here above the Rio Colorado.

The shadows were beginning to lengthen when we finally reached our boats at the junction. Camp was made under a large weeping willow tree, the only tree of its kind we remembered having seen on the journey.

While Emery prepared a hasty meal I made a few arrangements for embarking on the Colorado River the next morning. We were prepared to bid farewell to the Green River—the stream that had served us so well. In spite of our trials, even in the upper canyons, we had found much enjoyment in our passage through its strange and beautiful surroundings.

From a scenic point of view the canyons of the Green River, with their wonderful rock formations and stupendous gorges, are second only to those of the Colorado itself. It is strange they are so little known, when one considers the comparative ease with which these canyons on the lower end can be reached. Some day perhaps, surfeited globe-trotters, after having tired of commonplace scenery and foreign lands will learn what a wonderful region this is, here on the lower end of the Green River.

≈≈ NOTES

1. The Kolbs' photographic assistant.

2. This was John Jarvie, who ran the first post office and the only store in Brown's Park until his murder in 1909.

Now We're Safe, Now We're on the River: Bus Hatch's First Green River Voyage

Roy Webb

UTAH HISTORIAN ROY WEBB HAS WRITTEN EXTENSIVELY ON THE
GREEN RIVER AND THOSE WHO HAVE FOLLOWED IT. IN THIS ARTICLE
HE EXPLAINS HOW HATCH RIVER EXPEDITIONS, ONE OF THE DOMI-
NANT COMMERCIAL ENTERPRISES OPERATING ON THE GREEN AND
COLORADO TODAY, GOT ITS START AFTER A CHANCE CONVERSATION
IN THE UINTAH COUNTY JAIL.

Few names are as recognizable in the small world of river runners as Hatch River Expeditions. From the 1930's through today, there have been Hatch boats and boatmen, not to mention
quite a few Hatches, on the Green River. Commercial river running
boomed in the late 1960's. Virtually the entire first generation of commercial river runners who started their own companies got their start
with Bus and Hatch River Expeditions. All of his four sons Gus, Don,
Frank, and Ted, as well as uncountable numbers of cousins and nephews, worked on the river, and at least one, Ted Hatch, today runs the
highly successful Hatch River Expeditions Grand Canyon. Today
there are fourth-generation Hatch descendants working on the river, a
real dynasty, and tales of Bus and his life are still told around riverside
camps. Perhaps his greatest legacy, however, was the sense of sheer
fun that Bus and Alt and Tommy and Frank Swain and Cap Mowrey
introduced into river running. Before them, river running had been
serious business, and the accounts of many expeditions are downright
somber. Not so with the Hatch boys, who redefined river running
from a surprisingly sober venture to a floating, drunken party, ran
their cobbled-together craft with great panache and had a swell time
doing it.

But even a riverman such as Bus Hatch has to have a beginning and it came about in a surprising place; the Uintah County Jail. Bus's cousin, Frank Swain, like his father, Nick Swain, was a deputy sheriff for Uintah County. In September 1929, he was sent to LaSal, Utah, to pick up a prisoner wanted for non-support of his family. The story of Parley Galloway and how Bus learned to build boats is also well told in *The Middle Fork and the Sheepeater War,* by Johnny Carrey and Cort Conley (Backeddy Books, 1977). The prisoner turned out to be Parley Galloway, whose father, Nathaniel, was already something of a legend in Vernal. In the late 1880s, Nathaniel, or Than, as his friends called him, began running the canyons of the Green and Colorado rivers, prospecting and trapping beaver. He used boats of his own design, light, flat-bottomed skiffs that were very maneuverable. More importantly, though, he used them in a way that had never been tried. Rather than row with his back to the current, the traditional way to handle a boat, Galloway turned his boat around, facing downstream, so he could see where he was going and use his oars to control the boat in the roughest water. Nathaniel used his little craft and his revolutionary technique to run the Green, the Yampa, and even the Colorado in its roughest stretches, Cataract Canyon and the Grand Canyon. Sometimes with a partner, but most often alone, he traveled regions that just a few scant years before had been the haunts only of outlaws and hermits. Before his death in 1913, Galloway had spent more time on the Colorado River than any other man, and was known as the premier riverman of his time.

Parley learned how to build riverboats, and how to run them, literally at his father's knee, taking many trips with Nathaniel down the Green and its turbulent tributaries. When he was just a teenager, he ran the Green from Vernal to its confluence with the Colorado, and back up the latter to Moab with his father. In 1909, they ran the Yampa together on the spring rise. Parley successfully guided the Clyde Eddy party thorough Cataract Canyon and the Grand Canyon in 1926, even though he had never been down the Grand Canyon. On that trip, with a crew composed of inexperienced, "pink-wristed collegians," and an equally inexperienced leader, Parley was "the glue that held the group together," in one historian's phrase. So his river credentials were without question. His ethics, however, were another matter.

During long conversations with Parley in his cell in the Uintah County Jail, Bus and Frank listened eagerly to Parley's tales of the deep canyons of the Green and the Colorado—as Bus later put it, they spent as much time in jail as Parley did. Both Bus and Frank had read John Wesley Powell's account of his pioneering river voyages, and they were fascinated by the idea of navigating the river. Sensing opportunity in Frank and Bus's interest, Parley told the cousins that if they would collect some money Clyde Eddy owed to him and bail him out, he would help them build a Galloway boat and then guide them down the river. Bus and Frank agreed, and bailed Parley out of jail. He thereupon did "what he should have done, he skipped out," and promptly disappeared from the Uinta Basin, never to be seen again in eastern Utah. The two cousins were undeterred, however. They had built a boat once and could do it again. As for running the river through the mysterious canyons, by God, they would just do it on their own.

The cousins were not unfamiliar with the Green River, nor with boat-building, before their talks with Parley Galloway. They had built a boat for seining, and later used it for fishing and hunting trips around Stewart Lake and Horseshoe Bend. As early as 1927, Bus described one such hunting trip in a letter to his brother Alt, then a student at Brigham Young University:

The boat sure works fine. It is twelve feet long and hauls three men across Green River at once, in a "high wind" too. Sunday we went down to Horseshoe Bend. The bunch consisted of Frank Swain, Tom, Cap and myself. While we were across the river the wind came up and the waves on the river were sure rolling high. Cap, Frank, and myself got in the boat and crossed the river to the car. Frank got the short straw, and drew the job of rowing back across for Tom. By this time the wind was sure blowing like hell and the river was rolling high. We rowed that boat that day with paddles, Indian style, so [Frank] chose the best paddle and after a lot of coaxing and guying at him he got nerve enough to start. He put out to sea like Lindberg starting across the Atlantic, but wait, the waves sure raised hell with that boat. He got two-thirds of the way across. A big wave hoisted the boat way up and [his] heart went up under his chin and shut off his wind. The next wave took the boat in the face and splashed water all over him. His courage and reason and everything else he might have left him in a bunch. There is no retreat in history to equal the way old Frank pulled out. He ducked his head, socked the paddle into the water about six feet and the race was on. He paddled too much on one side and went in a circle. When he was in the third round he broke the circle and started back. I jerked out my Ingersoll [watch] but before I could shake it and get it started he hit the shore back on my side of the river. I never saw a boat travel so darn fast in my life, it stood up on its hind end like the bronc old Hessel rode hunting and how it did come. No one else ever made such speed and I'm sure the record will stand til hell freezes over and they can't equal it on skates either.

After they got through laughing at this display, they gave Frank a shot of moonshine to revive him. Then Bus and Frank made another attempt, but the waves were still too high. "We took off our shoes and put them in the bottom of the boat. We then checked our life insurance and put to sea again. When we hit the center of the river the old boat raised up, slapped the water like a cannon going off and we put back for shore like a spirit out of hell. We made it back OK and yelled across at Tommy, told him he would have to stay there until the wind died down if it took six weeks. Pretty soon," Bus concluded, "the wind calmed down a bit and we crossed and got him."

Fortified by this and similar experiences, and inspired by the long talks with Parley, the cousins were eager to try the canyons. In the little carpentry shop on the family homestead, Bus, Cap, and the others built a boat. Based on sketches made by Parley Galloway, it was sixteen feet long, with four feet of beam at the widest point. To withstand the shock of hitting rocks, the bow was carved from a solid piece of oak. There were two seats, so that the oarsman could row facing either direction; there were no watertight compartments. For supplies they took food in glass canning jars; for life preservers, they had inner tubes cut down at a local gas station so they would fit snugly under their arms. With their rifles, bedrolls, a couple of frying pans for cooking and bailing, and a sack of flour, they were ready to try the river.

Their first try was in August 1931. As in everything else they did together, Bus was the leader, and as he later noted, "appointed myself head boatman." Frank Swain, Tom Hatch, and Cap Mowrey were the passengers.

Bay Hatch drove them up to Hideout Flat, on the Green below Flaming Gorge, and arranged to meet them below the mouth of Split

Mountain canyon in four days. From their first moment on the river, they realized that the elaborate and expensive oak bow was next to useless; most of the rocks they hit were with the side of the boat, not the bow. Nor had they fully learned Parley's lessons. That and inexperience proved to be their undoing. Their first day, as Bus told it, "There was one rapid, a small rock in the middle of it, and I managed to hit that, so I was one hundred percent right there." Cap Mowrey later said the rock knocked a hole in the side of the boat "big enough to throw a cat through." But thinking fast, Cap clapped a pie tin over the hole and they were able to get to shore just as the boat sank. They repaired the hole with some strips of tin and tar, and continued on their way, a bit more carefully. Coming to Ashley Falls, they portaged that historic rapid, and ran Red Creek Rapid, just above Brown's Park, only after careful scrutiny.

In Lodore Canyon, they portaged Disaster Falls, the first major rapid. They tried to run Hell's Half Mile, the worst rapid in Lodore, but Bus lost control and capsized the boat. As they struggled with the overturned boat, they could see their food supplies in glass jars floating along beside them. As each one hit a rock, there was a "pop," as the jar broke. By the time they got to shore and righted the boat, they had nothing left to eat but a big onion and a couple of potatoes that Bus managed to grab. Fortunately, Frank Swain's old .30-40 Krag rifle was tied in and hadn't been lost. Spotting some mountain sheep looking on, he brought one down with a single shot. Their fishing tackle was just laying loose in the boat, so it was gone; onion and gamey, sandy mountain sheep meat was all they had to eat for the rest of the trip. Another loss to Bus was his feather pillow. He always said that he could sleep on a rock if he had a good pillow, and so had brought one from home. By the time they rescued it from the river, however, it took two of them just to drag it to shore. The pillow was left on a rock, another casualty of the spill.

As they sat around the campfire at Jones Hole, the others gnawing on gritty mountain sheep meat while Bus munched the onion, the cousins talked about river running. They decided that despite the mishaps, they wanted to explore the entire river, from the source, through the rugged lower canyons, to the Grand Canyon and beyond. They all had families and responsibilities—Bus had married Eva Caldwell in 1922, and already had three boys—but the lure of the canyons was still strong. They decided that when they could get time off from work, they would continue downriver. Starting the next year, they would explore the stretch from Ouray to Green River, Utah, then they would try the dreaded Cataract Canyon to Lees Ferry. After that, they would float the Grand Canyon, and who knows, even try the Amazon or the Yukon.

But first they had to get this trip over with. Two hard days on the river without any good food were beginning to tell; Cap noted that by the time they got to Island Park, "we's getting hungry enough to eat one another." There are nine miles of flat water to row to get through Island and Rainbow Parks, and they were so weak that they had to take turns rowing. The current is slow, and, of course, the wind was blowing upstream, as it always has. No one was home at the Ruple ranch, so they could get no supplies there. In Split Mountain canyon, they were beyond caring about how they navigated the many rapids, as long as they got through. By this time they had evolved a method for running rapids, whereby one of them stood in the stern and gave directions to the oarsman. This went against the Galloway technique, but it was faster, and that was what counted at this point. They finally reached the mouth of Split Mountain Canyon the last afternoon, and rowed down to Placer Point, where Eva and Frank Hatch were waiting with a big picnic lunch.

One realization to come out of the trip, besides the fact that glass jars were no good for carrying food, was that they needed better boats if they were going to attempt any more river explorations. While passing through Island Park, they had noticed something on the riverbank near the Ruple Ranch that made them forget about their growling stomachs for a while. It was a boat, and what a boat! Decked over, with watertight compartments fore and aft, room for plenty of supplies and a couple of passengers. It was about eighteen feet long, and four and a half feet wide, and with a flat bottom and enough rake to make it maneuverable in rapids. Bus' trained eye realized at once that this was a well-designed and well-made craft. How had old Hod Ruple come by such a sleek craft? The answer to that question involved none other than Parley Galloway.

In 1926, a couple of dudes from back east named Todd and Page decided to spend their vacation floating the canyons of the Green River. For a guide, they hired a man from southern Utah named

H. Elwyn Blake Jr. Blake had been a boatman for the 1922 USGS survey of the upper Green, and other government surveys, and was an experienced riverman. Blake's father, H. E. Blake Sr., had likewise been a pioneer riverman on the Green and Colorado; he was involved in attempts to start a steamboat line on the lower river around the turn of the twentieth century. For boats, Todd and Page bought two of the USGS boats, which were Galloway-style-craft—by now the standard on the river—and had Blake and another man, Curley Hale, put them back into shape. They had made it down the river in good shape until they got below Hell's Half Mile, when one of the boats was pinned immovably on a rock. They finished their trip in the remaining boat.

The next year, Parley Galloway and Frank Gerber were trapping down Lodore, when they found the abandoned boat. Freeing it from the rocks, Galloway took it down to Island Park and sold it to Hod Ruple, who used it for herding his cattle back and forth across the river. It was this boat that Bus and the others saw in Island Park. It had actually been another member of the party, Ogden "Og" West, who was rowing the boat when it wrecked, just below the Rippling Brook camp in Lodore. He froze at the oars and allowed the boat to drift onto a solitary rock in the middle of the river, where it was immovably lodged. Lost were provisions, bedrolls, cameras, exposed film, and other goods.

Bus wrote down the measurements of the boat, and as soon as he had time back home, set about building a copy. First he reduced the length to fifteen and a half feet. He felt that eighteen feet was too long. When he built in the watertight compartments, Bus used carbide cans, such as miners used. These had a screw-down lid with a gasket. Not only would they keep supplies and gear dry, they would provide extra floatation. Bus lavished extra care on the boat, making sure it would hold up under the beating that any boat gets running the rocky canyons. That October, Bus, Alt, Tom and a friend of Tom's named Chuck Henderson tried the new craft out with a run through Split Mountain. It worked perfectly, so Bus and Cap built another just like it. They were ready to make good on their pledge to explore the rest of the river.

Frank Swain had moved to Bingham in 1930 to take a job as security officer for Utah Copper Co. There he got to know the company doctor, Russell Frazier. In the summer of 1932, Frank and Bus took Frazier and another Bingham man, Bill Fahrni, on a fishing trip to Jones Hole. There the cousins regaled Frazier and Fahrni with tales of running the river. Of an exploring bent, Frazier asked to be taken down through Lodore. When he offered to pay for supplies and transportation. Bus and Frank agreed. This time the crew would consist of Bus and Frank, as boatmen, with Tom Hatch, Dr. Frazier, Bill Fahrni, and two other Salt Lake men, Rhinehard van Evers and Dr. Henderson, as passengers. They used their two new boats, whimsically named the What's Next? and the Don't Know and started from Hideout Flats the following September. They had clear sailing for the first four days, but in Lodore, they learned that the river was still in command in the canyons.

> On Thursday as they were going through Ladore [sic], the most hazardous canyon of the entire trip, they had the misfortune to lose one boat with all its equipment and provisions. Riding over Disaster Falls, where Captain Ashley's crew of seven men lost their lives by drowning in his famous expedition through the canyon, the boat passed over in safety but struck a huge boulder at the foot of the falls, turning the boat over and throwing it under four feet of water. Here it was held by the suction of the current.

Shaken by this experience, they lined the other boat down the left side of the rapid and then tried to salvage part of the supplies. But the current was too swift and the boat pinned too securely, and they had to give up the attempt after a day and a half. As the Vernal Express noted, "The sinking and abandoning of the one boat at Disaster Falls represented a loss of more than $500 to the party."

"Often the boats would ride in rapids more than 30 miles per hour," the Vernal Express reporter went on breathlessly. "Where the canyons walls suddenly narrowed and the racing river was confined to a narrow gorge, the sudden change would cause the water at the edge of the stream to raise into [the] air 10 to 15 feet and form a huge trough." In Split Mountain, the boat capsized, pinning Frank Swain and Dr. Frazier underneath. As Frank struggled to get free, he kicked Dr. Frazier in the head with his hobnailed boots, knocking him unconscious. But they soon revived him, and finished out the journey without any more mishaps. When they landed at Jensen, the bottom of the boat showed hard use, and there was more than sixty gallons of water in the bottom. The *Vernal Express* article about their trip concluded optimistically, however, noting that they were already planning another trip from Jensen to Lees Ferry the next year. Despite their bad experiences, they weren't through with the river yet. Nor was the river through with them.

Before they could plan any more trips, though, there was a lot of work to be done. The first order of business was to salvage the boat lost in Disaster Falls. In November, Bus, Frank, Cap, and Garn Swain took their remaining boat and floated down to the site of the wreck. There they found the boat intact, despite being pinned in the river for two months. Bus had brought 150 feet of steel cable, chains and two block and tackles; with this equipment, they soon had the boat freed. All it needed was some minor repairs—a testament to how well built the boat was in the first place—and it was ready to be taken down through the rest of the canyon. They rowed both boats out to the mouth of Split Mountain the next day, where they were loaded onto trucks and taken back to Vernal.

Bus had come a long way since the first trip down the Green a scant two years before. From open boats, clumsily run, he had progressed to sleek, state-of-the-art craft, and now possessed considerable skill at the oars of a river boat. As an article about their Cataract Canyon trip noted, Bus and the others had more than a thousand river miles to their credit, without any major mishaps. On all of these trips, Bus had been the unspoken leader. His boat ran first in the rapids, and he often ran all the boats through by himself. He was first to help with lining or portaging, or with cooking and other duties around camp. They had had their share of hardships and mishaps, yet through it all—the capsizes and the pinned boat in Lodore, the hot, hungry trip though Cataract Canyon—Bus maintained his sense of humor. When they did capsize a boat, or pin one on a rock, it was no big thing. They were on the river to have a good time, and no little inconvenience was going to interfere with that.

Sources of information for this story include *The Middle Fork and the Sheepeater War*, by Johnny Carrey and Cort Conley (Backeddy Books, 1977), personal interviews, *Vernal Express* articles, extant home movies, and *Life and Adventures of James P. Beckwourth*, anonymous.

The Marks of Human Passage

Wallace Stegner

In 1955 publisher and conservationist Alfred A. Knopf, alarmed by the Bureau of Reclamation plan to build a dam at Echo Park in Dinosaur National Monument and thus drown some of the wildest parts of the Green and Yampa Rivers, enlisted the aid of Wallace Stegner to edit a book of essays on the area in hopes of galvanizing the American public to oppose the project. Stegner not only edited the book but wrote its opening essay, in which he tracks the Monument's past and surveys its future.

Dinosaur National Monument is one of the last almost "unspoiled" wildernesses—which means it is relatively unmarked by man. Yet it is already, despite being one of the latest-explored parts of the continent, a palimpsest of human history, speculation, rumor, fantasy, ambition, science, controversy, and conflicting plans for use, and these human records so condition our responses to the place that they contain a good part of Dinosaur's meaning.

What shall we say of it? That it is a three-pronged district of about 200,000 acres, straddling the Utah-Colorado border a little south of where that border meets the southern boundary of Wyoming. That it is a part—one of the junior partners—of the National Park System begun with the reservation of Yellowstone in 1872 and confirmed by the establishment of the National Park Service in 1916. That topographically it is defined by the deep canyons of two rivers, the Green and the Yampa, which meet secretly in the sunny, sunken pocket of Echo Park and then together cut Whirlpool Canyon, Island Park, Rainbow Park, and Split Mountain Canyon, from whose mouth the water breaks out into the open Uinta Valley of Utah. That the plateau through which the canyons are cut is an eastward extension of the Uinta Mountains, one of the few east-west-trending ranges in the United States. That the larger of the two rivers, the Green, is the longest fork of the Colorado; and that it used to be called the Seedskeedee-

Agie, the Prairie Hen River, by the Crows, and by the Spaniards the Rio Verde. Its tributary the Yampa is even yet by some people and some maps called the Bear.

One can observe that Echo Park, at the heart of this reserve, lies at approximately 109° West Longitude and 40°31' North Latitude; that the altitude ranges from 4,700 feet at the mouth of Split Mountain Canyon to 9,600 feet at the tip of Zenobia Peak near the northeastern boundary; that the rocks exposed run in age from the Uinta Mountain quartzite of the Pre-Cambrian period to the Brown's Park sandstone of the Pliocene; that the life zones represented spread from the Sonoran in the canyon bottoms to sub-arctic on the higher ridges. The colors of the rocks vary from a rich red-brown to vermilion, from gray to almost sugar-white, with many shades of pink and buff and salmon in between. The cliffs and sculptured forms are sometimes smooth, sometimes fantastically craggy, always massive, and they have a peculiar capacity to excite the imagination; the effect on the human spirit is neither numbing nor awesome, but warm and infinitely peaceful.

Having assembled these facts, both objective and subjective, we have said very little. Even the dry facts are simply the generalizations of human observation, distillations of topographical, cartographical, geological, biological, and other work that men have done in the region. Describing a place, we inevitably describe the marks human beings have put upon a place, the uses they have put it to, the things they have been taught by it. Even the dinosaurs whose bodies grounded on the bar of a Jurassic river here 120,000,000 years ago, and whose petrified bones gave the Monument its first reason for reservation as well as its permanent and rather misleading name, were only rocks until human curiosity unearthed and studied and compared and interpreted them.

To describe Dinosaur one must begin by summarizing its human history, and human history in Dinosaur is quaintly begun in the completely human impulse to immortalize oneself by painting or pecking or carving one's private mark, the symbol of one's incorrigible identity, on rocks and trees.

The prehistoric people who inhabited the Green and Yampa canyons, and who belonged to the cultural complex known to archaeologists as the Fremont Culture, a laggard branch of the prehistoric Pueblo-

Basketmaker group, or Anasazi, are properly the subject of another chapter (IV) of this book. We may borrow them here only long enough to note that the pictographs and petroglyphs which they painted in red ocher or chipped with sharp stones in the faces of the cliffs mark the northernmost extension of the Anasazi Culture, and that these murals, together with the terrace camp sites and middens and the many storage granaries in caves, are among the earliest human marks in the area. To us, the most immediately fascinating of the relics the Fremont people left are these pictures, which record the game they hunted, the ceremonial objects they revered, the idle doodling dreams they indulged in, and—most wistful and most human of all—the painted handprints, and footprints, the personal tracks, that said, and still say: "I am."

These are all of Dinosaur's history for a long time; they reflect the period from about AD 400–800. Some archaeologists believe that on the Uinta and Yampa plateaus there may be evidences of the passage southward, sometime about the year 1000, of the Athapascan hunters who were the ancestors of the modern Navajo and Apache, but the origin of those camp sites is still speculative. Leaving out that possibility, there passed nearly a thousand years after the last of the Fremont people departed during which, as far as history knows, these canyons were only wind and water and stone, space and sky and the slow sandpapering of erosion, the unheard scurry of lizard and scream of mountain lion, the unseen stiff-legged caution of deer, the unnoted roar of rapids in the dark slot of Lodore and the unrecorded blaze of canyon color darkening with rain and whitening with snow and glaring in the high sun of solstice.

When the next man left a mark, he was a Spaniard, one of a watchful vanguard. The year was 1776. And nobody later reported seeing the mark he left; we know he left it only because Fray Silvestre Vélez de Escalante made an entry in his diary for September 14 as he was camped on the bank of the Green on his way to seek a route from New Mexico to Monterey in California.

"In this place," the explorer wrote (it was the day when the British were moving in to occupy New York, and General George Washington was preparing his retreat to Harlem Heights), "there are six large black cottonwood trees that have grown in pairs, attached to one another, and they are the ones closest to the river. Near them is another, standing alone, on whose trunk, on the side facing the north-west, Don Joaquin Lain with an adz cleared a small space in the form of a rectangular window, and with a chisel carved on it the letters and numbers of this inscription, *The Year 1776;* and lower down in different letters the name *Lain,* with two crosses outside, the larger one above the inscription and the smaller one below it."

There are still cottonwoods answering that description near the southern boundary of the Monument, a half-mile or so below the dinosaur quarry and Monument Headquarters. Almost certainly they are not the same ones, for cottonwoods are not long-lived trees; but if they are, as some people believe, they have proved a less durable or less inert base for immortality than the cliffs the Fremont people scribbled on: the living wood has overgrown and obliterated any inscription. Fortunately the passage westward of those first Spaniards, the discoverers of the Green River among much else, was also recorded in Escalante's diary, in the Word, the most durable of all materials. The Word thus bounds Dinosaur not only on its southern geographical border but at the threshold of its entrance into recorded history.

These Spaniards probably did no more than poke their noses into the canyons, though Escalante reported in his diary "two high cliffs which, after forming a sort of corral, come so close together that one can scarcely see the opening through which the river comes"; and Miera set down on his map a mountain he called Sierra Mineral that was split straight through by the river. Both journal entry and the Sierra Mineral are surely references to Split Mountain.

Except for that tempting glimpse, Escalante skirted the southern edge of the cut-up Uinta and Yampa uplifts. Other travelers would skirt them along the north, leaving a no-man's-land between the known routes called the California Trail and the Spanish Trail. The canyons were a barrier, not a highway. But the next mark that men made in them recorded an attempt to use the river as highway, and to link the Spanish-dominated country southward with the routes of trappers and mountain men just finding their way across the continental divide among the headwaters of the Green.

That next mark came forty-nine years after Escalante. Like Lain's inscription on the tree (and, for all we know, like the murals of the Fremont people), it recorded a name and a date.

"Ashley, 1825," it says. It is painted on a rock in Red Canyon, above Brown's Park and outside the present Dinosaur National Monument. It commemorated the first known penetration of the Green River's canyons by white men—the bullboat expedition of General William Henry Ashley and six mountain men from about the site of present Fontanelle, Wyoming, to somewhere in Desolation Canyon, below the Uinta Valley. The purpose, like Escalante's, was practical: the exploration of a route, this time for profitable fur trade and a more southerly rendezvous among the Utes. Like Escalante's, the route turned out to have serious defects, and was not soon used again. Moreover, the written accounts of the journey waited a long time to be made public. Nevertheless, history lost and then found again is still history.

Ashley had divided his party of mountain men into four brigades because Crows had run off many of his horses and left him overloaded. With six men and the bulk of the supplies, he pushed off from a point about fifteen miles above the mouth of the Sandy, hoping to open up the southern country to the fur trade. Into the teeth of the unknown—into the teeth, in fact, of wild and fearful rumors, such as the one promoted by his own employee and partisan James Beckwourth of an awesome "suck" where the river enters the Utah Mountains"—Ashley ran his laden bullboats. At Henry's Fork, where he appointed a rendezvous, and in Brown's Hole, where he found that several thousand Indians had wintered, he was in known country, or semi-known. But the run through Red Canyon's rapids had given them a good shaking and had made them unload and portage all their goods and lower the bullboats over one drop on rawhide cords. That was at Ashley Falls, named later by another explorer who had no idea who Ashley was; and that was where he took five minutes to paint his name on the rock.

The rest of his trip left no marks on the country. Through Lodore, which impressed them all with its gloom and scared them with its wild water, they went as unnoted as bubbles of foam; caught their breath in the lovely bottoms of Echo Park; ran or portaged through Whirlpool and Split Mountain canyons, still, of course, unnamed. In Split Mountain, Ashley was within an eyelash of drowning; his man Beckwourth later made claims to a heroic rescue. Actually when Ashley was running the canyons Beckwourth was clear over on the other side of the mountain with James Clyman's and then with Thomas Fitzpatrick's brigade.

Ashley's journal was not found and published until 1918. His scoot down the canyons in a flimsy pole framework covered with buffalo hide and calked with pitch was a casual episode in a career notable for fortitude and daring, and it had no effect on history because history never heard of it until much other history had overtaken and passed it. As it happened, the painted name and date on the rock by Ashley Falls stood there under rain and sun another twenty-four years before white men again came that way, and when they came they barely noticed the name and had no notion who had left it there.

They came on their way to somewhere else, part of the stream pouring across the northern passes bound for the gold fields of California in 1849. Their motive in running the river was not exploration, but impatience; their resource was not the cool daring of Ashley, but foolhardiness; and they knew nothing, neither geography nor history, to help or to deter them.

They were bullwhackers on a Forty-niner wagon train, fed up with dust and the poky plod of oxen, and displeased by the train-leader's decision to winter in Salt Lake City because of the lateness of the season. They said: By golly, if only a river would show up, and if they had a boat, and if it looked as if the water might flow to the Pacific, for a two-bit shinplaster they would... So the river showed up, and rumor said it ran to the Pacific, and at the edge, like something provided in a fable, lay a sunken barge that had been built as a ferry. They did not bother to think. They patched up the barge and loaded their gear into it, and when the wagon train pulled out for Salt Lake City the seven bullwhackers pried themselves off the mudbank and headed downriver.

God was good to them: at least He let them live. But He kept them pretty busy. At Ashley Falls they ran their barge among the rocks and couldn't budge it. Undaunted, they made two canoes out of pine trees and lashed them together to make a kind of catamaran. When that appeared insufficient to carry their stuff, they stopped and made another.

On those cobbled craft the seven somehow got through Lodore; within it, at Disaster Falls, they found a wrecked skiff and a note on a tree saying that their unknown predecessor was getting out to Salt

Lake by land. As trackless as driftwood, which they resembled, they floated through Whirlpool and Split Mountain and into the Uinta Valley, and through it, and on through Desolation and Gray canyons to about the site of modern Greenriver, Utah. Their taste for river voyaging was somewhat dampened, but their ignorance of geography—in which they were not alone in 1849—might even then have persuaded them to risk the river trail farther if the Ute chief Walkara, or Walker, had not taken pity on the misguided Mericats and talked them too into going overland to Salt Lake City, there to catch on with another wagon train. Their story was told many years later by one of their number, W. L. Manly, in a book called *Death Valley in '49*.

So except for the healed or rotted inscription in the cottonwood on its southern boundary, and the name of Ashley just outside its northern prong, Dinosaur had no recorded white history until past the middle of the nineteenth century. Escalante's discoveries had leaked into American consciousness indirectly, by way of Baron von Humboldt's 1810 map of New Spain, which was based partly on the map made by Escalante's companion Miera. But nobody had heard of Ashley or Manly, and it was reserved for the third man through the canyons to be their effective discoverer. He came with no other purpose than to know; he was in search of *this* country, not on his way somewhere else.

On May 12, 1869, the first transcontinental railroad train crossed the Green at Green River Wyoming Territory, and the first period of Western history was over. And as they crossed, the first transcontinental tourists reclining in the palace cars exchanged waves with the last continental explorers, who were calking their boats below the bridge. Those last explorers were Major John Wesley Powell's Colorado River Exploring Expedition, and they were not only closing one phase of the West but opening another. This one-armed veteran of the Union army, preparing his ten men and four boats for a raid on the unknown canyons, was later to have a greater effect on the development of the West than any other man.

He was probably, as Otis Marston points out in his story of Green River boating elsewhere in this book, not an especially good white water man; and, more than that, he was the first, so far as he knew. Though he had all the available information, including maps, he did not have much. He ran almost as blind as Ashley had, through a country still patched with guesswork and rumor. Though he saw Ashley's inscription in Red Canyon, he had no idea who Ashley was, and he misread the date as 1855 and guessed that Ashley must have been a prospector.

Powell was not the first explorer of these canyons; but he was the first explorer who "took." He brought the arts of written record along with him, he measured and mapped as he went, he left a trail that led backward into the broad migration track of western civilization. Working his four heavy, awkward, overloaded boats laboriously down and over and around rapids and falls, he named what he passed, and behind him the canyons stretched northward to the railroad, forever now a part of human knowledge.

He passed and misread Ashley's daub, passed Brown's Park (then called Brown's Hole) with its tracks of Indian and fur-trader and rustler and horse thief and its ruins of old Fort Davy Crockett, earlier called Fort Misery, left over from fur-trade days. Once he dropped through the Gate of Lodore, which is for practical purposes the northern river entrance to the present Monument, the map and its names are his: the Canyon of Lodore, Disaster Falls, where he lost a boat, Triplet Falls, Hell's Half Mile, Echo Park and Steamboat Rock, Whirlpool Canyon and Island Park and Split Mountain. The accounts written by himself and the men of his party for various newspapers were the first reports on that country, except for Jim Beckwourth's monumental lies, that the world at large saw. The photographs taken by his photographers E. O. Beaman and Jack Hillers in the next few years were the first pictorial record, and brought the canyons to the parlor stereoscopes of the nation. Powell's own *Report on the Exploration of the Colorado River of the West* remains one of the great Western adventure stories, as well as a cornerstone of early geology.

The Major hung on to this country which he had opened. He ran the canyons again in 1871, and he was exploring the area by land all through the seventies. He clarified the whole region of the Plateau Province, stretching all the way from Wyoming to modern Lake Mead, and in person or through his collaborators he gave it not merely a map and names, but much of its geological history and an explanation of its forms. Reading the rocks of this country so strange, so unstudied, and so perfectly exposed by the cutting edges of the rivers, he produced a second monograph, *The Geology of the Uinta Mountains of*

Utah and a Portion of Country Adjacent Thereto, and in that book and its predecessor, the *Exploration,* laid the foundations for much of the modern science of geomorphology. In the area east and south of Dinosaur, among the White River and Uinta Utes, he began the studies of the native tribes that eventually made him, in the words of Spencer Baird of the Smithsonian, the one who "knew more about the live Indian than any live man."

The real discoverer of the Dinosaur Canyons was the man who brought knowledge to them, and that man was Powell. Though Clarence King's Survey of the 40th Parallel worked across the northern edge of the Uintas in the late sixties, and both F. V. Hayden and the celebrated paleontologist Othniel C. Marsh had touched the fringes a year or two later, it was Powell who penetrated the country and made it his own. King, Hayden, and Marsh all persist on the map as names of high Uinta peaks, but Powell's mark is all over the map. He is the *genius loci* of Dinosaur, as of all the canyons of the Green and Colorado. Schoolmaster to the nation, explorer, enthusiast, planner, and prophet, he probably affected more lives in the West than any of our Presidents have, and it was from the canyons of Dinosaur that he drew much of his early knowledge and the hints that a long career would develop into policies of land and water and settlement vital to half the continent.

But it was not Major Powell who got the Dinosaur canyons preserved as part of the National Park System, and not he who gave the Monument its somewhat misleading name. That, or the beginning of it, was the work of another enthusiast, less illustrious but quite as dedicated, named Earl Douglass.

Douglass, like Powell, was a frontier farm boy, self-made, partly self-educated. When he came into the Uinta Valley he was already a distinguished field geologist, paleontologist, and botanist. He had worked with Marsh at Yale and botanized with C. G. Pringle in Mexico; he had discovered the mammalian fossils that dated the controversial Fort Union deposits in Montana; he was the discoverer of the duckbill dinosaur, and one of the first authorities in the world on Tertiary mammals. He first conducted a search through the Uinta Valley because a hunch told him that giant bones reported by sheepherders meant a real deposit, a regular dinosaur quarry, somewhere near. And he was encouraged in his bone-hunting by Andrew Carnegie, who sent him out on a personal commission to find things to fill the Carnegie Museum's Hall of Vertebrate Paleontology in Pittsburgh, and win people to education with something as big as a barn.

Douglass found his dinosaur deposit in August 1909, when he stumbled across a row of Brontosaur vertebrae weathered out in relief in an exposed wall of the Morrison formation below the mouth of Split Mountain Canyon. He worked the quarry under the most primitive conditions for fifteen years, scraping and blasting and chiseling at the rock, removing and labeling the bones, packing them in homemade plaster of paris cooked out of the local gypsum ledges, hauling them to the railroad dozens of miles away and shipping them back to the Carnegie Institute—700,000 pounds of them altogether.

He filled not only Carnegie's hall but many another; in almost any good paleontological museum the world around you are likely to encounter the bones of dinosaurs, big or little, carnivorous or herbivorous, that were grounded on the Jurassic bar where Monument Headquarters now stands, and were patiently picked out of the rock 120,000,000 years later by Earl Douglass and his helpers.

In a very real way, Douglass gave his life to that dinosaur graveyard. He put his best years into it. His unfinished stone house, part of the dream he had of an irrigated homestead on the banks of the Green, still stands there with the wind lonesome through its window and door holes and the lizards alert on its sills—as eloquent an archaeological monument as any the Fremont people left. Within a little fence, under homemade headstones below the dune-like Jurassic foothills of the Uintas, lie the bodies of his father and sister. These things give him a dry and whispering vested interest in the place; his innocent, laborious, enthusiastic spirit persists there.

He is also the reason why the Dinosaur Monument exists, for he found it so hard to protect his diggings from souvenir-hunters that he had to do something. At first he tried to take out a mineral claim, but found that bones, even petrified ones, were not among the minerals. So he appealed to the Carnegie Museum, and the Museum took its influence to Washington, and on October 4, 1915, Woodrow Wilson by proclamation set aside the eighty acres around the quarry as Dinosaur National Monument.

The quarry is still part of the Monument, whose headquarters building sits next door. Eventually, with funds, there will be a roofed over natural museum in the pit, with the bones of one or several dinosaurs exposed in high relief and in place, and with dioramas to show the Jurassic swamp world partially and accidentally preserved across scores of millions of years.

But the dinosaur quarry which gave the Monument its name is no more than the front yard of the people's park here established. Back of his natural schoolroom, which until it can be properly developed must remain a dusty hole in the side of a sun-smitten ridge, is the living laboratory of the Green and Yampa canyons stretching all the way from the mouth of Split Mountain to Steamboat Rock, and from that natural dividing cliff up the Yampa to Lily Park and up the Green through Lodore to Brown's Park.

The canyons were added to the Dinosaur National Monument by proclamation of Franklin D. Roosevelt on July 14, 1938, in a move which was part of the national rescue operation to save eroded range lands and mined Dust Bowl fields and endangered watersheds and half-spoiled wilderness areas from total ruin. The consciousness of national guilt and mismanagement, and the press of necessity, were strong then; they are less strong now, when partially successful rescue work and a rainier cycle have temporarily healed some of the scars of the thirties. To this moment, at least, the Green and Yampa canyons have been saved intact, a wilderness that is the property of all Americans, a 325-square-mile preserve that is part schoolroom and part play-ground and part—the best part—sanctuary from a world paved with concrete, jet-propelled, smog-blanketed, sterilized, over-insured, aseptic; a world mass-produced with interchangeable parts, and with every natural beautiful thing endangered by the raw engineering power of the twentieth century.

We live in the Antibiotic Age, and Antibiotic means literally "against life." We had better not be against life. That is the way to become as extinct as the dinosaurs. And if, as the population experts were guessing in November 1954, the human race will (other things being equal) have increased so much in the next three hundred years that we will have only a square yard of ground apiece to stand on, then we may want to take turns running to some preserved place such as Dinosaur. *How much wilderness do the wilderness-lovers want?*

ask those who would mine and dig and cut and dam in such sanctuary spots as these. The answer is easy: *Enough so that there will be in the years ahead a little relief, a little quiet, a little relaxation, for any of our increasing millions who need and want it.* That means we need as much wilderness as can still be saved. There isn't much left, and there is no more where the old open spaces came from.

Perhaps, when the Jurassic equivalent of a hornet stung a dinosaur somewhere out along his eighty or ninety feet of tail, it may have taken him ten or fifteen minutes to get the word. Even when he had a regional organization, the so-called "second brain" of the Stegosaurus, he was mentally retarded; his reactions were slow, with results that we can read in the rocks of the quarry in Dinosaur National Monument.

It should not take us so long as it took Stegosaurus to get word that is vital to us. There is some evidence already that we run the risk of an over-specialization as fatal as that of the sauropods—we may over-engineer ourselves. The vital wilderness, the essential hoarded living-space, the open and the green and the quiet, might not survive the bulldozer as readily as they survived Ashley's bullboats and Manly's bullwhackers.

A place is nothing in itself. It has no meaning, it can hardly be said to exist, except in terms of human perception, use, and response. The wealth and resources and usefulness of any region are only inert potential until man's hands and brain have gone to work; and natural beauty is nothing until it comes to the eye of the beholder. The natural world, actually, is the test by which each man proves himself: I see, I feel, I love, I use, I alter, I appropriate, therefore I am. Or the natural world is a screen onto which we project our own images; without our images there, it is as blank as the cold screen of an empty movie house. We cannot even describe a place except in terms of its human uses.

And as the essential history of Dinosaur is its human history, the only possible destruction will be a human destruction. Admittedly it would be idiotic to preach conservation of such a wilderness in perpetuity, just to keep it safe from all human use. It is only for human use that it has any meaning, or is worth preserving. But there is a vast difference among uses. Some uses use things *up* and some last forever. Recreation, properly controlled, is a perpetual use, and a vital one. It is possible to make such a wilderness as Dinosaur accessible without ruining it, and more than possible that its value for human relief from twentieth-century strains and smells and noises will prove greater than its problematic, limited, and short-term value for water or power, especially when those values can be had at other sites without violating this unique and beautiful canyon sanctuary.

We have learned something of what we risk when we mess around with nature's balances. If we destroy even so apparently worthless and harmful an item as down timber in a forest, we destroy the home of insects and grubs that are the food of certain birds. Destroying their food, we drive the birds out or thin them out, and in doing so we remove one of the principal policing agents. Deprived of its winged police, our nice cleaned-up forest may be infected with sudden devastating pests, more virulent and less controllable than anything that nature's checks and balances have permitted before.

Eventually we may learn that it is quite as dangerous to remake without sufficient precaution the total face of the planet, to turn our bulldozers and earth-movers loose just because we can.

Back in the canyons of the Green and Yampa, and in the pockets along side streams, there have been hermits and squatters and isolated ranchers from the 1870's on. One of them, old Pat Lynch, heard about Echo Park from his friend Major Powell and settled there probably in the seventies. During many years in the canyons he spread himself; he was a one-man Occupation of what was called locally Pat's Hole. He had cabins and cave shelters in both Echo Park and Castle Park; a cave on the Rial Chew ranch on Pool Creek still contains some of his personal belongings and his sapling bed. Castle Park seems to have been the real Pat's Hole, headquarters of Pat's occupation, for in the possession of Charley Mantle is a notice which says: "To all who this may consarn that I Pat Lynch do lay claim on this botom for my home and support. Wrote the 8th month of 1886 by P Lynch."

Pat was the first white man to use the Yampa and Green river canyons, and he used them both for his livelihood and for his pleasure. He did not neglect immortality: his private petroglyph, a ship under full sail, is pecked into the cliff in Castle Park to link his spirit with Fremont man and Ute Spaniard and fur-trade partisan. He was a cultural horizon: University of Colorado archaeologists excavating Hell's Midden found a whole clearly defined layer, already covered with silt and dirt, containing the suspender buttons, cartridge cases, and other artifacts and relics of Pat Lynch's authentic life.

But the most characteristic of the remains he left is one that might be used as a motto by all the increasing users of the canyons who have come after him. In a cave that had been one of Pat's shelters, the Mantles found a note. It said, in the brogue that cropped out even in Pat's writing:

> If in those caverns you shelter take
>
> Plais do them no harm
>
> Lave everything you find around hanging up or on
>   the ground.

That is all conservation is about. That is all the National Parks are about. Use, but do no harm.

It is legitimate to hope that there may left [*sic*] in Dinosaur the special kind of human mark, the special record of human passage, that distinguishes man from all other species. It is rare enough among men, impossible to any other form of life. *It is simply the deliberate and chosen refusal to make any marks at all.* Sometimes we have withheld our power to destroy, and have left a threatened species like the buffalo, a threatened beauty spot like Yosemite or Yellowstone or Dinosaur, scrupulously alone. We are the most dangerous species of life on the planet, and every other species, even the earth itself, has cause to fear our power to exterminate. But we are also the only species which, when it chooses to do so, will go to great effort to save what it might destroy.

It is a better world with some buffalo left in it, a richer world with some gorgeous canyons unmarred by signboards, hot-dog stands, super highways, or high-tension lines, undrowned by power or irrigation reservoirs. If we preserved as parks only those places that have no economic possibilities, we would have no parks. And in the decades to come, it will not only be only the buffalo and the trumpeter swan who need sanctuaries. Our own species is going to need them too.

It needs them now.

The Dinosaur National Monument

Earl Douglass

In 1909 paleontologist Earl Douglass discovered one of the world's great collections of fossilized dinosaur bones along the Green River near Split Mountain. Douglass was instrumental in the successful effort to preserve the area as Dinosaur National Monument, which would eventually be expanded to incorporate the wildest parts of the Green and Yampa Rivers. In this previously unpublished manuscript, Douglass explicates the geology of the region, details the explorations that led to his discovery, and calls for its preservation for the benefit of generations to come.

When one enters a great natural history museum like those in New York City, Washington or Pittsburg [*sic*], he is lured there by curiosity, interest in nature, or that something in his being which is attracted by the mysterious or thrilled by the marvellous. Among many other interesting things, he sees bones, skulls, skeletons and restorations of huge, strange or bizarre beasts, some of which, it is claimed, once inhabited the earth before man lived or wrote histories. He asks or thinks, "Where in the world did those things come from?" The giant whales, he knows, came from the deep, dark, hidden wastes of the ocean—and "who knows what unheard of things are still there?"

He finds that the greater number of the seemingly absurd burlesques on animal life came from "way out west." "O, yes," he thinks, "that explains it. Anything could come from there."; and he goes away satisfied, in a way; yet it is likely that at times after this his mind is "at seas" with the whales or is roaming over that land of wonders, where all impossibilities seem easy. He has at least a foundation for that imaginary world which all of us build. How much is true, in this land of dreams, and how much is fiction, and which is the more fascinating and marvellous? Let us go to the ancient burying place of some of these strange animals and try to read the story that is told there; then each can judge for himself.

Teeth and bones of large animals, different from any now living; were found in Europe about one hundred years ago, and some of them were so large that the naturalist, Richard Owen, named them Dinosaurs, (Greek *deinos,* terrible and *sauros,* lizard). They were not lizards or *like* lizards—they were not like anything now living, but they had to have a name, so the poor little lizards were called upon to furnish a name for what we now know was one or more mighty races. They were classified as an order or subclass of reptiles but some believe that they, like the mammals, should be put in a class by themselves. In fact a more careful study seems to show that what we call "dinosaurs" belong to two or more unrelated orders of animals.

About fifty years ago, bones larger than those which had been found in Europe, were discovered in the Rocky Mountain region. Professor O. C. Marsh of Yale College became much interested in these. In the region of Como Bluffs, in Wyoming, he opened several quarries where the bones of dinosaurs were imbedded in the rock. One of his best quarries was north of Canyon City, Colorado. He did not usually find complete skeletons with the bones articulated, but he found many parts of skeletons. As in Ezekiel's "valley of dry bones" the bones of the same kind—if not of the same individuals—came together "bone to his bone", a few at a time until Professor Marsh began to see what "manner of beasts" these animals were. Out of these ancient rubbish heaps slowly developed the bony-plated, spike-tailed *Stegosaurus* (covered-lizard), the huge long-necked, long-tailed *Brontosaurus* (thunder lizard), the fierce, sharp-toothed and sharp-clawed *Allosaurus* (leaping-lizard) and others.

From these bones which Marsh had assembled he made pictorial restorations. They were not perfect, as he did not have all of the bones, and nearly all of the skulls were disarticulated or more or less crushed, but he was the only man who knew much about the American Dinosaurs. His scientific work and scientific ideas formed a splendid basis for the work of those who followed, and one of his greatest services to science was the development of the proper methods of quarrying and shipping the bones of these immense animals.

Dinosaur National Monument, map by Norton Allen,
from *Desert Magazine*.

≋ Some of the Carnegie Museum's Explorations in the West

After spending many years in collecting fossil mammals—camels, three-toed horses, rhinoceroses, mastodons, and many others, in the Upper Tertiary deposits of western Montana, I made a request of Doctor Wm. J. Holland, the director of the Carnegie Museum that I be sent to Utah to make a collection of fossil mammals from the Uinta (lower Tertiary) formation there. In the spring of 1908 I started for this field.

I produred [*sic*] a team and outfit in Grand Junction, Colorado. My brother-in-law accompanied me. From Mack, a station on the Denver and Rio Grande railway and the southern terminus of the narrow-gage [*sic*] Uinta Railway, we drove to Achee which is at the foot of that great escarpment which seemed to shut out the long-dreamed-of hunting ground of the fossil collector. While we were looking at this great rocky curtain and wondering how we were going to get over it we saw two dark lines of smoke arising from just below the top of the rim, then a dark thread, and the truth suddenly struck me and I exclaimed, "Great Heavens! Is that where the train comes from?" "Heaven" was the right word, for the train, a double header, was just starting down from the sky up in the region of Baxter Pass.

We were advised to ship our wagon over the pass on a flat car, and it was good advice as it was enough for the horses to climb the steep slope without the wagon and load. It was only about three miles to the top of the pass by the trail, while the railroad—said to be the steepest in the world without a cog-rail—twisted and "squirmed around", as it climed [*sic*] a distance of seven miles to the top of the pass. It seemed like a great serpant [*sic*] that had tried to climb over and had given it up.

Some of us have an instinctive belief that there is something great and wonderful behind the farthest forest or hill or ridge that we can see. This has often led me on and on to return weary and hungry after dark. Though we laugh at the bear that "went over the mountain to see what he could see", we cannot help having a fellow feeling for him. When I had reached the summit of the pass where I had hoped to get a view of the "promised land," we could see, stretching below, and far away to the northward, a labarynth [*sic*] of rocky canyons and escarpment; and into this confusing maze the little railroad found its way.

Why does this railroad climb over this immense rocky wall into this wilderness of badlands, rocky canyons and semi-arid wastes? We shall see.

At Dragon, which was then the terminus of this railroad—fifty-five miles in length—there was a dense, black smoke issuing in clouds from a large, straight, perpendicular fissure in the sandstones of the canyon wall. One could easily imagine that a great saw had cut this fissure into the earth and a black substance in a liquid or plastic form had poured in and this had dried and hardened. Possibly it was from the fancied resemblance of this substance to congealed dragons blood that this vein was called the Black Dragon. The filling of the fissure was a black, jetty material and resembled cannel coal but was much more bright and shiny. It could be plainly seen that it would burn. The find [sic] dust will explode something like gunpowder and this was the cause of the fire in the vein. It is the dried, asphaltic, residue of petroleum and is called Gilsonite from the pioneer who was one of the first to call attention to it. It was derived from the immense and far famed deposits of oil shale above and below the sandstones in which it occurs. It was to transport this gilsonite—useful for many purposes—that this little railroad was built. In a canyon south of Dragon a stream of natural lubricating oil and water flows from a fissure in the sandstone rocks.

From Dragon we followed the Uintah Railway Stage Line to White River which flows westward through the Uinta Basin and enters the Green River, which is really the upper portion of the Colorado River. For 25 miles more the White River has cut a picturesque canyon through the Green River shales and the overlying Uinta Deposits. The shales are nearly or quite 1000 feet in thickness and yield, by distillation, as high as 90 gallons or more of oil to the ton.

But the Green River deposits are interesting in another way as they contain such wonderful records of the life of the far off time when they accumulated as sediments in the marshes, lakes and rivers. In them are found remainds [sic] of fish, turtles, lizards, birds (about the rarest of vertebrate fossils), and hosts of plants and insects beautifully preserved. Nearly all of the orders of insects, as bugs, beetles, flies, mosquitoes, ticks, dragon flies, moths, etc. have been found. Countless billions of the larvae of insects—especially those of the Diptera (flies) were entombed entire. In places these form a considerable portion of the rock and there seems little doubt that they contributed their part to make the shales so rich in oil.

Fossil leaves and stems are found in great abundance in many formations, but here we find fossil fruits, singly and in clusters, and fossil flowers with all of their minute parts showing. Even thin microscopic sections have shown the minute, fertilizing, pollen grains.

After crossing the White River we ascended a canyon in the Uinta sandstones which are younger than the Green River beds and immediately overlies them. These sandstones are "shot through" with immense parallel veins of gilsonite, each vein "showing up" for many miles in length and one vein attaining a thickness of 18 feet.

North of the canyon is a region of desert prairies with outlying buttes and mesas, and beyond this, to the northward, a wilderness of badlands collored [sic] yellow, brown, green, gray and red. It was in this region—we did not know just where—that we hoped to find the remains of extinct mammals found nowhere else. We camped in a stone cabin by a gilsonite vein—the Cowboy—and began to search the sandstone ledges in the surrounding buttes, mesas and the bare badland areas—and not without success. We remained in this camp for five months and obtained two four-horse loads of fossils in the rock. Complete skeletons of the larger mammals—the Titanotheres or *giant beasts*—had not been found here but later the Carnegie Museum Expedition discovered a pocket of bones and skulls in a sandstone cliff and two skeletons and several skulls were quarried out. One of these skeletons forms the splendid slab-mount of Dolichorhinus (long nose) now on exhibition in the Carnegie Museum.

During the summer of 1908, Doctor Wm. J. Holland, the Director of the Carnegie Museum and an old friend of Andrew Carnegie, came to visit us in our camp and to look over the fossil grounds. He was much interested in the big dinosaurs and he went with me to some bluffs near Green River where Mr. B. Burton—who was superintending the construction of a gold-dredge boat by the river—had shown me some large bones. One of the bones which we found there would probably weight [sic] nearly 800 pounds. There were many "scattering" bones, but, as we did not find very good indications of complete skeletons, Dr. Holland hardly thought that the prospect warranted extensive excavating. On our return we crossed the river on a ferry and followed a wagon trail between the Green River on the south and the unique walls of uplifted rocks on the north, which encircled, on the westward, the bare, rugged, fantastically carved Split Mountain uplift. Instead of seeking an easier route through softer rocks on the west side of this uplift, the Green River has cut a deep canyon through the older and harder rocks in the heart of the mountain. We little thought as we rode along admiring the unique scenery and remarking that it was different from anything that we had scene [*sic*], we were passing within a half mile of just the thing the Carnegie Museum and other museums had sought for many years—a greater burying ground of prehistoric monsters than had been found—one which contained complete skeletons and perfect skulls of the great dinosaurs.

I returned to the Carnegie Museum in the autumn of 1908, and when the winter had nearly passed and the warmer days made the fossil hunter long for the wild free mountains and badlands of the west, Dr. Holland said, one day, "Douglass, you'll have to go to Utah again. You made a good collection and you have only begun." The possibility of finding big dinosaurs was discussed, as well as other alluring prospects.

In the summer of 1909, I discovered fossil mammals in the Wasatch (lower Tertiary) of Western Colorado and made an excursion into the Uinta deposits forty miles further west than the region where we had collected the previous year. On returning to Myton, Utah, I received a letter from Dr. Holland which made me decide to go at once and make a search for dinosaurs. I went to the region east of Vernal and followed the formation in which we had seen the remains of dinosaurs the year before. Many fragmentary bones were weathered out on the surface but on excavating it was found those still buried in the rock were borken [*sic*] and disassociated. These were of no value to us as it was complete or nearly complete skeletons that was needed at the time, both for study and exhibition. After a search of about two weeks I was pretty much disheartened as to the prospect there, but there was still a little section which I had not looked over.

I returned the next day and found a sandstone ledge which contained many weathered and broken bones. I followed it down to the bottom of a deep gulch and up the steep slope on the other side. When I had reached the top of the ridge, near the termination of the sandstone ledge, there suddenly appeared to my vision seven large joints of the tail of a huge dinosaur, weathered out on the face of the steeply sloping southern surface of the outcrop. It looked far better than anything I had seen and the position of the bones gave the impression that a whole skeleton was buried there. I reported it to Doctor Holland. He was much interested. It was seen that it would be expensive work—that of quarrying out such an immense skeleton, freighting it "across country" sixty five miles and sending it by the narrow gage and main line railroads to Pittsburge [*sic*], but Mr. Carnegie said, to go ahead and see what was there.

Work, with a force of men, was begun the first of September. The tail was followed forward in the direction in which the bones of the body should be. The huge pelvis was found in place, but in excavating beyond this to see if the joints of the dorsal region (the back) were in place, there came a sad disappointment. There was a break, but a little further to the west a series of bones extended a distance of about 20 feet. After working around these it was discovered that they were the articulated bones of an immense neck. Just below this the dorsals were uncovered and most of them were articulated. The limbs and ribs were found near but disarticulated. There was a year of hard work, planning and excavating before it was certain that we had a skeleton complete enough to mount on its feet, but the first impression that there had been a nearly or quite complete animal buried there was correct, and, in 1914, its skeleton was mounted in a life-like position in the Carnegie Museum. It was the first individual skeleton of this kind to be mounted on its feet with so little restoration.

Before this skeleton was out, another, as complete but smaller, came to light. In this nearly all of the parts of the skeleton, including the ribs, were articulated, and before this was out other bones and parts of the skeletons showed up. As we stripped the bone layer new bones and skeletons were ever coming to light, so we were lured on year after year by the discovery of more complete skeletons and perfect skulls than had been found elsewhere. While some of these furnished the nearly complete bony framework of dinosaurs partly known, others were forms not previously discovered. The place which scientists had long sought had been found, so why discontinue the work. The great dinosaurs and the age in which they lived were little known. Few other institutions could afford the expense. Mr. Carnegie had taken a special interest in this work and had furnished the means to do it "out of his own pocket". It was not the American spirit to leave any part of past history dark if the records were accessible. Now was the opportune time. The future will almost certainly show Mr. Carnegie's wisdom and justify Dr. Holland's judgment and enthusiasm in continuing the work as long as he did.

The significance of this quarry does not lie wholly in the fact that two museums and one university have shipped to their store rooms 350 tons or more of fossils in the rock and are working them out slowly and painstakingly, in their laboratories, for exhibition and study; that many years later scientists will study and compare the many different forms brought to light; that they will read the secrets recorded in the surrounding rocks; and new volumes will be added to our knowledge of the world and its past history. Of as great, or greater, importance to us is the fact that in our democratic civilization knowledge and science are valuable in proportion as they are taken into the consciousness of the people.

As stated in the beginning of this article, many go into the great museums to satisfy the natural craving for the marvellous, but the strange things which they see, surrounded by more or less artificial settings, make their thoughts and imaginations fly away toward the setting sun from whence these marvels came; when they actually, come to this great burying ground of the past, set in the midst of vast lonely distances, surrounded by plains and badland wastes with their background of mountain hights [*sic*]—when in the midst of this seemingly almost unreal workd [*sic*] they behold, exposed on the rocky cliffs the great skeletons of animals which are supposed to have lived millions of years ago, it is then that they get such a stirring up and rearrangement of their thinking powers as they have never experienced before. They begin to see that while they had been dreaming what was not so a greater world that was real was hidden from view.

What should be done with this world-wonder so that it may give the pleasure and profit which it is capable of furnishing?

The answer seems clear and definite. I have been with the quarry from the first and have talked with many people in varied ranks of life and I have yet to hear a dissenting voice from those who have seen the quarry when large portions of skeletons were exposed.

A natural museum should be made by uncovering the bones and skeletons in relief upon the ledge thus making a great "panel mount." This should be housed for the protection of the skeletons and the comforts and convenience of sight-seers and students.

The quarry has been left in an ideal condition for such a display. There is a block of the bone layer 125 feet in length and 25 feet or more in height which could be uncovered at a minimum expense. The zone which contains the bones has been taken away from three sides of this area—east, west and above. Bones and skeletons were numerous all around the area and they were seen extending into it [when][1] the work stopped, so there are no doubts that the further excavating would uncover an abundance of bones for display.

The rocks are dipping here to the southward, away from the main axis of the Uinta Mountains, at an angle of 60 degrees—30 degrees from perpendicular—so that when the picture is uncovered one can sit or stand and gaze at it at ease as one would study or admire a great painting. No other place yet discovered could be made to furnish such an exhibit. No other known quarry has such a superabundance of material to uncover.

When this plan is carried out—and it seems sure to come sooner or later—this monument with its unparalleled settings will be a Mecca for geologists from all over the world—a natural geological school. Not only is the formation which contains the dinosaurs beautifully exposed, but a succession of stratified deposits more than 40,000 feet in thickness and showing formations which originated in oceans, deserts, seashores, inland seas, lakes, marshes, rivers, flood plains, and sand dune areas—reaching from what is to us the dawn of life to the present—is exposed as an open book ready to be read by enthusiastic investigators. As yet we have interpreted but a few words and sentences of this great book.

≋ NOTES

1. A gap occurs in the text here.

Shall We Let Them Ruin
Our National Parks?

Bernard De Voto

ANOTHER LEADING WESTERN WRITER, HISTORIAN, AND CONSER-
VATIONIST WHO PLAYED A LEADING ROLE IN THE STRUGGLE AGAINST
THE ECHO PARK DAM PROJECT WAS BERNARD DE VOTO. THE ARTI-
CLE EXCERPTED HERE, WHICH CALLS FOR PRESERVATION NOT ONLY
OF ECHO PARK BUT OF AMERICA'S WILD RIVERS AND THE NATIONAL
PARK SYSTEM AS A WHOLE, FIRST APPEARED IN THE JULY 22, 1950,
ISSUE OF THE *Saturday Evening Post*.

No one has asked the American people whether they want their sovereign rights, and those of their descendants, in their own publicly reserved beauty spots wiped out. Thirty-two million of them visited the National Parks in 1949. More will visit them this year. The attendance will keep on increasing as long as they are worth visiting, but a good many of them will not be worth visiting if engineers are let loose on them.

The entire National Park System comprises an area less than three quarters of 1 per cent of the area of the United States. It contains only sites that are universally acknowledged to be supreme in beauty, grandeur and spectacle. They were set aside to the sole end that they should be preserved as they are, that there should always be places where Americans could have the inestimable experience of untouched wilderness, unspoiled natural beauty and unmarred natural spectacle. That end is now in danger of being subverted by engineering construction. No one can doubt that the public, if told all the facts and allowed to express its will, would vote to preserve the parks from any alteration now or in the future. But the public is not being told all the facts; it is not being given a chance to express its will.

Most people who have seen the Grand Canyon consider it our supreme natural spectacle. What would it look like if the Colorado

River at the bottom of the gorge, the river that carved the gorge, were to be made a dry stream bed?

Down near the Arizona-Utah boundary is Rainbow Bridge, the most famous and most beautiful of all the natural bridges, a high, superbly symmetrical arch of stone, long ago set aside as a National Monument. The water of a storage reservoir may undermine it and bring it down. Should we permit that to happen?

After the Green River flows out of Wyoming to cross parts of Northwestern Colorado and Northeastern Utah, it roars and riots through a series of deep, narrow canyons, one of which is named Lodore. If a dam were to transform the tempestuous Green in Lodore Canyon into a lake 500 feet deep would you drive 2000 miles to sail a dinghy there?

These and other areas of unmatched beauty or sublimity, which were made National Parks or National Monuments so that they could be preserved untouched forever, are in danger of being ruined by engineering projects. Should we let them be ruined?

The National Park Service is a bureau of the Department of the Interior, where, in appropriations, it is overshadowed by the Bureau of Reclamation, which builds dams. Though the Park Service has other duties, its primary job is to administer the National Parks and Monuments. The act of Congress which created it directed it "to conserve the scenery and the natural and historic objects and the wildlife therein, and to provide for the enjoyment of the same in such manner and by such means as will leave them unimpaired for the enjoyment of future generations."

These words are perfectly clear and they enact into law a policy that goes all they way back to the establishment of Yellowstone National Park in 1872. In fact, it goes back further, to a handful of citizens of Montana who first explored the Yellowstone country and who, though they might have homesteaded all its marvels for themselves, decided spontaneously that it must belong to all the people of the United States. The Act of Dedication of this, the first national park any nation ever set aside, established Yellowstone Park "as a public park or pleasuring ground for the benefit and enjoyment of the people," and directed the Secretary of the Interior to preserve "from injury or spoliation...all timber, mineral deposits, natural curiosities or wonders" and to retain them "in their natural condition."

The legally enacted policy cannot be misconstrued: the parks and monuments are to be preserved as they are naturally, without deface-ment. It has been maintained so far, though not without hard effort. Because some of these areas contain valuable minerals, timber, water resources and water power, there have been many attempts to get the law changed so that they could be exploited. These attempts, which would ruin the parks if they succeeded, have heretofore usually been made by private groups intent on getting hold of public resources for their own profit.

In the last few years, however, a curious development has brought the National Park System under attack by two public agencies. Each of them has about a third of a billion dollars of public funds to spend every year, and so can exert incomparably more pressure than any corporation that ever cast a covetous eye on the wilderness beauties which were set aside for posterity to enjoy. One of these agencies is the Bureau of Reclamation, the other the Corps of (Army) Engineers. Their campaign of attrition raises fundamental questions about our grandchildren's heritage of wilderness scenery. It also involves serious issues in regard to the power of Federal agencies to subvert public policy. How the campaign works and what hinges on it can be clearly seen in the current effort of the Bureau of Reclamation to get autho-rization, which is now not legally possible, to make over Lodore Can-yon in Colorado.

The canyon was named and first traversed by the adventurous one-armed geologist, John Wesley Powell, on his exploration of the Green and Colorado rivers. It was on June 8, 1869, that he took his boats into this deep and narrow gorge. Confined between sandstone walls that are alternately overhanging and set back in terraces, the Green here becomes an unimaginably violent chaos of rapids, falls, whirlpools, sucks and chutes. This twenty-mile stretch is one of the most hazardous—and most spectacular—parts of the so-far-untamed Green River.

Before entering Lodore Canyon, the Green flows tranquilly through a mountain meadow called Brown's Park. At the lower end of the can-yon it emerges into another beautiful, high-walled valley which Pow-ell named Echo Park. Massive rock formations rise from the floor of Echo Park, and here the Yampa River flows into the Green from the east, having just emerged from a narrow, twisting canyon wholly unlike Lodore, but equally overpowering. The Green then flows westward through two more canyons. The setting of these four canyons is a landscape of brilliantly colored, fantastically eroded mesas, buttes, mountains, gulches and high basins. A panorama of fantasy, overwhelming to the imagination, this high rock desert has certain resemblances to the Bryce Canyon and Zion Canyon country and to Cedar Breaks, all in Utah, and to the setbacks and vistas of the Grand Canyon, which is in Arizona. But as each of these tremendous spectacles is, it is unique, of its own individual character and quality. It is one of the great scenic areas of the United States.

In 1938, Lodore Canyon, Yampa Canyon, Echo Park, the two subsidiary canyons and their rocky desert setting—327 square miles all told—were made public domain to the National Park System. About a third of it is in Utah, two thirds in Colorado. If the area had been called, say, Green River National Monument, its nature and importance would have been self-evident in the name. But a National Monument already existed at its western edge, a small tract of eighty acres which had been set aside to protect the greatest known deposit of Mesozoic fossils, especially dinosaurs. The new reservation was added to this and the whole received the name of the original small part, Dinosaur National Monument. As a result, during the effort to keep a magnificent scenic wilderness from being defaced, many people have supposed that only the quarry where dinosaur fossils are excavated is at stake, though, as a matter of fact, the quarry has never been endangered.

When the monument was established, most of Brown's Park was left outside the boundaries. The exclusion was made because, years earlier, the Reclamation Service—now the Bureau of Reclamation—had declared Brown's Park a possible site for a reclamation project—that is, for a reservoir from which water could be pumped to irrigate a small area in Eastern Utah. The Bureau of Reclamation has by now abandoned whatever intention it may have had of so using Brown's Park. But it has undertaken to construct a hydroelectric-power development in Dinosaur National Monument. Both the laws which govern power projects and those which protect the National Park System forbid the construction of power dams in National Parks and National Monuments. There are, however, various ways of skinning a cat if you are good with a skinning knife. No one has ever said that the Bureau of Reclamation isn't.

In 1943, the First Assistant Secretary of the Interior made a "reclamation withdrawal" covering most of Dinosaur National Monument—that is, he officially declared it an area which could be used for reclamation projects. The "withdrawal" was almost certainly unauthorizable and therefore of no force. Furthermore, it was so smothered in administrative routine that, though it would destroy the monument, the National Park Service did not learn of it when it was made. On the basis of this questionable and semicovert withdrawal for reclamation—for irrigation—the bureau then began to plan a power development, which is prohibited. It proposed to build two dams with attendant power plants, one at Echo Park, the other at Split Mountain, farther down Green River. The estimated cost of the project is $207,000,000.

The dams cannot be built as the law now stands. They can be built if the law is changed—if pressure sufficiently powerful can be brought to bear on the Secretary of Interior so that he will be forced to recommend their construction, and then on Congress, so that it will amend the acts which now apply. The Bureau of Reclamation has enormous sums to spend in local communities for direct and indirect fiscal benefits; it generates political pressure as expertly as it does electric power. As soon as its plans for Dinosaur Monument were published, an agitation to breach the fundamental policy of the National Park System was set up in Utah and three neighboring states. It would be naïve to suppose that the bureau had no part in organizing this agitation; it was already well organized when the plans were made public.

The National Park Service first heard of the project as a daydream of the Bureau of Reclamation in connection with a vast plan for the transformation of the West called the Colorado River Project. The Green River is, of course, part of the Colorado River system. It was, so to speak, a theoretical, just-possible expedient to be tentatively considered in case equivalent results could be secured nowhere else in the Colorado River basin—and to be considered then only after exhaustive study and only after consultation with the National Park Service.

In spite of this understanding, *and without consulting the Park Service or obtaining clearance from the Secretary of the Interior*, the bureau laid the Dinosaur Monument project before the bodies that administer the interstate agreement which apportions water from the Colorado River. In February of this year those bodies recommended the immediate construction of Echo Park Dam. This would require legislation from Congress to authorize construction that is now prohibited in the monument—and the heat was on. Especially, the heat was on the Secretary of the Interior, one of whose duties is to protect the public interests—your interests—in the National Park System. The Western block worked smoothly. When Secretary Chapman ordered a public hearing, four Western senators and five Western congressmen appeared to add their testimony to that of embattled mayors and chambers of commerce that the nation would be well served by the abandonment of the policy which has protected the National Parks.

The hearing disclosed that not only heat had been generated but much fog, or smoke screen, as well. The Echo Park and Split Mountain project is solely a power development, but it received much support it otherwise might not have got because it has been represented in the West, where irrigation is a sacred word, as an irrigation project. Again the people of Utah have come, or have been led, to believe that water which the state has been allotted from the Colorado can be got to a still theoretical and prodigiously expensive reclamation project in Central Utah only from the reservoirs which the Bureau of Reclamation has planned in Dinosaur Monument. Actually, the bureau's own plans show that this water is to be taken from another project, farther up Green River and outside the monument. Utah and neighboring states have come, or had been led, to believe that these dams are indispensable for storage water allotted to them from the Colorado. Actually, the bureau plans to provide most of this storage at another dam far to the south of the monument, and the rest of it—if any more is needed for the allocations—could be provided at other sites outside the monument.

Finally, Utah believes that the sites of these dams are the only ones where power for its still-theoretical project could be generated, whereas there are many feasible sites outside Dinosaur Monument. And at the public hearing, Gen. U. S. Grant, III, himself an engineer, showed that the use of one of these other sites would reduce the cost of the project by a third. Nevertheless, the various appeals mentioned above have been blended to make a really formidable confusion.

No Western state would receive any benefit from the construction of these dams inside the monument that could not be insured by alternative construction outside it. What about the people of the United States as a whole, whose property the monument is? On behalf of sectional and even local interests, the general public will have to pay the non-recoverable cost, always a large fraction of the total cost, of a $207,000,000 project. In return it will suffer the permanent ruin of an area of great natural beauty.

For it will be permanently ruined. If you cut down a forest, Nature will probably grow another one in the course of a few centuries, but if you change a river, a mountain or a canyon, you can never change it back again. The downriver dam in Dinosaur Monument would defile the mountain park country along and below it substitute a placid reservoir for the turbulent river above. The other one, Echo Park Dam, would back water so far that throughout the whole extent of Lodore Canyon the Green River, the tempestuous, pulse-stirring river of John Wesley Powell, would become a mere millpond. The same would happen to Yampa Canyon.

Throughout both canyons the deep artificial lakes would engulf magnificent scenery, would reduce by from a fifth to a third the height of the precipitous walls, and would fearfully degrade the great vistas. Echo Park and its magnificent rock formations would be submerged. Dinosaur National Monument as a scenic spectacle would cease to exist.

A specious argument which has been used in connection with this assault on Dinosaur Monument is also a steadily increasing danger to other parts of the National Park System. We long ago passed the point where reclaimed Western land could repay the cost of the projects that reclaimed it, as it was originally intended to do. If it costs several hundred dollars an acre to make land worth fifty dollars an acre, the rest of the cost must be charged to something besides reclamation. If the project includes the production of electricity, the sale of power will take care of part of the remainder. If it includes flood protection—and, nowadays, try to find any dam on any babbling brook that is not supposed to—whatever fraction of the remainder can be allocated to flood control can be written off altogether, since the whole country benefits from reduction of flood losses. But honest cost accounting ends right there; no additional economic justification can be found.

Hence the Bureau of Reclamation has begun to publicize a shimmering but carefully unanalyzed value which it calls "recreation."

If the bureau can successfully allege that its projects create facilities for recreation, then it can charge to them as much of the uneconomic cost as it is able to get away with. Nobody doubts that the American people need facilities for recreation and will need more. But what kind, where, at what cost, and who shall pay for them? Should we write off $10,000,000 of the cost of an irrigation project because it will provide bass fishing for one North Dakota county? Should Philadelphia and Birmingham be taxed to provide sailboating for Las Vegas?

If it is able to force the Echo Park project through, the Bureau of Reclamation will build some fine highways along the reservoirs. Anyone who travels the 2000 miles from New York City—or 1200 from Galveston or 1000 from Seattle—will no doubt enjoy driving along those roads. He can also do still-water fishing where, before the bureau took benevolent thought of him, he could do only white-water fishing, and he can go boating or sailing on the reservoirs that have obliterated the scenery.

But the New Yorker can go motoring along the Palisades, boating in Central Park, sailing at Larchmont and fishing at many places within an hour of George Washington Bridge. No one will ever drive 2000 miles to row a boat; no one will ever seek recreation in a National Park except the kind for which the "pleasuring ground" was created— the unique experience of awesome and wonder that an untouched wilderness spectacle provides. The only reason why anyone would ever go to Dinosaur National Monument is to see what the Bureau of Reclamation proposes to destroy.

Unquestionably, the national interest requires the parks and the monuments to be preserved unmarred, as they were intended to be.

No emergency serious enough to justify invading the National Park System arose during either World War. No emergency is in sight now. But with as much time for planning as might be required, with promising and perhaps better alternatives only cursorily investigated, the Bureau of Reclamation is able to threaten Dinosaur National Monument with destruction. And probably the bureau's hand was not idle in a California agitation that has succeeded in introducing into

Congress a bill to investigate all possible power sites in Kings Canyon National Park. This park preserves the most magnificent mountain country in California outside Yosemite Park. Its boundaries were drawn so as to exclude areas which ought to have been included, but which were left out precisely because they were valuable power sites. The Engineers threaten Mammoth Cave with a dam which even Kentucky does not want. They threaten Glacier Park with a dam which they formally agreed not to build.

If any of these attempts should succeed, the law which protects the parks will be circumvented and there will be no protecting any of them from similar impairment thereafter. The parks do not belong to any bureau, any group of planners or engineers, any state or section. They belong to all of us. Do we want them? Will our grandchildren want them?

Dinosaurs, Parks, and Dams

David Brower

AT THE TIME OF THE ECHO PARK DAM CONTROVERSY, DAVID BROWER WAS EXECUTIVE DIRECTOR OF THE SIERRA CLUB AND PLAYED A PIVOTAL ROLE IN DEFEATING THE PROJECT. IN THIS ARTICLE, FIRST PUBLISHED IN *Pacific Spectator* IN 1954, BROWER POINTS OUT THE FLAWED RATIONALE FOR THE DAM AND THE THREAT IT POSED TO THE INTEGRITY OF THE ENTIRE NATIONAL PARK SYSTEM.

Absorbed as he was with the climax of the Civil War, Abraham Lincoln could hardly have known how far-reaching a step he was taking when, in 1864, he signed the bill which ceded Yosemite Valley to California as the first park to be preserved for the nation as a whole. This was a major step in the growth of the national park idea. Eight years later Yellowstone became the first national park per se, and more were soon added. Other nations, looking upon this idea and finding it good, followed suit, themselves setting aside some of the finest of their own scenic assets for the use and enjoyment, without impairment, of present and subsequent generations. Of this land they said in effect: This is a national park; to find as it was, to leave as it is.

The entire concept, and the National Park System which it bore, is now being challenged. The test is in a controversy seething over Dinosaur National Monument, astride the Colorado-Utah border between U.S. Highway 40 and Wyoming. The monument itself is named for an 80-acre fossil quarry set aside in 1915, by authority delegated to the President by Congress under provisions of the National Antiquities Act of 1906. The name gives no hint of what the present boundaries, today encompassing more than 200,000 acres, were extended in 1938 to preserve—the magnificent canyons of the Yampa and Green rivers, spectacularly carved through the front of the Uinta Mountains, part of the Rocky Mountain chain.

The trouble, to put it one way, is that the Yampa and Green are tributary to the Colorado, and that plans to develop the erratic Colorado's resources of water and power happen to include two dams within Dinosaur National Monument, at Echo Park and Split Mountain, which would flood all the 100-odd miles of the monument's unique canyon country beneath the waters of two fluctuating reservoirs. Echo Park dam, the more immediate threat, would be 525 feet high, would store 6,460,000 acre-feet of water in 107 miles of reservoir when full, would have an installed power capacity of 200,000 kilowatts, and would irrigate nothing.

Four bills—three in the House and one in the Senate—are now before Congress to authorize five of the ten dams the Bureau of Reclamation thinks necessary in its Upper Colorado River Storage Project, devised to enable Wyoming, Colorado, Utah, and New Mexico to meet their commitment under the Colorado River Compact of 1922 and thereupon to consumptively use about half of the Colorado's waters in the upper basin states.

The box score is a little perplexing. The upper basin states and the Bureau of Reclamation want ten dams (plus participating water-using projects). The current legislation calls for five dams. The Secretary of the Interior is currently favoring two—Echo Park and Glen Canyon— plus Navajo dam as a part of a participating project. The administration, through the Bureau of the Budget, has not yet agreed to any. Conservation organizations across the land do not object to a sound Upper Colorado storage project, but they insist that it must not encroach upon the dedicated lands of the National Park System, which the Secretary of the Interior is required by law to protect.

The basic plan of the Upper Colorado Project, published in 1950 and not substantially altered since, has been reviewed by several agencies. Basically the upper basin states favor it. California thinks the financial aspects are unsound and illegal, the engineering studies are vague and uncertain, Colorado River Compact interpretations are erroneous, and the quantity and quality of the lower basin's water are in jeopardy. The Corps of Engineers calls the 1950 report "a preliminary treatment of a plan" and questions both the engineering and the benefits. The Department of Agriculture tactfully objects to having been left out of the agricultural planning, as well as to the incompleteness of the study and the accounting methods proposed. A federal power engineer points out that the power output has been miscalculated and indicates that Echo Park power could only be sold at a loss; moreover, the upper basin is charged neither for the loss of power at Hoover Dam—the equivalent of what would be produced by about three and a half years' flow of the entire Colorado River that must be lost from the filling of the upstream reservoirs—nor for the subsequent loss from upstream depletions. The Fish and Wildlife Service questions the alleged benefits to fish and wildlife. The Geological Survey states that water-resource data fall far short of presenting an understanding needed for the storage plan. And the National Park Service has said that the effect of the two dams in Dinosaur upon geological, wilderness, and related values of national significance would be deplorable.

Conservation organizations (including the American Planning and Civic Association, the Federation of Western Outdoor Clubs, the Izaak Walton League of America, the National Audubon Society, the National Parks Association, the National Wildlife Federation, the Sierra Club, The Wilderness Society, and the Wildlife Management Institute) have argued that the Bureau of Reclamation's own figures show that alternate dams or combinations will fill the storage and power needs and at the same time spare the National Park System from an invasion that would set a dangerous precedent. They feel that the planned intrusion upon Dinosaur poses the gravest threat to that system since its creation in 1916, and that dams in Dinosaur would not only destroy the park value of one of the finest units in the system but would also speed the expressed desires of government and private agencies to dam the waters of other important park units—Kings Canyon, Mammoth Cave, Glacier, Yellowstone, Grand Canyon—or to cut redwoods in California and rain forest in Olympic, or to build aerial tramways at Rocky Mountain and Rainier.

The Secretary of the Interior's own Advisory Committee on Conservation recommended in April 1953: "The Echo Park and Split Mountain Dams in Dinosaur National Monument should be eliminated from the Upper Colorado River Storage Project as violations of the National Park System. We recommend that all available data on alternate sites for these dams, including economic factors, be made public."

The second part of the recommendation was the committee's suggestion for a way out. The conservationists' alternate proposals, most
of them advanced by Major General U. S. Grant III, who had forty-
two years' experience with major dams in the Corps of Engineers,
were dismissed by the Bureau of Reclamation without adequate explanation. The committee therefore felt that if the public must pay to
spare its park system, the public should know exactly what the cost
would be, and should have a chance to check the accounting. Since the
previous Secretary of the Interior had been convinced that Echo Park
and Split Mountain dams "absolutely are not necessary," the committee thought this opportunity for review all the more important.

But they got nowhere, and on December 8, 1953, read a revised
recommendation to Secretary McKay: "We believe that the Bureau of
Reclamation has misunderstood our Recommendation...that in this
type of situation a summary of the facts supporting the Bureau's
viewpoint and a similar summary of facts warranting rejection of the
principal alternate plans should be made available as a public document. The offer to make field data available at a regional office does
not meet this requirement in the opinion of your Committee."

The Secretary made no further comment. Eight days earlier he
had, it was discovered later, approved the recommendation of Under
Secretary Ralph O. Tudor that Echo Park dam be built. Testifying
before the House Subcommittee on Irrigation and Reclamation January 18, 1954, Mr. Tudor put it this way: "In the final analysis, the
increased losses of water by evaporation from the alternative sites is
the fundamental issue upon which the Department has felt it necessary to give any consideration to the Echo Park Dam and Reservoir...
The difference in evaporation between Echo Park and the other most
favorable dam site is about 108,000 acre-feet [less per year at Echo
Park]." That was enough water, he felt, to supply all the needs for a
city the size of Denver: and in a water-poor, scenery-rich land, the
need for water should have precedence over the need for parks. "We
can't eat scenery," a Utah delegation was telling congressmen; neither
could they drink it. And they were thirsty for the National Park
System's acre-feet, although subsequent testimony showed that the
Colorado River states (including California) were losing more than
20,000,000 acre-feet of water per year through wasteful irrigation
methods.

Other testimony pointed out something else—that one alternative, a higher Glen Canyon dam, could provide necessary storage with 185,000 acre-feet less annual evaporation loss than Mr. Tudor had testified would result. Indeed, there would be a net gain of at least 20,000 acre-feet per year, and possibly a lot more when the admittedly poor evaporation data used by the Bureau were refined. Mr. Tudor's mistake—or the mistake of whoever did the arithmetic—was just another, if spectacular, example of the incompleteness of the 1950 report—a report being used, General Grant has been forced to infer, to undermine the National Park System. And to perpetuate, not the parks, but Reclamation's expressed love of pushing rivers around.

In spite of all this testimony, Secretary McKay was still out to save enough water for a city the size of Denver when he addressed the Los Angeles Chamber of Commerce on February 2, 1954. He added something new: the Department wanted to do at Dinosaur what had been done at Lake Mead—give millions a chance to look at a dam and reservoir (a chance the millions already have in hundreds of places)—heedless of the great distinction between national parks and recreation areas. California's Millerton Lake, Mr. McKay thought, was another splendid example of what Dinosaur's destiny should be—the same Millerton Lake which his national park study team thinks could well be out of the system, its recreation administered by the state.

If the test of a national park must be its popularity with automobilists, then Dinosaur may not fare too well—and the San Francisco Bay Bridge, Hollywood Freeway, and Holland Tunnel should become national parks (and the New York subway system, which saves automobilists from themselves, a recreation area). If, on the other hand, the test of a park lies in the quality of experience—unmechanized experience with the magic of the natural world—then an unaltered park at Dinosaur is, and can always be, as rewarding a source as any of the great national parks.

Implying that Dinosaur's quarry is its chief reason for being, the dam proponents monotonously reiterate that the dinosaur bones will be safe—a point conservation organizations have known all along, and which was never an issue. The proponents then advance other arguments.

This problem has received careful consideration, Mr. McKay writes. But apparently not enough consideration to withstand the scrutiny his Advisory Committee on Conservation has twice urged be given.

"The beauty of the Monument will by no means be destroyed," Mr. McKay's form letter tells those who have protested to President Eisenhower (who, in his State of the Union message, promised to protect the national parks and monuments). But the Park Service has stated just the opposite. The beauty of the Dinosaur canyons would suffer just as much as the beauty of Yosemite Valley would suffer from a 500-foot dam and a fluctuating reservoir behind it; just as Hetch Hetchy's beauty and national-park usefulness were destroyed.

The canyons can't be seen by enough people without a reservoir, the next argument goes. Yet last summer alone, when for the first time people in numbers were at last learning of the ease and safety, and the inspiration, of drifting down the rivers, there was more river travel through Dinosaur's canyons than in all the years before put together. People of ages from four to seventy-seven floated through and enjoyed it, half of them taking six leisurely days for the trip, camping out along the river under the box elders and cottonwoods, exploring the side canyons and caves for evidence of prehistoric Indians, watching the wildlife, relaxing in a beautiful river wilderness beyond the highway's noise and exhaust. And the river trips were at nominal cost— about $10 per day on the river, including prepared meals, leadership, and lodging in a sleeping bag on a grassy beach. These were only the vanguard of thousands upon thousands who could share the same resource—millions in the course of time, if it be left for them.

About 3,000 people drove the primitive roads that lead to a few key points—Echo Park, Castle Park, Island Park, Harper's Corner, and Round Top. Moderate improvement of the existing roads and trails would provide adequate conventional access; the river trail would—and should—remain the unique contribution of this park.

Probably 20,000 drove the short dusty road from U.S. Highway 40 to Monument headquarters. Bumps and mud prosper where an irrigation ditch spreads wastefully over the road. What doesn't prosper is the Headquarters Museum, long appropriation-starved, with its meager exhibit of dinosaur bones, its shadeless and well-worked fossil quarry near by. In its hot and cramped interior there is scant suggestion that this place deserves monument protection at all, much less any suggestion of the great canyons far beyond the ken of the highway-fixed traveler. But for all its shortcomings the museum gives facts. In near-by Vernal, however, if the traveler hears about Echo Park, it is only as "Utah's last waterhole," although none of the reservoir would be in Utah, it would not bring water to Utah, and its parent project would give Vernal highly saline Green River water in exchange for the clear mountain water now running down its gutters.

Would the alternates result in a substantial loss of power? Some of them would, some wouldn't. But power, according to Mr. Tudor, isn't the criterion anyway. Steam generators, fired by the ailing coal mines (diesel locomotives don't use coal) of Utah, Wyoming, and Colorado, could supply power when, where, and as needed, probably at less cost, using up a resource no less renewable than the fast-silting reservoirs, which are all that can be built on the Colorado until upstream soil conservation and range-management practices are instituted in earnest.

Some Utah congressmen strain hard at another point, that Echo Park dam wouldn't be a damaging precedent. Chief basis for this point is that a Park Service employee swore in 1950 to having promised in 1936 that the enlargement of Dinosaur National Monument would not interfere with needed storage and power development in the area. If that was his promise, it can be variously interpreted, and there was no authorization to promise Echo Park dam; in any event it can be presumed to have been superseded by the presidential proclamation of 1938, which provided, in enlarging Dinosaur, only for a reclamation withdrawal below Brown's Park and within the northern four miles of the Monument, a site the Bureau of Reclamation has apparently now abandoned.

The hue and the cry. The claim and the counterclaim. What can the layman, who wants parks, but who doesn't want to see an area die of thirst, believe?

Perhaps he can believe that the national park idea, nurtured these ninety years, should not be abandoned without compelling reason. Secretary McKay stated this, in essence, in October 1953. How to define "compelling"? The public can well join the Advisory Committee in asking that this definition be spelled out. When one Secretary has said Echo Park dam and the invasion are absolutely unnecessary, his successor, and the bureau which supplies his figures, should be expected to have something more compelling than an erroneous estimate of water loss and a wish to duplicate Lake Mead.

The intelligent layman could also ask for answers to the objections by other government agencies. He might further wonder how fervently the federal government should support, at financial risk to all the nation, a 1922 river-allocating compact which in 1954 emerges as a costly device to lift Colorado River economy by its bootstraps. Or to take what four Peters are using in the lower basin (population 12,000,000), and can continue to use at their own expense, in order to give it to one Paul in the upper basin (population 3,000,000)—a Paul who hasn't used it yet, but thinks he can if Uncle Sam will stake him to it and throw in Dinosaur free.

What are the stakes? A billion and a half dollars, give or take a few million, for the initial phase; as much again for the ultimate phase; and all this, using January 1953 prices in January 1954. Three billion then, multiplied by two, if the fifty-year record of the Bureau in exceeding its estimate is used as a reasonable multiplier.

Yes, the intelligent layman, to whom parks are part of the full life, however intangible their value, is entitled to ask if there isn't some other solution, and to ask for the status quo until it has been clearly proved that there is no other solution.

There remains a vital question about parks and their relation to the solution. As our steadily increasing population, which we are reluctantly becoming mature enough to recognize for its potential jeopardy to our way of life, progressively trims our budget of natural resources, we shall have to seek a real solution if we are to balance our budget. Seek, or have poverty forced upon our children's children. The question, then, is this: Shall we use up the last one percent of land set aside in parks and wilderness and then seek a natural-resource solution, having postponed the reckoning a few decades? Or shall we seek sooner, and arrive at a solution with parks still on hand, for whatever they can contribute to the future of a culture?

The bones of those dinosaurs, hard by two of America's most superlative canyons, remind us that these were creatures whose bulk outstripped their brain. Now we are faced with a dinosaur's foot, with fair suggestion of the bulk to follow, right at the door of our National Park System. The least we can do is to push that foot back and to give the next generation a chance to choose whether its culture is to be of bulk or of brain.

The Battle for Echo Park

Russell Martin

Numerous books have been written about the Echo Park dam controversy, but one of the most compelling accounts of the struggle appears in Western novelist and historian Russell Martin's book *A Story That Stands Like a Dam: Glen Canyon and the Struggle for the Soul of the West,* which examines the complicated trade-off that saved Echo Park while dooming Glen Canyon.

It was President Woodrow Wilson who in 1915 had designated 80 acres of land on the Utah-Colorado border as a national monument, his sole purpose being the protection of an important paleontological resource—whole dinosaur skeletons embedded in a shale and sandstone bluff. With Harold Ickes's encouragement,[1] Franklin Roosevelt had enlarged the monument two decades later, increasing its size by 2,500 percent, preserving in the process more than 100 miles of the canyons of the Green and Yampa.

Although Howard Zahniser, executive secretary of the Wilderness Society, had never heard of Dinosaur National Monument before the Bureau of Reclamation announced its intention to inundate much of it, he had done much of the quick, frantic organizing in opposition to the plan that preceded Interior Secretary Chapman's hearing in 1950, and in the intervening months since then he had assembled seventeen member groups into a large and rather unwieldy organization calling itself the Citizens Committee on Natural Resources. Additionally, Zahniser had enlisted the support of Edward Mallinckrodt, Jr., a wealthy St. Louis chemicals manufacturer and, like himself, a passionate defender of wilderness. The fight to save Dinosaur would be very expensive, Zahniser was well aware, and with Mallinckrodt, he had secured an important patron.

Mallinckrodt, a member of the Sierra Club, had been disappointed that the club hadn't been involved in the early opposition to the Echo

Park Dam proposal. Regardless of whether people like Walter Huber *liked* the rough desert country of Dinosaur,[2] it was a national monument and it deserved protection. When Mallinckrodt took his case to David Brower, the club's new executive director—its first full-time staff member—he discovered he already had a committed ally.

Soon after he had left the Sierra Club's board of directors to become its paid staffer at the end of 1952, Brower had published an article in the *Sierra Club Bulletin*, which he edited, called "Folboats Through Dinosaur," an account by club member Stephen Bradley of a family float trip through the monument on the waters of the Green, and he had been invited to view the home movie of the journey filmed by Bradley's father, Harold. The article and the short film were an inspiration to Brower; he was a mountaineer, an alpine man, and had little experience in boats or in desert country, yet the Bradleys had made the river and the canyons come alive for him. The trip sounded like a terrific adventure, and surely Dinosaur must be a marvelous place. Brower vowed that the following summer he too would float through the Canyon of Lodore, through wide and pastoral Echo Park, where the Yampa spilled into the Green, through Whirlpool and Split Mountain canyons; he would see and experience Dinosaur for himself, and in the meantime, the Sierra Club—at least in the body of its executive director—would begin to work to save it.

Brower had no background in political organizing, but he did have a lifetime of experience in coordinating group expeditions into the back country, so he began to battle to save Echo Park by doing what he knew how to do. By the early summer of 1953, he had scheduled three Green River trips through Dinosaur, each one including sixty-five people, most of them club members. Five dozen or more people was an enormous number to send down the river in a single boating party, but with the assistance of Bus Hatch, operator of a commercial river-running business in nearby Vernal, Utah, the hearty adventurers from Berkeley and Bolinas, from Mill Valley and Menlo Park were ecstatic when the river washed them out—sunburned and mud-caked—at Split Mountain campground at the end of the 44-mile run. On one trip, seventy-three-year-old Harold Bradley, a Green River veteran and the recently retired head of the University of Wisconsin medical school, was along as proof that this strange sport of river running wasn't limited to daredevil adolescents. On another,

Brower was joined by two of his sons, still children. And on that trip, Brower himself got into the movie business, working with photographer Charles Eggert on the raw footage of what would become an invaluable visual aid, a twenty-eight-minute film entitled *Wilderness River Trail*, demonstrating what a dam and reservoir in Dinosaur would destroy.

In the summer of 1953, the Green and Yampa rivers were floated by far more people than had ever done so before, and tourists arriving in cars across the rutted dirt roads that led to Dinosaur—people who had been told by the *Saturday Evening Post* and by the dependable *Reader's Digest* that Dinosaur was a terrific place—crowded the monument's meager campgrounds. But Dinosaur's visitors did more than make curious kinds of pilgrimages. When they returned home, they wrote letters, thousands of letters. They showed slides and snapshots to their friends and neighbors and encouraged them to write letters. The publications of the Wilderness Society, the Audubon Society, the Izaak Walton League, the Wildlife Federation, and the Sierra Club encouraged their members—those few who actually had visited Dinosaur and the many who had not—to write letters! By the time its hearings on the CRSP [Colorado River Storage Project] were scheduled to begin in January 1954, the House Subcommittee on Irrigation and Reclamation was receiving hundreds of missives a day, arguing not so much against the CRSP itself as against the idea, the *very idea* of building a dam in Echo Park. Although the chambers of commerce in Vernal, Utah, Grand Junction, Colorado, Farmington, New Mexico, Flagstaff, Arizona, and dozens of other towns did their best to counter with letters of their own—letters that fairly pleaded for the gargantuan federal project—the congressional mail was estimated to be running 80 to 1 in opposition.

Western congressmen were dumbfounded. How had all these people from watery Massachusetts and humid Ohio gotten bent out of shape by some canyon out in Colorado? Bureau of Reclamation engineers and administrators were mystified, and some of them were a little hurt. Heretofore they had been heroes; they had constructed great dams that had helped to feed and shelter the burgeoning nation; their dams had helped this country weather a depression and win a war. But now, as they tried to do no more than continue their wonder work, they were being made out to be destroyers, killers of landscape.

It was difficult to understand, but it didn't make sense to panic. The hearings would put Echo Park into perspective and would clarify the critical importance of the project to the states of the upper Colorado basin. The hearings, much like dams themselves, surely would calm the conservationists' rough rhetorical water. David Brower had never testified before a congressional committee or battled the Bureau of Reclamation. The House CRSP hearings were going to be a baptism by fire, no doubt, and it made sense to him to observe them from gavel to gavel rather than just to arrive in time to make his own statement. At Howard Zahniser's invitation, Brower checked into Washington's Cosmos Club and prepared to stay a while as the hearings were convened on January 18, 1954.

A parade of administration witnesses opened the nine-day proceeding, beginning with Under Secretary of the Interior Ralph Tudor, an engineer who had designed the San Francisco Bay Bridge before accepting the call to government service. And rather than commence with an overview of the proposed project, Tudor jumped directly to the defense of Echo Park Dam, claiming it was fundamental to the success of the project as a whole, explaining that alternative sites would result in unreasonable water losses from evaporation. When sympathetic California Congressman Clair Engle asked him if taking Echo Park out of the CRSP would be "like taking the engine out of the automobile," Tudor said it would be "like taking the pistons out." But the under secretary also wanted to make it clear that Interior's endorsement of Echo Park did not mean that it would allow a developmental assault on the national parks. After all, Conrad Wirth, a respected park service administrator since the days of the Civilian Conservation Corps, was currently its director, and Wirth wouldn't sanction any attack on the system.

Tudor was followed by Ole Larson, a Reclamation regional director based in Salt Lake City. Larson agreed that Echo Park Dam was "the wheel horse of the upper basin," and stated that despite its best efforts, the Bureau had been unable to find an acceptable alternative to the "remarkable storage vessel" created by the canyon topography of Dinosaur. Then came in long and sometimes tedious succession Reclamation numbers—men arguing in support of the project's economics, and congressmen, ranchers, and civic leaders from Colorado, Wyoming, and Utah claiming that it was dry as dust out west and that the only antidote to drought was a CRSP that included Echo Park. G. E. Untermann of Vernal explained that as far as "saving" Dinosaur was concerned, the people who lived nearby didn't want to be saved. "We want to be damned," he declared.

After six days of supporting testimony, it was time to hear from "the abominable nature lovers," as Utah Senator Arthur Watkins had termed project opponents during his own testimony before the House subcommittee. Yet if the subcommittee members were expecting to hear next from a bunch of sob sisters, they were indeed surprised when gentlemanly General U. S. Grant III began his testimony. Grant, an officer of the Army Corps of Engineers for forty-three years, pointed out that the Federal Power Act of 1920 prohibited private power companies from developing projects inside national parks and monuments. It made no sense, he continued, for a government agency to be allowed to do what private enterprise could not, "namely to do irreparable damage to a scenic area set aside after careful study." The CRSP, *in toto*, was "not a well-worked out, balanced project," the general declared, his physical presence, his courtly manner, as well as his name and his professional renown, lending a special credence to his statement. "The hard fact is that the Bureau of Reclamation has already made site surveys and other preparatory work—including propaganda—to such an extent that it does not want to make similar studies of alternative sites," he charged.

The succession of opposition witnesses was long, if not necessarily always as impressive or eloquent as General Grant. Joe Penfold, speaking for the Izaak Walton League, said it seemed duplicitous for Reclamation engineers to reject alternative sites as too wasteful of water when an estimated 25 percent of all the water the Bureau delivered was currently lost through seepage in unlined irrigation canals. Howard Zahniser curiously chose to give a dramatic reading of the Robert Southey poem from which the Canyon of the Lodore had derived its name. And when it was David Brower's turn, the rookie witness, representative of the lowly and largely unknown Sierra Club, began by comparing the danger to Echo Park with the one great developmental disaster his organization could never forget.

Cranking up a still-montage film called *Two Yosemites* to show to his captive audience, displaying before-and-after photos of the Hetch Hetchy Valley with a show-and-tell kind of flourish, Brower got right to the heart of his concern. "If we heed the lesson from the tragedy of the misplaced dam in Hetch Hetchy, we can prevent a far more disastrous stumble in Dinosaur National Monument," he told the members of the subcommittee. Then he issued a kind of challenge: "I know, and I will bet Reclamation knows, that if the river disappeared in its course through Dinosaur, or was somehow unavailable, a sound upper Colorado storage project could be developed elsewhere." That was the strategy Brower, Zahniser, and the confederate conservationists had agreed to pursue—not to oppose the CRSP as a whole, but rather to acknowledge the need for water and power in the isolated upper basin in tandem with their claim that other reservoirs in other canyons would be as beneficial as the one proposed for Echo Park. But Brower astonished the assembled congressmen—who tended to view Bureau reports, with their complex and seemingly impenetrable jumble of computations, as semisacred texts—when he went to a blackboard and pointed out that, in the case of these critical evaporation rates they were talking about, the engineers couldn't correctly add and subtract.

In arguing against alternatives to Echo Park—in particular, a conservationist proposal to increase the height of Glen Canyon Dam and thereby store the water now slated for Echo Park—Reclamation engineers had claimed that such an alternative would result in an annual loss by evaporation of 165,000 acre-feet of water more than would Echo Park. Yet Brower, who coyly defined his arithmetic as the simple, ninth-grade variety, pointed out that in making the comparison, the engineers had forgotten to subtract the evaporative amount caused by Echo Park (assuming it wasn't built) from the evaporative total of the proposed alternative. Instead of causing far more evaporation than would the dam and reservoir at Echo Park, Brower demonstrated with a piece of chalk, a higher Glen Canyon Dan would result in 2,610 acre-feet less evaporation and, he paused for emphasis, the resulting Glen Canyon reservoir would store 700,000 acre-feet *more*.

It was startling testimony, but it was true. Under Secretary Tudor subsequently admitted to the subcommittee that *somehow* Reclamation's figures had been in error. In nine days of testimony pro and con Echo Park, Brower's had been the most powerful. The neophyte had successfully chipped a hole in the rhetorical Echo Park dike. Perhaps the dam in Dinosaur *wasn't* the pistons, the engine, the whole damn drivetrain of the CRSP. Perhaps the way to bring the legislation on board, wondered some subcommittee members, was to forget about Echo Park.

President Eisenhower had held a press conference in March to recommend officially the construction of the Colorado River Storage Project, including both Echo Park and Glen Canyon dams, so by the time the Senate Subcommittee on Irrigation and Reclamation held *its* hearings at the end of June—most of the same people saying much the same thing as they had in January—the CRSP steam roller appeared to be moving inexorably forward. Letters in opposition were still arriving by the bundle, but the House Interior Committee nonetheless had reported its CRSP bill favorably to the full House. The Senate, where western senators had far more power by sheer force of numbers, was widely seen as a kind of home ground for wayward water projects. And as far as Utah Senator Arthur Watkins was concerned, the principal goal of the Senate hearings was to crush this higher Glen Canyon alternative that the conservationists had hoisted before the House. Watkins, often acting as temporary subcommittee chairman, often the only senator present in the Senate Office Building hearing room during the six long days of testimony, had planned to ferret out what seemed to be obvious about this fellow Brower: he wasn't an "honest conservationist" as the others were. He was a *Californian*, and as such was surely in cahoots with the Colorado River Board of California, the Los Angeles-based organization that was fighting the CRSP simply to keep as much of the Colorado's water as possible flowing downstream for as long as possible. Those water-stealing bastards weren't fighting a fair fight, Watkins was convinced. The San Francisco conservationist was nothing more than a pawn of the L.A. water boys, and their opposition to Echo Park was simply a smoke screen.

Although Watkins found that Brower was very willing to admit that he had one hour-long meeting with Northcutt Ely, attorney for the Colorado River Board, he otherwise withstood the senator's challenge. No, neither he nor the Sierra Club was in regular communication with the board; no, they had never discussed common strategy; no, the board had made no contribution to the club or to its efforts in opposition to Echo Park; and no, Senator, the Sierra Club and all the allied conservationists were interested only in protecting Dinosaur

National Monument, not in sabotaging the whole of the CRSP. Watkins finally surrendered and left Brower alone to state his case, a second time, that the Bureau had a better alternative, that as long as little Rainbow Bridge National Monument, tucked high in a side canyon 50 miles upstream from the dam site, was protected, Reclamation ought to build Glen Canyon Dam to the very rim of the canyon walls.

Realizing that Brower and the conservationists, in their push for the higher Glen Canyon Dam, had found a real opening, Interior Secretary McKay sought in the fall of 1954 to diffuse their arguments. The Interior committees of both houses had approved Echo Park and the rest of the CRSP in the spring and summer; in late July, President Eisenhower, in Colorado on vacation, had flown over Dinosaur and pronounced that on visual inspection there seemed to be no reason not to dam it. Neither body of Congress had voted on the CRSP prior to adjournment, but if the conservationists could be held at bay until early in the next session, and if this Glen Canyon business could be put to rest, it still appeared that Echo Park could be built.

What the secretary did was to write privately to the Sierra Club representative, explaining, almost as if he were sharing a secret, that while, yes, raising the height of Glen Canyon Dam was an interesting possibility, the Bureau of Reclamation had discovered sadly that it wouldn't be feasible. In his November letter, the secretary stated that the sandstone that would support the dam's weight was "poorly cemented and relatively weak in comparison to most high dams." It simply couldn't be trusted to support a 700-foot-high structure, and therefore Echo Park still would be needed.

In his response to the secretary, Brower reminded him of an earlier Reclamation report that had dispelled the U.S. Geological Survey's concern about the underground basins beneath Glen Canyon and that had endorsed the dam's foundation material as "remarkably free of structural defects." Brower implied, but didn't go so far as to charge, that Reclamation and the Interior Department were again playing fast and loose with the truth. Then, having learned very quickly how you fought these political fights, he made the letters public.

Elsewhere on the public relations front, the conservationists were planning something extraordinary. With the assistance of Alfred Knopf, a New York publisher and chairman of the Interior Department's Advisory Board on National Parks, they were preparing to publish a book devoted entirely to Dinosaur National Monument. It would be a piece of propaganda, of course, but it would be an elegant one. Entitled *This Is Dinosaur*, and containing dozens of black-and-white and color photographs, the book would be an eloquent explanation of why Echo Park and all of Dinosaur were so important. Wallace Stegner had agreed to edit the text, which would include essays by himself, Knopf, geologist Eliot Blackwelder, wildlife biologist Olaus Murie, archaeologist Robert Lister, pioneer river-runner Otis "Dock" Marston, and journalist David Bradley. Together, the several essays would be a kind of celebration of the book's subtitle—*The Echo Park Country and Its Magic Rivers*. A book like this, an unabashedly conservation-minded picture book, had never been published before, but in the face of what threatened Dinosaur, and with Knopf's generous underwriting, it was certainly worth the risk. If it made enough money to help continue the political battle, so much the better; but even if the book lost money, if it alerted more Americans to what was in danger, well, that would be a success in itself.

Although David Brower's name was in no way associated with the book when it appeared in January 1955, its pages nonetheless bore the watermark of his increasing commitment to the Echo Park struggle. The book had been his idea, and it was he who had approached Stegner about playing a major role in its creation. Stegner, a Sierra Club member, had been strongly in favor of the organization's forays into the world of power politics under Brower's leadership, and he supported the book as a tool in the campaign. He had once been enamored with Hoover Dam, but twenty years later, he had begun to regard desert dams with great suspicion, and now he cautioned Brower that there really wasn't any way to win this battle. In recent years, he had twice boated through Glen Canyon. The trips had been overwhelming experiences, and Glen Canyon, he could attest, was even more remarkable than Dinosaur. A high dam in Glen Canyon, even if it somehow spared Echo Park, would be a tragedy.

Brower's first trip floating the Green through Dinosaur had been the most profound wilderness experience of his life, and he told Stegner that he couldn't imagine that *any* place could be more beautiful, more wondrous than Dinosaur. Yes, Glen surely was another glorious canyon, but unfortunately, it had never received federal protection and that was what this battle really was all about. It was too much to hope that they could scuttle the entire upper basin project, but if together they could save Dinosaur, that in itself would be something very significant. They just didn't have the resources, the time, or the political muscle to fight on every front.

Understanding the sad practicality of that argument, Stegner willingly devoted his talents to the Dinosaur projects, and in the foreword to *This is Dinosaur* he stated its purpose: "If the American people, through Congress, choose to authorize the proposed dams and take the losses, they can do so. Our book attempts no more than to show— so far as words and pictures can show a region so varied and colorful—what the people would be giving up, what beautiful and instructive and satisfying things their children and their grandchildren and all other Americans from then on would never see."

Wayne Aspinall knew when he opened his copy of *This Is Dinosaur*, sent to him in January 1955, courtesy of Alfred A. Knopf, that things were going from bad to worse. What four or five years ago he had presumed would be a brief whimper of opposition to Echo Park dam site had turned into a roar, a carefully orchestrated howl of protest that showed no sign of abating. Following the House subcommittee hearings a year before, his staff had counted the letters commenting on the CRSP, and only 53 of 4,731 of them were in support of the dam. With no little amount of maneuvering, the western Colorado congressman had succeeded in favorably reporting the bill out of the full Interior committee, but only by a tenuous 13 to 12 vote. And now, the conservationists had published a book all about how terrible a dam in Dinosaur would be, and a copy had been sent to every member of the House, every Senator, most of the high-level people over at Interior, and to every newspaper editor between Boise and Albuquerque. Colorado Senator Eugene Millikin had assured Aspinall that the bill was secure in the Senate, but in the House, where the West's influence was spread mighty thin, it still looked like a hell of a scrap, and this book wasn't going to help matters a bit.

Aspinall, a small, bespectacled ex-schoolteacher—quick to grin but testy, nearly venomous at times—had grown up beside the Colorado River, the Grand back in those days, in the small fruit-growing community of Palisade, Colorado, and nothing had been of more import to him during his many years of public service than reclamation. Now, as chairman of the House Subcommittee on Irrigation and Reclamation, he wielded the kind of power that could get dams built where dams were needed, yet it was the kind of power that had been nurtured by compromise, by a kind of legislative realism that was legendary among his colleagues.

Early in the CRSP struggle, Aspinall had issued a dire warning about the conservationists: "If we let them knock out Echo Park, we'll hand them a tool they'll use for the next hundred years." But now, with his House head count a little worrisome, and with the conservationists clearly appearing to be gaining strength, he was beginning to wonder whether Echo Park Dam might have to be sacrificed to save the CRSP. Echo Park was in Aspinall's district—it would be *his* dam—and he certainly did not want to lose it. Neither did he care for this David Brower, this cocksure young Californian who was constantly disputing the best men in the Bureau of Reclamation, and who must have played a part in this fancy coffee-table book he had been sent. Yet maybe Brower would have to win this one. Increasing the height of Glen Canyon Dam—assuming the boys at the Bureau could make it work—would accomplish much; the upper basin would get the gigantic storage facility it had to have, as well as a colossal hydropower dam that would pay for a large supporting cast of irrigation projects. If it came down to it, Aspinall already knew heading into a second round of hearings in March 1955, designed to counter the swelling opposition to the project, that he could live without Echo Park.

The Senate's second CRSP hearings were showcased by the Bureau of Reclamation, its administrators and engineers making it as plain as they could that Glen Canyon was a good and safe place to build a dam. Yes, the Interior secretary had made statements about possible limitations on the height of the dam, but those concerns couldn't be addressed in detail until the project was authorized and extensive field tests were completed. The conservationists monitoring the testimony were incredulous. Reclamation was claiming that first Congress should approve the CRSP and *then* it would figure out exactly what kind of dam it could build in Glen Canyon, was that correct? That was indeed correct, responded Reclamation Commissioner Dexheimer, and it was long-standing Bureau procedure. And the senators seated on the dais plainly were undisturbed by what seemed to the conservationists to be the prospect of buying a pig in a poke.

But when the House hearings opened four days following the close of the CRSP proceedings in the Senate, southern California Congressman Craig Hosmer—no fan of a CRSP in any form—pounced on the subject of Glen Canyon. He had it on good geological authority, he told the committee, that the sandstone forming the walls of Glen Canyon was so porous it was a virtual sieve. As water backed up behind Glen Canyon Dam, it would leak so swiftly into the rock that the reservoir might never fill and "the country might be stuck with the most enormous white elephant in history." Chairman Aspinall winced as Hosmer continued his assault, announcing that other experts had proved that electricity generated by atomic power would soon be the cheapest electricity to produce, so cheap it might not even be metered, and certainly far cheaper than the hydroelectricity that would come from Glen Canyon. And as if that weren't enough, Hosmer next hauled out the Bureau's own project cost-benefit statistics demonstrating that although the four upper-basin states would receive $137 million in benefits from the CRSP for only $75 million in revenue contributions, every other state in the nation would lose money, a deficit totaling more than $3 billion when you factored in the loss of investment interest. "For instance," Hosmer shouted, "the state of New York will receive, according to the Bureau, $77,398,000, but the taxpayers of New York will have to fork out $493,600,000 for the project. Who does the Bureau of Reclamation think it's kidding?"

Congressman Aspinall was beside himself. Why was he worried about the wacky conservationists when a member of his own subcommittee—a Californian whose plain purpose was to reserve the whole of this great river for his own and his neighbors' swimming pools—was attacking the bill with a tomahawk?

The Senate Interior Committee favorably reported the Colorado River Storage Project bill on March 30, and after three days of debate on the floor of the Senate—including fervent, often eloquent oration in opposition by Senators Paul Douglas of Illinois, Hubert Humphrey of Minnesota, and John Kennedy of Massachusetts—Senate bill S. 500, authorizing the construction of six dams and storage reservoirs, including those at Glen Canyon *and* Echo Park, and twelve participating irrigation projects, at a cost of $1 billion and change, passed by a vote of 53 to 28. It was a resounding victory for Reclamation and for the senators from the Rocky Mountain states.

Wayne Aspinall didn't celebrate, however. He knew, by doing no more than counting noses, that the House version of the bill the Senate had just passed couldn't even survive the Interior Committee. The *New York Times* editorialized against Echo Park, but not against the whole of the CRSP, in early June, and a few days later, Aspinall reluctantly did the same in a subcommittee executive session. Although the Californians on the subcommittee kept up their efforts to kill the entire project by voting to *keep* Echo Park, Aspinall prevailed, and the dam in Dinosaur National Monument was deleted from the bill. Then, on July 8, the House Interior committee favorably reported it, still *sans* Echo Park, by a vote of 20 to 6.

But even with that kind of showing in the Interior Committee, Aspinall was reluctant to bring the bill to the floor of the House for debate. His current estimate was that House Democrats would split about evenly on the legislation, but Republicans would vote it down three to one. "I would rather have such an important bill given full debate and rational consideration when the emotions of the members are not as high-strung as they are," he explained. But there was more to his reluctance. The conservationists now were claiming that deleting Echo Park from the House bill was nothing more than an end run to get it passed. Plans were already laid, they contended, to resurrect Echo Park Dam in a House-Senate conference committee. A little time was needed to calm down the conservationists and get them behind this bill of their own making, Aspinall understood. And time also would help the old general in the White House. He still staunchly supported the project, and he, no doubt, could eventually persuade the recalcitrant House Republicans to shape up, but even Ike could do nothing overnight. So, on August 2, Congress went into recess without taking further action on the CRSP, and the battle for Echo Park stretched out a little longer.

During the five years that Echo Park had been under ever-increasing national scrutiny, Americans had poured into the place that theretofore had been frequented only by a handful of dinosaur buffs and scientists. In the summer of 1955, 45,000 people visited the monument, an estimated 1,000 of them traveling through it on the bucking backs of the rivers. Members of conservation organizations, journalists and newspaper people, congressmen and their staffs, and even the odd rancher or uranium miner determined to demonstrate his open-mindedness floated the Yampa and the Green during the runoff-swollen months of early summer. Dinosaur, for the first time since those great, fated creatures themselves roamed the region, had become a busy place.

But Glen Canyon, on the other hand, remained a relative refuge for silence. Reclamation geologists and survey crews had made occasional forays into the canyon, taking core samples in the riverbed at the two sites proposed for the dam, drilling drift tunnels into the looming walls. A few boatmen who had worked for Norman Nevills had escorted paying customers of their own down through the canyon each summer—some of whom actually tried to generate a bit of congressional enthusiasm for making the place a national park—and Art Greene had ferried a few more upstream to Rainbow Bridge. Yet although the dam proposed for Glen Canyon would be far bigger than the one at Echo Park, its reservoir vastly larger, no one fighting the political fight from either side had paid any personal attention to the place. Neither the Interior secretary, nor the high-ranking appointees at Reclamation, nor the solons who ultimately would decide the canyon's fate, nor more than a smattering of the legions of conservationists who were encouraging them to dam it had ever traveled to Glen Canyon.

During the congressional recess in December 1955, California Congressman Craig Hosmer finally went to have a look. Accompanied by John Terrell, public-relations man for the Colorado River Board, a couple of independent geologists, and a cameraman, Hosmer set out to prove that nobody had any business building a high dam in such a geologically suspect setting. Despite the Senate vote, the conservationists were doing a good job in their efforts to scuttle Echo Park. If Hosmer could lead a last-ditch effort to impugn the rocky integrity of Glen Canyon, perhaps neither dam would be built and the Colorado would continue to flow unchecked to California.

Using Art Greene's Marble Canyon Lodge as a base, for three days the four men helicoptered in to the dam sites, poked about with pick hammers, photographed everything that captured their interests, and hauled back out of the canyon gunnysack loads of sandstone and shale. In the evenings, warmed by Art Greene's piñon fires and his inexpensive whiskey, they surveyed their booty and pronounced it precisely what they had come looking for. By the time President Eisenhower had delivered his State of the Union address on January 5, 1956, Congressman Hosmer had mailed a small sample of Chinle shale to the editor of every daily newspaper in the nation, and each of his colleagues in the House was a recipient as well, the congressman attaching a note with every chunk suggesting that fun could be had if the bearer dropped it into a bit of water.

David Brower, Howard Zahniser, Joe Penfold, and other leaders of the confederation now known as the Council of Conservationists paid little attention to the congressman's largess. They were in the midst of negotiations with Wayne Aspinall that would result in the prohibition, plain and simple, of a dam in Echo Park. In late October, the conservationists had gotten wind of a secret meeting scheduled in Denver at which governors, congressmen, and water-board members from the upper-basin states would try to figure out how to pass a House bill without Echo Park, then make sure that the Senate's CRSP bill (Echo Park included) prevailed in the conference committee. In order to head them off, Zahniser had come up with some quick cash, flown to Denver, and taken out a full-page ad in the October 31 edition of the *Denver Post*, the "open letter" making it very clear that unless Echo Park *irrevocably* were deleted from the CRSP, the conservationists and their allies would launch an all-out attack, this time not just on the Echo Park proposal, but on the entire upper-basin project.

It was no bluff, the politicians recognized, and they knew by now that they were dealing with formidable foes. Despite the objections of Senator Arthur Watkins and the rest of the Utah delegation, who still clung to Echo Park as if it had been ordained by Brigham Young (which, from a particular Mormon perspective, it *had*), Colorado Representative Aspinall declared to his assembled colleagues that he could strike a deal with Brower and his bunch if they would capitulate on Echo Park. On November 2, the Upper Colorado River Commission, with the blessing of the several states' elected officials, formally rejected the proposal to build a dam inside Dinosaur National Monument. Then, following a series of meetings and correspondences, and the revision of the house CRSP bill—now containing language stipu-lating that "no dam or reservoir constructed under the authorization of this act shall be within any national park or monument," and mandating "adequate protective measures to preclude impairment of the Rainbow Bridge National Monument" from the reservoir behind Glen Canyon Dam—Brower, Zahniser, and company drafted a letter to Aspinall on January 23, 1956, withdrawing their opposition to the Colorado River Storage Project.

On Wednesday, March 1, President Dwight Eisenhower held a press conference to make two brief announcements. First, he would be a candidate for a second term in office. And second, Congress should "get busy and get on with" passage of the CRSP. The follow-ing day, however, California Representative Hosmer held the floor in the House of Representatives and held the president at bay, announc-ing that the geologists with whom he had journeyed to Glen Canyon had discovered that, yes indeed, water backed up by the dam would flow into gargantuan underground basins capable of hoarding 350 million acre-feet of water; the Navajo sandstone that formed the can-yon walls was so porous that 15 million gallons of water a day would flow around the dam's abutments; and the Chinle shale that underlaid the Navajo formation would literally disintegrate when it came in contact with water, causing the canyon walls to avalanche into the reservoir pool, filling Glen Canyon with wet rock instead of water.

Congressman Hosmer did not paint a pretty picture, and he had graphic show-and-tell assistance from Florida Representative James Haley, who poured water into a glass containing a piece of Chinle shale and quickly produced mud, warning the House of the dire con-sequences the Chinle formation would bring about if the dam were built. But Representative Stewart Udall, a first-term congressman from Arizona and therefore a staunch supporter of the Glen Canyon site, had his own piece of stone in tow. As he rose to speak in support of the grand benefits of Glen Canyon Dam, he dropped a little cyl-inder of sandstone—part of a core sample from the dam sites, he explained—into a water glass. At the conclusion of Udall's glowing remarks, he drank the clear water from the glass to great guffaws and hearty applause. Moments later, he and his colleagues voted 256 to 136 in favor of the CRSP and its centerpiece dam in Glen Canyon.

Despite the deletion of Echo Park Dam, David Brower had been tempted to keep up the opposition. The Bureau of Reclamation's indecision about the specifications for a dam in Glen Canyon, the geologists' accusations, and the *cost* of the whole thing seemed reasons aplenty to kill the entire project. But the Sierra Club's board of directors had informed him in January that, with the Aspinall-engineered compromise, *its* fight, and therefore his fight, was finished. And so Brower, certainly not as jubilant as some of his fellow conservationists, but nonetheless satisfied with the certainty that they had accomplished *something* of enduring value, left the Cosmos Club for the last time and returned to San Francisco. Howard Zahniser, who would quickly shift gears to begin congressional lobbying for a law designating and protecting wilderness lands throughout the nation, pronounced the final version of the CRSP an unqualified victory. Joe Penfold of the Izaak Walton League said the bill now was a sound one, and he praised Aspinall and other congressional realists "for their successful efforts in reaching an accord with us." Ansel Adams, head of a Sierra Club–affiliated lobbying group called the Trustees for Conservation, said his organization gladly could now support the upper-basin bill because of its "reaffirmation of the national park principles." Newton Drury, who had been director of the National Park Service back when the struggle began, and who had prophesied that "Dinosaur is a dead duck," expressed his astonishment at the outcome, and his great admiration for the people who had proved him wrong.

It had taken more than half a decade, but the band of mountaineers and bird-watchers, tree-huggers and river rats had blocked the concerted efforts of the Eisenhower administration to turn the canyons of Dinosaur into a slackwater lake. Forty years following John Muir's failure to save Hetch Hetchy, they *had* preserved Echo Park— forever, it seemed—and they successfully had made the case that preservation itself could be a kind of wise use. But they had done something perhaps even more astonishing. They had called into question the competency and the integrity of the Bureau of Reclamation, an agency that theretofore had been a symbol of government service at its finest. They had sown seeds of suspicion about precisely how the federal bureaucracy regarded the public's lands, and they had demonstrated that conservation battles could be waged and won within the political arena. In the process, too, they secured the overwhelming transformation of Glen Canyon.

≋ NOTES

1. Secretary of the Interior.
2. Former president of the Sierra Club.

The Other "Place No One Knew"

Roy Webb

IN THE FINAL CHAPTER OF HIS BOOK *If We Had a Boat,* GREEN
RIVER HISTORIAN ROY WEBB COMMENTS ON THE COMPARATIVE
SILENCE THAT ACCOMPANIED THE INUNDATION OF FLAMING
GORGE AND PRESENTS THE REMINISCENCES OF A FEW WHO KNEW IT
AS IT WAS.

Much has been made among environmentalists of the loss of
Glen Canyon to a Bureau of Reclamation project in the
early 1960s. Volume after volume has been written about its
lost wonders, poems penned, songs composed about the beauties of
the canyon forever drowned by the waters of Lake Powell. Radicals
agitate for its destruction and even, in fiction at least, hatch plots to
accomplish that end. Environmentalists bemoan its fate as their greatest defeat, even though they actually had more than a little to do with
that fate.

Glen Canyon was not the only one to be affected by the Colorado
River Storage Project, however. At the same time, a sister to Glen Canyon Dam was being built on the Green River, about midway between
the town of Green River, Wyoming, and the Uinta Basin. And even
though the canyons and river to be inundated were of rare beauty and
filled with rich historical heritage, not a word was said when the gates
of Flaming Gorge Dam were closed and the Green began to back up.
The salvage survey conducted for Glen Canyon produced shelves of
documents, thousands of photographs and hundreds of feet of movie
film; Flaming Gorge, Kingfisher, and Red Canyons rated one fifty-
page document. No songs, no films, no poems, no radicals plotting its
destruction.

What follows, then, are some descriptions of this stretch of the
Green River as it was in the days before the Green was known as a
trout fishery and Flaming Gorge a playground for motorboats. This
is not to moan or complain or bewail the fate of the Green, for the

dam is a fact and given the state of the world will probably be holding back the Green long after man has reduced himself to ashes. This is simply a reminder that there was once a river below those cold, green waters; that Glen Canyon was not the only "place no one knew."

Just below this fork (Henry's Fork) we entered the mouth of the first canyon and encamped amid the cottonwood trees surrounded by bluffs 1200 ft. high and on one side nearly perpendicular. It is the grandest scenery I have found in the mountains and I am delighted with it. I went out to see the country this morning and found it grand beyond conception. The river winds like a serpent through between nearly perpendicular cliffs 1200 ft. high but instead of rapids it is deep and calm as a lake. It is the most safe of any part we have yet seen for navigation.

— GEORGE Y. BRADLEY, 1869

From this point (the west cliff of Kingfisher Canyon) had a fine view of the Green winding around at the base of bright red cliffs to the northwest with the wooded valley of the Kingfisher Creek [Sheep Creek] and the crystal stream winding in the midst....Bold rocks of grey sandstone tower on the right; on the left, crags and rocky slopes with scattered cedars, pinons, and firs.... The Kingfisher comes in on the right through a narrow canyon valley with steep walls, the valley itself filled with alders and willows completely hiding the creek. Then the creek emerging from its own canyon meanders across the little park, its banks fringed with willows. The river flows at the foot of the cliff on the left and is hedged by a border of willows from the meadow on the right. Looking down the river the walls seem almost to close where the river turns to the left around Beehive point.

— JOHN WESLEY POWELL, 1871

Flaming Gorge hard into view, the right side a dark red flame below in the morning sun with a grey cap of sandstone overtopped with brown, the whole cliff rising to 1000 feet. While on the left the quiet green of a lovely grove of cottonwoods heightened by its contrast the beauty and grandeur of the scene.... Kingfisher is a beautiful clear stream that ought to contain trout. When we came to the cliff and looked down its valley I thought it as lovely as we ever saw.... The valley is thick with cottonwoods, willows, alders, and box elders. The water is clear of a slight reddish tinge, cold, and where it empties into the Green the color of the two streams is brought into vivid contrast.

— ALMON HARRIS THOMPSON, 1871

Just below the mouth of Henry's Fork [the river] doubled to the left and we found ourselves between two low cliffs, then in a moment we dashed to the right into the beautiful canyon, with the cliffs whose summit we had seen, rising about 1300 feet on the right, and a steep slope on the left at the base of which was a small bottom covered with all cottonwood trees, whose green shone resplendent against the red rocks....The canyon was surprisingly beautiful and romantic. The river seemed to flow with an impetus it had exhibited nowhere above....At the foot of the right hand wall...we beheld our first real rapid, gleaming like a jewel from its setting in the sunlight which fell into the gorge, and it had as majestic a setting as could be desired. For myself I can say that the place appeared the acme of the romantic and picturesque....Flaming Gorge is the gateway, Horseshoe the vestibule, and Kingfisher the ante-chamber to the whole grand series.

— FREDERICK S. DELLENBAUGH, 1871

Passing through Horseshoe...we found deep, placid pools, and sheer, light red walls rising about four hundred feet on either side, then sloping back steeply to the tree-covered mountains....[I]n Kingfisher Canyon were a few of the fish-catching birds from which the canyon took its name. There were many of the tireless cliff-swallows scattered all through these canyons, wheeling and darting, ever on the wing....It is a picture to tempt an artist....[L]ittle openings, or parks with no trees, are tinted with a beautiful soft gray; "brownstone fronts" are found in the canyon walls; and a very light green in the willow-leafed cottonwoods at the river's edge....The river glistens in the sunlight, as it winds around the base of the wall on which we stand....

We remained until noon of the following day at Ashley Falls, exploring, repairing, and photographing this picturesque spot. The canyon walls here dropped down to beautiful, rolling foot-hills eight or nine hundred feet high, tree-covered as before but more open. The diversity of rocks and hills was alluring.

— ELLSWORTH L. KOLB, 1911

[T]he north wall of Flaming Gorge, with its vivid hues of red, brown, and ocher, rises like a huge flame of fire ahead. The gorge…forms a very impressive entrance to the series of canyons below….Through the Flaming Gorge and Horseshoe Canyon box elder trees are scattered along each bank where the walls offer any footing and pine trees dot the slopes, extending down to the water's edge. In places the solid rock walls are almost vertical and rise several hundred feet above the river. The gray shades of the rock with the generous sprinkling of pines and the river winding its way between the walls form a constantly changing panorama. [Kingfisher Canyon] is wonderfully beautiful. The river is like a placid lake, and the beautifully colored canyon walls with their green trees clinging to the slopes are perfectly reflected in the river as in a huge mirror.

— RALF R. WOOLLEY, 1922

Flaming Gorge, Horseshoe and Kingfisher Canyons were short and rapid free, filled with sunshine and songs of countless birds, and with the call of geese and ducks high overhead. Many deer and beaver could be seen along the tree-lined shores.

— BUZZ HOLSTROM, 1938

Below here Red Canyon begins, crags and narrowing rock walls presenting a dramatic view synchronized to roaring cataracts. Along the narrow bottoms are tall western yellow pines.

— AMOS BURG, 1938

The countryside continues to be sumptuous. Above all, there was the arrival in front of a pink mountain where debris was strewn with little bushes, lavender in color and with a trifling of yellow due to the flowers. Then, all of a sudden, an imposing, mysterious overwhelming wall bright red and dark, at the same time, without vegetation, none— a face completely stripped, closed, proud and high, rich in its only substance and which gave the impression of silent majesty.

— ANTOINE DE SEYNE, 1938

We are all terribly impressed by the unusual beauty of this, Horseshoe Canyon. Not alone is the change so great from the barren canyons above here, but this canyon is outstanding.

— NORM NEVILLS, 1947

Flaming Gorge is very beautiful. It is colored red and yellow with a greenish tinge. Below Flaming Gorge we encounter a small ripple. Next is Horseshoe Canyon with many pines and rocks looking like they do at the Natural Bridges National Monument....Very brilliant walls between Horseshoe and Kingfisher Canyons....Red Canyon is dark red, studded abundantly with yellow pine trees....The scenery here is very spectacular and the rapids, although rocky, do not have any big waves at this stage of water.

— HARRY P. SPARKES, 1951

[C]amp was set up in Carter's Canyon [Carter Creek] that afternoon. It was a lovely camp setting with rushing streams of cold water on two sides emptying into the Green....[T]he scenery was picturesque....The weather was ideal, and the waters quite exciting with a variety of rapids and spots of quiet.

— CONEE CLEMENS, 1962

I remember Carter Creek as being a beautiful place where a stream came in there....But the living space was the bottom of the canyon...where all the deer were—the animals, the geese and all of these; the wildlife was along the bottom. So when you put in the dam there and flooded it, it essentially killed all the living space for the animals. There were a lot of animals there....The beauty of the canyons seemed to be the bottomlands of the river—the immediate bottomlands...you take a picture of the canyon the way it was and then—and it's a beautiful picture—and then if you take the scissors and cut off the bottom third, that's what it looks like now.

— DON HATCH, 1984

One characteristic of those canyons—those are probably the most ideal places for beginning river runners to get going. They were fairly big waves [but] easy and straightforward. It was very beautiful....We worried a lot about Ashley Falls but it was pretty simple....A good part of that area was forested.... I remember one morning having mist hanging over the canyon, hanging over the forested walls; it was... one of the loveliest sights I've seen on the river.

— CAL GIDDINGS, 1984

A Recent Year

Philip L. Fradkin

PULITZER PRIZE-WINNING JOURNALIST PHILIP FRADKIN HAS WRIT-
TEN WIDELY ON NATURAL RESOURCE ISSUES IN THE WEST. IN THIS
EXCERPT FROM HIS BOOK *Sagebrush Country,* FRADKIN USES A TRIP
DOWN THE YAMPA AND GREEN RIVERS TO EXAMINE THE CONTRO-
VERSY THAT ERUPTED IN 1985 OVER THE PROPOSAL TO ELEVATE
THE STATUS OF DINOSAUR NATIONAL MONUMENT TO THAT OF A
NATIONAL PARK AND TO COMMENT ON THE CONFLICTS INHERENT
IN THE DESIRE TO BOTH PRESERVE AND PROVIDE ACCESS TO OUR
PUBLIC LANDS.

Nineteen eighty-five was not the best of years for the administrators who oversaw Dinosaur National Monument at the
eastern end of the Uinta Mountains. Then again, it was not
the worst of years. What can be said with certainty is that the year
began on the wrong foot, and the remainder of it was spent hopping
about trying to catch up; which pretty well summarizes how public
lands in the West are administered.

Joe Kennedy, the monument's superintendent, thought up the idea
about changing the monument's name to the more prestigious desig-
nation of a national park. The legal difference is that a monument is
established by an executive order of the President while a park has
to clear all the hurdles of the legislative process. But Kennedy—a
large, lumbering southerner who was fairly new to the area—was not
knowledgeable about western ways. Emotional subtleties that were
rooted in history, not legal technicalities, were the real issues in the
controversy.

Kennedy ran into a buzz saw of opposition that chewed him up
and came just short of spitting him out in the process. The man was
dazed by his encounter with the realities of the West, and eventually
he left for his native South.

The superintendent operated out of the administrative headquarters of the monument some two miles outside the small town of Dinosaur, Colorado, and a world apart in terms of orderliness from the disorder of the typical western hamlet. As the headquarters is physically removed from the town, so are the employees of the federal land-management agency distanced from the surrounding population. Park Service employees are transferred frequently and live and work in bureaucratic ghettos separated from their constituencies. They are remote, uniformed entities whose primary loyalty is to their careers and their agency. The stone walls of the monument headquarters are a bulwark against the unpredictable qualities of life as it is lived outside, not an invitation to enter.

The year began this way.

The superintendent had been looking at publications printed on slick paper whose carefully composed photographs seemed to pop out of the page and beckon the reader into a four-color scene that could never be duplicated in real life. Those fantasy pictures in books and magazines, be they written in English, French, Japanese, or German, depicted the "crown jewels" of the National Park system: such places as Yosemite, Yellowstone, Grand Teton, Glacier, Rocky Mountain, and Grand Canyon national parks. If the publication was particularly thorough, as was one published by Sunset Books, there might be a mention in smaller type of Aztec Ruins National Monument, Capulin Mountain National Monument, Capitol Reef National Monument (whose status was changed after publication to Capitol Reef National Park), and Dinosaur National Monument.

The accompanying descriptions told the story of relative status. Grand Teton was described thus: "Favorite park of many who know them all; once the gathering place of fur traders and trappers, in a setting of majestic beauty; its spires attract mountaineers from everywhere." Dinosaur, on the other hand, was located on a "semi-arid plateau in Colorado-Utah with deep gorges, rapid waters, and rich skeletal deposits of prehistoric reptiles." There was this warning concerning the national monument: "Back roads sometimes hazardous." In distant cities choices for summer vacations were made from such publications.

Kennedy had those publications stacked in his carpeted office, and looked at them and showed them to visitors, along with a Utah

State University graduate student's thesis on the drawing power of the differing land classifications. A national park ranked higher than a monument, and national forest lands were considered third best. Federal lands rated higher than state lands. What Kennedy clearly saw was that national-park status meant bigger type size in such publications, more visitors, larger budgets, and more personnel. Park status could be a bureaucrat's dream come true, and Kennedy admitted that he had initiated the proposal, at least partially, for such reasons.

So the superintendent and his staff in the first month of that year put together a three-page summary entitled "The National Significance of Dinosaur National Monument." The document cited the richness of the dinosaur bone deposits, the drama of the Green and Yampa river canyons, the uniqueness of the Uinta Mountains (incorrectly termed "the only east-west mountain range in North America"), the sanctuary for such threatened species as the peregrine falcon, and the human history extending from the ancient Frémont Indian culture to the Escalante expedition to the river journeys of William Ashley and John Wesley Powell.

For some reason the Park Service's concept of the monument's history stopped in 1869, the year Powell and his men first descended the Green and Colorado rivers. This proved to be a decisive mistake for Kennedy. Had he carefully examined the historical record after it had been prematurely terminated, he would have found that similar attempts to change the monument's name failed in the early 1950s, when conservationists and dam builders fought over the destiny of the monument, and by implication the remainder of the national park system, in the first classic confrontation of the modern conservation movement.

Nothing that was publicly visible celebrated this western bloodletting in the monument. The locals, who had been around longer, were aware of that bitter controversy; and their emotional actions that year could be traced back to the prior disappointment of having the proposal for a cherished dam, which they thought meant prosperity, defeated by the actions of outsiders, whether Park Service personnel or conservationists. Both were equally distrusted, feared, and disliked. So, in a sense, Kennedy was thwarted by history before he even began his quest.

Grumbling began to be heard to the west in Vernal, Utah, following the initial proposal to change the status of the monument. So the following month another document from the administrative headquarters found its way into the surrounding communities. This paper attempted to answer the concerns of the natives. No, such a name change would not dash hopes for greater energy developments in the area. A stricter air-quality standard for the surrounding desert, which might scuttle plans for future energy projects, was not automatic. Nor was the name change related to the issue of eliminating grazing in the national monument, or other restrictive management plans that might be put into place. Congress and the states of Colorado and Utah would have to rule on these matters. The document did not state that, if more people could be moved to visit a place because of a name change, the same shift in nomenclature might cause politicians to view it differently. This subtlety did not escape the locals.

The paper ended with a soothing thought: "For those of us who work at Dinosaur, the name change means greater national and international recognition. For the local communities a name change means that residents can take greater pride in their national park and enjoy the added income of more park visitors spending their money locally." Tourists represented a $1.3 billion industry to Utah; and the federal government was something of a mother lode itself, since its expenditures accounted for slightly more than 50 percent of all public monies spent on outdoor recreation in the state. For rural counties, such as Uintah County in the northeast corner of Utah, which were in the grip of a recession because of fading energy-related projects, the benefits of tourism were being rediscovered.

It was a good ploy; but the locals, when confronted with the alternatives, still put their faith in industrial development, though it was declining. Their choice was not logical, but it was consistent with the illusive search for quick mineral wealth that pervades the history of the West.

The best way to experience Dinosaur is to float down the Yampa and Green Rivers. The most dramatic landscapes in the monument are the canyons of the two rivers, which form sinuous transportation corridors through the high, rolling plateau country and mountains of the 211,141-acre national monument. These uplands are duplicated elsewhere in the West with great regularity and greater grandeur. It is the canyons, and dinosaur quarry, that are different.

Located at the eastern end of the Uintas, the monument is drier than the remainder of the range because it lies in the rain shadow of the higher mountains. But the elevated desert has a certain austere drama. The nakedness of the landforms reveals the tremendous forces that wrenched this land in eons past. The land, with the twisted rivers forming the baseline for such observations, was torn this way and that by powerful forces and tilted on its side to reveal not only the bones of the past but almost a complete geological record of its existence. Both revelations drew the finest scientific minds of the nineteenth century to this remote region.

Science has given way to recreation. Currently eleven thousand persons float down the two rivers each year. When they begin their trip and when it ends, the equipment they take with them, where they eat and where they sleep, how they dispose of their wastes, and other essential matters are determined by a set of regulations known as a river management plan. In 1972 there were 17,000 boaters on the river. After that year the waters within the national monument began to be rationed because of congestion and deterioration of the surrounding countryside by thousands of sets of tracks and the detritus people left behind. Studies were undertaken, public hearings conducted, and in 1979 the plan was adopted. A lottery was held each year to determine who among private applicants could take a river trip. There were eleven commercial operators whose allotments were determined by historical use, and Don Hatch of Vernal had the largest slice of that pie.

The two seasonal rangers I would be traveling with for the next few days had a number of duties to perform. They would be maintaining twenty-one campgrounds, performing rescues if needed, checking permits, giving interpretive talks, making wildlife observations, and answering questions, such as why do we have to conform to all of these regulations in the wilderness? (Answer: So it may continue to appear to be a wilderness. The major deception of the West is that each visitor believes he or she is the first, when along these two rivers habitation has extended back some 9,000 years, at the very least).

I met Bill Ott and Jim McChristal at the maintenance yard behind the monument's headquarters. It has always amazed me how much mechanized equipment is needed to keep a so-called natural area in its natural state. The monument is not in its natural state, nor has it been for some time. So machines are necessary to patch roads, repair pickups, make trail signs, collect trash, and fix motors attached to boats that patrol a supposedly motorless river.

Both men were seasonal rangers, Bill being the senior of the two. He had a background in microbiology and river running. Jim came to rivers via a career as a technical writer for an aerospace firm. Both were in their late thirties and were part of the back-to-the-land movement that had invaded the West in the previous decade. While some of those footloose people had left the territory to seek more secure employment, others, like Bill and Jim, had found a temporary niche there.

On the hour-long drive to Deerlodge Park at the eastern end of the monument the two men talked with Elaine Adams, another seasonal ranger and the driver who would return with the vehicle. They used a combination of Park Service and river argot. The discussion ranged from Park Service jobs, pay, and housing, to river boats, oars, and rapids. "Cat" translated to Cataract Canyon and "Deso" referred to Desolation Canyon in their discussion of hazardous drops elsewhere that would not be encountered on this trip.

The best way to see Dinosaur National Monument is to float the sixty-two miles from Deerlodge to Split Mountain campground. The rapids are not fearsome, as are those in the Grand Canyon, and the steady movement of the current from east to west through the twisting, ribbed canyons provides a movable walkway through the landscape.

The weather was unsettled. A series of spring storms were traversing the high desert. The temperature the night before had been below zero, and today it was clear but chill. The spring flood stage of the Yampa was just beginning to subside, leaving driftwood among the cottonwoods in the flats above the slippery riverbank at Deerlodge Park, where we launched the rafts. The Yampa still has a seasonal ebb and flow, it being the last major tributary of the Colorado River system that has no major upstream impoundments or diversions. However, there have been more than twenty major proposals to change the river's free-flowing status. The West refuses to remain still.

After checking the permit of another party that was also readying to depart, we shoved off in the two rubber boats at 11:50 a.m. On the river there was a radio check with headquarters, and the base operator asked for my address and telephone number. Next of kin, I supposed. We passed some cows grazing peacefully on the north bank of Deerlodge Park shortly before we entered the confines of the canyon.

Just beyond the Grand Overhang there were constant reminders of the ever-present cattle culture. We passed four bloated cow carcasses, this being one reason why we carried our drinking water with us.

Reminders of past cultures intermingled with the present one. Remnants of the Fremont Indian culture and the leavings of Shoshoni and Ute Indians were scattered along this stretch of the river. Mantle Cave, a short hike from the river, was a prime site for Indian artifacts. At a nearby ranch, a private inholding within the monument, modern artifacts were strewn about the yard. A covey of snowmobiles were beached in the sagebrush and scattered about were irrigation pipes and rusting fuel drums, and other ranch trash. Archaeologists had sifted through the Indians' junk piles in the cave. Today's junk would be tomorrow's find.

The only rapids of any consequence, Warm Springs, were passed without incident; and we ended that day at Echo Park, whose green lushness encased within rock walls recalled estate lands in wet northern climates rather than the parched canyonlands of the West. As we stood on the bank after unloading the rafts, a single kayaker flashed by with an offhand comment and a wave of his hand between hasty paddle strokes. He was insouciance personified. There was nothing the two rangers could do about the illegal river runner. Their boats were too slow and their radios ineffective from that isolated enclosure.

Such illegalities were a problem that year. The position of a certain segment of river runners was not much different from that of other users who were testing the limits of restrictions on public lands. What the boaters wanted was a larger piece of the river, and their target was the Park Service regulations that halved the permits between private parties and commercial outfitters. The river runners contended that the lottery they were subjected to was not equivalent to the outright granting of a permit to a commercial concessionaire. "Can you imagine calling an airline to reserve space during the busy holiday season and being told to apply to a lottery? Like airline seats, river permits should be available by advance registration," they maintained.

To test the law in an American tradition that goes back at least as far as the Boston Tea Party and forward to the recent Sagebrush Rebellion, ten river runners publicized their pending attempt to run the river without permits and then quietly slipped downriver in a raft and several kayaks one night of the Fourth of July weekend. Park Service rangers observed their departure and then used megaphones to direct the river runners to come ashore. The boaters proceeded downriver and came up against a Park Service flotilla of two motor-driven craft. The rafts were boarded and towed ashore. Two of the kayakers evaded the net and made their way to Echo Park.

Those who were apprehended upstream and the two who landed at Echo Park were taken before a federal magistrate. Some were released, some fined, and the two who had a free but apprehensive night and day on the river later went to trial and were fined and jailed for a few days. The federal judge noted that the Park Service had a difficult choice to make between preserving the natural resources and providing the very public access that might result in frayed lands and rivers.

The name change controversy came up on the river.

Dave Whitman, who had just joined the monument staff as Chief of Interpretive and Visitor Services, met us at Echo Park, having been trucked in from above. Whitman wanted to get the feel of the river that has carried so much history along with it on its headlong rush through the Uinta Mountains.

Sleeping, eating, and cavorting about in the nearby campground was a noisy group of Denver high school students. We planned to meet the students and their teachers at the Jones Hole campground that night for an interpretive talk around a campfire. The get-together would be a significant "visitor contact" for the rangers, and they could log it as such.

The noontime departure was in a broad swing around Steamboat Rock, radiant in the bright sun, and then another gentle arc brought us into a zone of darker, more constricted rock, where Bill Ott told me to watch carefully for a two-inch pipe and some writing on the rock wall to the left. We saw no pipe or writing, and Bill guessed that the high water had obscured those fitful reminders of the dam fight of the fifties. But on the opposite bank there was a rock cairn, which I took to be a remnant of that conflict. The mystique of the Park Service had not been well served by its secretive maneuverings during the administrative and legislative battles. Other forces had been in the forefront.

The weather was threatening and the run from Colorado into Utah and on to the Jones Hole campground was uneventful. We beached the two boats, made camp, and ate all the leftovers, which, when lumped together, vaguely resembled Chinese food. The two seasonal rangers stationed at Jones Hole and a visiting ranger from Rocky Mountain National Park joined us. Shortly before nightfall we marched over to the students' camp in what must have been an imposing procession.

There were about twenty students and five instructors, comprising half of the senior field-studies program of the Jefferson County public schools, an outgrowth of the more loosely organized alternative-school concept of the seventies. The emphasis was on direct experience with the real world, which meant being involved in an urban project, working on a farm in eastern Colorado, hiking through the desert wilderness of south Texas, and running the rapids of the Yampa and Green rivers—all the time applying the more traditional subjects of English, Social Studies, Science, and Physical Education to what was being encountered around them.

The students, now reaching the end of the course and the safe years of high school, were exuberant about what they had learned. There had been lessons in independence, teamwork, limitations, denial, danger, solitude, fitness, and compromise. The hope was that from this smorgasbord of learning they emerged with independent minds. There would be a test tonight.

The students sat in a circle, some reclined on foam pads, and a few gave each other back rubs. It was that kind of crowd. There were crickets nearby, a great horned owl in the distance, and the constant, reassuring murmur of the river, of whose boating history Bill Ott spoke in learned detail.

Then Dave Whitman, who had been to all the appropriate training schools, took over. His formal training was apparent. He captured the immediate attention of the students by stating in a decisive tone, "How about stretching?" The suggestion did three things at once. It established his presence, his consideration, and the fact that he was in charge now.

After the students sat down, Dave asked: "When you picture a dinosaur, what do you think about?"

Nothing like a little audience participation to start things off, I thought. There was silence, and finally a few tentative answers like big, cold-blooded, ancient.

Well, said Dave, dinosaurs were the reason for this park. He then launched into a short discussion of the ancient beasts and ended by asking, "What do you think of our park?"

The answers ranged from "great" to "beautiful."

"It is a national monument now, but we think it has most of the qualifications for a national park. Would you like to see it a national park?"

The pitch was out in the open. The question that Dave had asked had all the badly disguised subtlety of priests asking visitors in a cathedral if they believe in God.

There was a chorus of yeses that I found disappointing, given all the work that had gone into developing independent minds within the past year, But, in their defense, the students were in the grip of a revival-meeting mentality. Whitman said he would let their leaders know to whom to write, and thus another national-park constituency was born.

I then spoke to say that the Park Service ranger had not outlined all the current considerations that were involved in such a decision— the monument's history and the history of the surrounding mountains and deserts that made up this distinctive entity called Sagebrush Country. Perhaps the students should immerse themselves for a while in that web, I suggested, before rendering an opinion.

From the silent faces that surrounded me in the firelight I did not sense a great deal of assent to my remarks. It was easier to feel than to think, and plenty of feeling was going on in the West that year.

Echo Park Through Split Mountain

Ann H. Zwinger

In her book *Run, River, Run,* naturalist and artist Ann Zwinger recounts in copious detail her trip down the Green River from its source in Wyoming to its confluence with the Colorado River. This chapter describes Zwinger's passage through Split Mountain Canyon with an Outward Bound group and explores the geological and human history of the area.

Here lie a Green River raft, a pump, ten paddles and life jackets, assorted duffel, food bags all over the ground. It is May and of course it's raining and since this is an Outward Bound trip, the seven of us are expected to get it all together and on the river. Our instructor is Mark Leachman, slender, quiet, bearded, hidden beneath a high-crowned, broad-brimmed hat. He is a very, very good boatman and an excellent teacher. When he says, "Listen up!" we *listen*. There are twenty-eight of us in all on this trip, among them my daughter Sara.

We have been issued rain suits, heavy slickers almost totally waterproof except for the shocker that goes down the front of your neck when you're leaning back to backpaddle in a rapid. Since it's raining, we have them on, sweating through trying to get the raft inflated. Uninflated, it looks like a mistake: an amorphous wrinkled flotsam, no front, no back, all middle. When the first pontoon is full, it sits there like a lopsided doughnut. As we pump air into the other side, the raft rises out of some primordial vulcanized sleep to become something resembling a boat. At command, the seven of us carry, drag, lug, and stumble it onto the bank edge and push it over. It plops in with a large smack, tugging with the current.

Next come the big Coast Guard–approved bright orange life jackets. The extra bolstering in front makes everyone look like orange pouter pigeons. They are constantly in the way: you can't get things out of your pocket, you can't get things into your pocket, you can't lean over far enough to pick up something dropped in the bottom of the raft. Amazingly, after a few days, one does acclimate well enough to be almost efficient, in an elephantine sense. But not yet. Still, we somehow all manage to get into the raft without getting into the river first.

It is my first experience with paddling a raft. It handles like—well, nothing in my experience. I am reminded of the description by Andy Hall, the young bullwhacker who served as boatman and cook on Powell's first expedition. In Hall's idiom, his boat would "neither gee nor haw nor whoa worth a damn" as if it "wasn't *broke* at all!" This raft does not crease the water as a sailboat does, or arrow it as a canoe; it seems more to pivot, and were it not so heavy, to skitter. We practice the six simple commands: forward, right, left, back, rest, and hold. It seems impossible to believe that at the end of this trip Mark will have us running rapids with style and respect for the river, and with the elation that comes with accomplishing something new and difficult with éclat.

At Echo Park, the river, out of Lodore, makes a hairpin turn around the prow of Steamboat Rock before it enters Whirlpool Canyon. Steamboat Rock comes down to the water in an elegant line, almost the same color as the flat swirling river, but more variegated: the weathered beige of the Weber Sandstone is bannered with gray, tinged with yellow, scrubbed with black, strung with desert-varnish pennants. Manganese and iron oxides, with other trace elements, are dissolved and carried in rain water. When rain and surface water drain over rock surfaces, they redeposit these minerals on the rocks in dark, often shiny, streaks. When it rains, many areas of the cliff face may remain dry, but rivulets gloss the streaks of desert varnish, following patterns that have carried rain water for centuries. The deposition of desert varnish is slow, measured in hundreds of years, especially in this arid country where rainfall is so sparse.

Steamboat Rock is massive and monumental, rooted in the Mitten Park Fault, a spectacular example of drag faulting. The rock formations in the fault are compressed upward, so twisted and gnarled that the rock almost loses its quality of rockness, as Baroque architecture passes into sculpture. The drag is pronounced, particularly on the upthrown side on the left, rock strata bent in the direction of the thrust. Several hundred feet of the Uinta Mountain Group, which disappeared just upriver in Lodore, are pulled up into view again. Weber Sandstone twists upward like the bare ribs of some Norse boat; the gray limestones stand vertical, on edge. The contrast between cold gray and sandy red, between vertical and horizontal, clearly revealed because there is no obscuring vegetation, illustrates the process of drag faulting as clearly as a textbook diagram.

The fault's name? Pat Lynch named this small park after his mule, Mitten.[1]

Whirlpool Canyon is bounded by the Mitten Park Fault on the east and the Island Park Fault on the west. The afternoon wind coming around the corner of Steamboat Rock is sufficient for sailing. We rig our rain jackets with paddles in the sleeves, use two more paddles as centerboards, and sail down the river. But, as we turn into Whirlpool Canyon, the head-on wind is so strong that, even with eight people paddling, the raft seems to plow back upstream. Alongside, short sticks entrapped in the vortices of the eddies whirl around as if stirring a witch's brew. Having picked up the Yampa River, the Green charges in Whirlpool with vitality and nerve.

Whirlpool Canyon is the antithesis of the sunny, sandy openness of Echo Park, where the water is flat, the rocks golden sandstone. The waves are high and fast and lurch upstream. The wind makes it difficult to maneuver, exhausting to paddle, and cold in the shadows. I put on my wool mittens and they rub my hands raw where they're sunburned, an occupational hazard of boating. Spray spatters my sunglasses. No one talks, except usually quiet Allie, who is captain and keeps yelling tersely, "Keep paddling!" The raft bucks through big, malicious waves. The boat hangs between wind and water, poised, seemingly going nowhere. Only the cliffs seem to move, ever so slowly, upstream. The ancient brooding rocks come right down to the water, striped like a Dobos torte or slabbed with ripple-marked sandstones stacked like cards against the canyon wall.

About three miles downstream the river widens enough so that sand beaches intervene between river and wall. Two Canada geese nest on one of these. They stalk with necks extended, wary, facing away from the raft, suspicious but unwilling to fly. Finally, complaining in anserine irritation, they take off in a great sweeping arc. With eggs in the nest they do not remain away long, and even before we are out of sight they are back down.

We pass "Stateline Rock," where boaters assure passengers that they are leaving Colorado and entering Utah. And then, Jones Hole ahead. It has been a long day of paddling for me, perched in an awkward position, and I am sure I will be sore, stiff, and a walking wounded. Instead, as I half jump, half-fall off the raft, some peculiar elation hits: I have survived another day on the river's terms, and weary as I am, my only regret is that I have to put the paddle down. The river pours by and I want to go with it.

Jones Hole Creek empties into the river, having cut a narrow canyon into the sandy-red Lodore Formation, whose cliffs now flank the river. Like Lodore, the lower part of Whirlpool Canyon is steeper, flaring at the top to a mile and a half across. In autumn, big groves of cottonwoods let the sun shaft through to leaves on the ground, an underfoot goldness. In spring, violets make a Botticelli carpet under the trees just leafed out into pale yellow-green, and one spring the cicadas sang green rondeaux. In spite of the fact that as a campground it is woefully overused, it is still a Midas place.

I walk to a ledge at the far upstream end of Jones Hole. It is just big enough for a sleeping bag, about six feet above the water, floored with abrasive gray limestone embedded with shells. When I slept there last October, a boxelder smoldered as red as the cliffs across the river, and in a crevice, a small rosette of distilled-lavender asters bloomed. It was a solitary spot in a vast canyon, right above the river that purled quietly beneath, facing a cliff outlined with stars. That night a misting rain fell, then cleared, and the stars came thinly through, small raindrops breathing down even as the sky blackened.

I awoke to a loud clanging: one of the boatmen was out on the basketball-sized cobbles that pave the river bed, trying to get wash water. The river had dropped a foot or more during the night, baring almost thirty feet of shoreline. The sun rose behind a cloud, turning it blinding white, an incandescent river morning.

But this year a surge of high water has dumped a pile of logs and brush that leave room only for chipmunks and ground squirrels.

Powell named the creek here Bishop Creek, after his chief topographer on the 1871 expedition, and Jones Hole after Stephen Vandiver

Jones, the assistant topographer. But it seems not to have been called Jones Hole by local residents until after an episode involving Charley Jones in 1883. In an attempt to reclaim his wife and children, who had left him, Charley Jones knifed a hired man. Thinking he had killed him, Jones holed up for the winter in this remote canyon that now bears his name, going out the next spring when he discovered that the man had not died.

Jones Hole Creek runs muddy today, a colder brown than the river; it cuts into the Green like a scimitar, curving downstream, maintaining its separate identity as far as I can see. The Island Park Fault that terminates Whirlpool Canyon downstream swings northward, and it is in this zone of weakness that this creek runs. The creek used to be prime fishing; one of Powell's men reportedly caught 20 trout here, and Galloway, in 1909, reportedly snagged a total of 129. Fishing has declined with the increasing popularity of the campground and large boating parties that enjoy wading and splashing in the creek. Trout are almost never caught in the main stream of the Green in this reach, for it is too silty; rainbows and browns in Jones Hole Creek have not been introduced and are thought to have come in from the Yampa or Upper Green River before Flaming Gorge Dam closure. And Jones Hole Creek was certainly fished by prehistoric Fremont Indians who frequented the area.

A short walk upstream still leads to a wall of Fremont drawings—a walk through thickets of waist-high rustling horsetails, through garlands of butterflies, yellow violets and wallflowers, gold parsleys and twinpod, starflowers and opulent drifts of pale blue chiming bells, along a stream brightened with yellow monkey flowers and clumps of watercress. On a sandstone wall, high above the creek bottom, are the drawings, both pictographs and petroglyphs. The latter are chiseled into the stone surface, while the pictographs are painted with hematite pigment, applied with a twig or branch, fingers, or a yucca-fiber brush. The wall is long, and there are many figures arrayed over the surface, placed with no interrelationships, no perspective, among them a square-shouldered human figure with a horned headdress about fourteen inches high, stiffly drawn, a typical Fremont representation. The animals are more naturally limned: cleft feet of deer, long curling horns of mountain sheep, added to a simple rectangular body. Circles and a careful pattern of triangles arranged in rows, a grid of holes pecked out

of the rock, some spatter marks, a series of circles—enigmatic, evoca-
tive. A rough rectangle is divided into squares; to its right, which is
upstream, is a zigzag, a common abstraction for water. The two forms
together, and their orientation, imply a net set for catching fish.
Although there is no historical evidence whatsoever for interpretation,
it is hard to ignore the implications of such widespread symbols ori-
ented to the landscape in which they occur.

The Fremont Indians who produced these wall paintings lived in
this area between AD 300 and 800 or 900, the northernmost extent
of a culture found first along the Fremont River (now called the Dirty
Devil, the name originally given it by Powell) in south-central Utah.
Long considered a "peripheral" and offshoot culture, it is now recognized as having had a fully-achieved cultural pattern that spread over
most of Utah, with recognizable regional variations, two of which
occurred along the Green River drainage. The Fremont lived a semi-
nomadic existence with few material goods, and probably began the
practice of agriculture when corn, squash, and beans were introduced
into the region. Storage cists of corn are tucked away in protected
caves and overhangs, or in pits in the ground provided with covers.
The Indians also gathered many wild seeds, bulbs, and nuts, among
them rice grass, prince's plume, yucca, beeplant, wild onion, prickly
pear, squawbush, and mariposa lily.

Small points and snares are the tools of the hunter, and as in other
prehistoric cultures, the Fremont wasted little. They wove strips of
fur into a net of fiber cords to make light, warm robes. From bone
they made awls and punches that hold, even today, firm and heavy in
the hand, useful, sturdy objects. Also from bone they fashioned coun-
ters for games, smooth on one side, sometimes decorated on the other.
Some have holes drilled in them and were undoubtedly worn as orna-
ments, and no wonder—they are small, light objects in the hand,
clicking together pleasantly, scattering with a winsome clatter like
thin dominoes.

Pottery is the mark of a civilization that needs vessels for cooking,
storage, and carrying. The Fremont made a utilitarian plain gray ware
out of alluvial clay and tempered it with whatever was at hand, and
shaped it into ollas and pitchers. So seldom are they decorated that a
small pitcher I saw, sitting on the shelf in the University of Utah
anthropology laboratory, attracted my attention because of the plea-

sure and care an Indian hand took—molding small clay disks, perfo-
rating each with a small hole, and applying them in a neat overlapping
row. The Fremont Indians made fine baskets; a bundle of fibers, often
yucca, wound around a split willow rod core and sewn together to
form a closely-woven container. Both baskets and pottery were sometimes lined with gilsonite, a tarlike substance found in the Uinta
Basin that made them waterproof.

Unique to the Fremont culture are small clay figurines, probably
made for religious purposes, and an ingenious moccasin design. The
figurines, like the pottery, are gray; they are unfired, decorated with
a fingernail imprint for an eye, a pinched-out nose. The lower part is
unfinished, serving as a handle perhaps, and one fits into my hand
as if planned, a miniature face staring upward with an inscrutable
expression.

Moccasins were made of mountain-sheep hide, designed so that
the dew claw forms a kind of hobnail. Never mind that this made the
seams come on the foot at all the points of wear and that a great
amount of industry was probably expended in keeping them patched;
what intrigues me is that glimpse of patterned perception that saw, on
the fleet foot of a mountain sheep, a glimpse of human utility.

On a bright May afternoon the raft cavorts through the remainder of
Whirlpool Canyon with great good humor, bucking the rollercoaster
waves head on. Strictly speaking, these are not rapids in the sense of
rocks and falls that require precise maneuvering. Although the waves
are big, there are no hidden rocks or surprises, just an increased drop
in a narrowing channel that pushes the water into foaming haystacks.
None of the rapids in Whirlpool are named except for one unofficially
called "Greasy Pliers," obviously a boatman-named rapid commemorating the loss of that indispensable tool. Our raft wallows over the
waves like some huge inchworm, and at any one moment the crewman
in front of me may be three feet above or three feet below, paddle out
of the water or submerged nearly to the top.

The rock formations disappear in order as we travel downstream,
first the Lodore Formation, then the intervening limestones, and finally Weber Sandstone coming down to water's edge, forming cliffs
full of crusader castles and old fortifications from ancient deserts—
and who knows what intrigues and machinations go on inside or what

veiled eyes watch through slotted windows. Reddish at the base, gray-white to tan toward the top, the cliffs rise, divided into bays; trees grow within the hollows but not on the edges, emphasizing the knife sharpness of the ballasts between. The lightness of the water and the fantasies of the rock give as light-hearted a character to the lower part of Whirlpool Canyon as the dark rocks give somber aspect to its entrance.

The Island Park Fault marks the end of Whirlpool Canyon. Island Park itself separates Whirlpool Canyon and Split Mountain, and the river meanders and braids across it, as if it had all the time in the world, looping a length of seven miles across three air miles, a peaceful cul-de-sac between two racing gorges, named by Major Powell for the numerous islands around which the river flows. Some are sand-bar islands, flat, like a piece of tan paper pasted on the water; others are bigger, carrying cottonwoods and brush, or sprigged with a row of this year's tamarisk, that make a thin green haze, last year's row farther back and a little taller, studded with cocklebur and annual grasses.

Henry C. Ruple, who originally homesteaded Island Park, came here about the same time as Pat Lynch. The latter used to tie a few logs together and float and walk down Whirlpool Canyon to visit the Ruple Ranch. At the conclusion of the visit, he borrowed a horse from Mr. Ruple and rode back up to his current lodging on the Yampa or Green. There he let the horse go, and it would find its way back to the Ruple Ranch.

Before Flaming Gorge Dam was built upstream, the river froze over in the winter, thick enough to drive a team of horses across, temperatures down to 40° F. below for six weeks at a time. G. E. Untermann and his wife lived here for several years, Mrs. Untermann having been a Ruple before her marriage. Mr. Untermann tells of the winter of 1936–37, when he chopped holes in the ice so cattle could drink; the last ax blow would release a fountain of water that froze on boots and trousers on contact, and had to be whacked with the flat of the ax to make movement possible. Three to four inches of new ice froze in the holes every night. Sometimes the ice would cut off cottonwoods along the river as neatly as a buzz saw.

In the springtime, newly green cottonwoods edge an island stretching flat with sagebrush. The water is peaceful, reflecting the sky in a lavender blue. Vortices ease out from the bank, a flat swirling that is soporific to watch; there are intimations of the lower Green in this quiet, wide river. And then Island Park ends as it begins, with a fault. The rock strata rise and curve above a loose talus slope to crenelated cliffs, rock faces broken, ledges and sharp slopes sprinkled with trees, and in the far, far distance, a ridge with a thin dotted line of spring snow.

If Lodore is an anomaly, Split Mountain is incredible. From the air one can see how the river hooks into the mountain at one end, runs for some five miles right down the middle, then angles out at the other end, as it entered. Calling it Craggy Canyon in 1869, Powell took a second look and changed it to Split Mountain two years later, and it is precisely that, a mountain cut by a tensile copper wire of a river.

Split Mountain is small as mountains go, about ten miles long and five wide. As an entity it was probably contemporaneous with the main Uinta Mountain uplift. As at Swallow Canyon, the river is superposed. Split Mountain simply did not exist as a positive geographical entity when the river first flowed above it millennia ago. Probably the whole Rocky Mountain region at that time had only mild surface relief, more rolling than mountainous. The river flowed across and then through softer rock layers left now only in the adjacent valleys. When it reached the underlying Weber Sandstone, it continued to cut downward in the same channel. The river has cut through all the sedimentary formations that record a rising and falling of the land, some sediments laid down underwater and some not, some on the oscillating shore, some continental, some marine. The way in which these sediments eroded provides the panorama of Split Mountain.

Split Mountain is a morning canyon: of all the Green's canyons, it is the most upbeat, a pure delight of sun and water and rock. (I have felt this way even while running it on a dark, freezing, foot-soaked, hand-numbed October evening, shivering and stiff.) At its entrance the Island Park Fault soars upward in massive ribs, a rising line that is infectious. Split Mountain is one glorious chute, rapid after rapid, with just enough time to get your breath in between before the line of foam and the din downstream announce another. The river drops 140 feet in seven miles, a drop that ensures fast rapids, and the river profile shows four sharper inclinations, all named: Moonshine, SOB,

Schoolboy, and Inglesby. Like the rapids of Lodore, these were boat-man-named some forty years ago by Bus Hatch, one of the best boat-men on the river when only wooden boats were used. Moonshine is named for Moonshine Draw on the left, obviously commemorating some illicit activities on the mountainside. SOB was, in a wooden craft, that kind of rapid to run; Schoolboy, because after much fretting Hatch considered it that easy. And Inglesby commemorates a dentist who went overboard here. They can be run in succession, bright rapids, spanking rapids, sunshine rapids, and best of all morning rapids.

Of the times I have relished Split Mountain's rapids, perhaps it is on the Outward Bound trip that I enjoy them most. We have worked together for five days, have learned the raft's temper and the river's power, and now begin to concentrate on the refinements of running. Mark draws diagrams in the sand and we talk over how best to run, what position the raft should be in on entrance, what landmarks there are to orient by, the danger spots. About two hundred yards beyond the entrance to Split Mountain lies Moonshine Rock, an immense boulder fallen off a high slope or tumbled in by Moonshine Draw. From the river, at high water, the rock shows only as a large, omi-nously slick surface. On its downstream side is a stationary wave with a hole of sobering dimensions. A short chute of slick swift water fol-lows, and then the tongue of the rapid itself; in midstream are the rocks that must be slipped around, and then the river jogs straight into the cliff and piles up against the wall in an entrapment to be devoutly avoided. The rafts' attitude going into the tongue should be about forty-five degrees, a strong pull out of the current to avoid the wall, and then into haystack tail waves that pile up in sleek, opaque café au lait pyramids.

We adjust life jackets to breathless; during rapids, the bottom and midships fastenings are cinched in tight to prevent the jacket from popping over your head in case of being thrown out. (In that case, proper procedure is not to swim but to face downstream, knees slightly bent to act as shock absorbers against the rocks.) We pile into the raft, backpaddle to get to midriver upstream, edging into position, already sweeping so swiftly downstream that we immediately enter the pour-ing tongue. We swivel to confront the rollers. The raft bucks; a sheet of water comes point-blank over the bow. Everyone paddles even though the paddle may be biting thin air because stopping means a loss of control. Water pours over the side, cascades of spray and splash inundate everyone, no time for anything but putting the paddle in the water, bracing, watching the paddle in front of you, keeping the beat, pushing back tons of water, switching to one back stroke to turn, pulling away from the cliff and out of the current and suddenly—it's over, in seconds, too swift for exhilaration. That comes with looking back over what you've come through and the sight of another rapid in a thin rim of unfurling white on the river horizon ahead. Moonshine is a rapid I got to captain, although not to my satisfaction—I have not yet learned to allow for the time lag in the raft's response. At this moment I want only to go back and do it over and do it better while it is fresh in my mind, with more style, more precision.

I look back through hexagons of water on eyelashes, flaring with sunlight, to see caramel waves breaking upstream. I feel surfeited with sun and spray and dazzle and May. In the brief quiets between rapids, when there is time to wipe sunglasses and look about, I savor the heightened awareness that rapids bring, that make one more responsive to this total world of rock and sunshine and river. Split Mountain ends with sedimentary beds canted downward at a steep angle, a definitive satisfying end. At the boat landing we unlash gear, tip the rafts up on their sides and slosh them clean, open the valves and let the air out. We fold them and carry them to the truck, six river days encapsulated in a neoprene packet.

The rest of the group goes home, but my husband, Herman, and boatman Clair Quist meet me at Split Mountain and we shove off in Clair's ten-man raft within the hour, my continuity of river unbroken. The elation of Split Mountain persists almost as long as the view of it lasts downriver, but my knowledge of having cleft through that mass of rock on a beautiful May morning, suspended on a crystalline lather of spray, remains with me still.

≋ NOTES

1. For more on Pat Lynch, see "The Marks of Human Passage" in this volume.

Two-Snake Days

Ellen Meloy

ELLEN MELOY'S BOOK *Raven's Exile* PRESENTS A RECORD OF ONE OF THE EIGHT YEARS SHE AND HER HUSBAND, MARK, SPENT AS RIVER RANGERS IN DESOLATION CANYON ON THE GREEN RIVER. THIS SECTION ILLUSTRATES THE HARSH CONDITIONS FACED BY THOSE WHO VENTURE INTO THE LOWER CANYONS AND THE CHANGES FLAMING GORGE DAM HAS IMPOSED ON THE LOWER SECTIONS OF THE GREEN.

The Tertiary is airborne.

The wind roars upcanyon at fifty miles an hour, launches tables and tents across gravel bars, smashes birds against boulders, snaps tree limbs from cottonwoods as if they were dry linguine. The top three inches of Arizona blast through Desolation in a hurricane of high-velocity sand grains that engulf the raft and filter through the tent mesh at night, blanketing sleeping bags, hair, and eyelashes with fine rose-beige powder. Wind, the Navajo say, etched the whorls on our fingertips. This wind redesigns the whorls.

Desolation's spring windstorms never begin with a benign nuzzle of tamarisk fronds or thin clouds veiled across canyon rims, portending an imminent front. They never curl around the nape of the neck, softly lifting tendrils of hair, teasing the nostrils with pungent aroma of sagebrush. Desolation's spring winds erupt with an abrupt, thunderous bellow of jet engines. They funnel upriver, gain speed in the narrow chasm, careen around bends and oxbows, shriek down straightaways, rouse sand clouds hundreds of feet into the air. Defying a current so forceful, it effortlessly moves submerged boulders downstream, the winds turn the river surface back on itself, pushing it upstream in a bank-to-bank roll of whitecapped breakers. Of all the world's notorious winds—foehn, Santa Ana, mistral, khamsin—Desolation's winds most resemble the Australian brickfielder, dust-bearing storms from the continent's interior, and the sand-laden simoom of the Sahara.

Desolation's winds can last a few hours. They can also blow for a week without ceasing.

Although rapids have become more frequent—deep lateral chasms now intersect the mainstem every quarter mile, spilling debris fans into the river—progress against the wind is slow. We take turns at the oars, advance ten yards, then lose twelve during a scrambling, Marx Brothers switch. The wind churns water into three-foot waves that break over the boat, soaking us. Ravens roll on the ground, howling with laughter.

We ricochet downriver past Dripping Springs, slip down the riffles and rapids above Wild Horse Canyon, whose elegant dunes are obscured by the haze of windborne sand, and pull over to chat with a party of river runners hunkered down on a sandbar, their faces sunburned the color of lobsters at the boil behind bright-colored cones of sunblock on their noses. A doleful bearded fellow slumps low in a boat, talking softly to his dog.

"Aha!" I tell Mark as we approach. "Kononpaiochi. People of the North, the people who do not comb their hair."

"The wind stole our hats," says one boater with a blue nose. "Blew them to Wyoming."

"Another gust turned that raft upside down in the water," a yellow-noser laughs, pointing to a fourteen-footer. "A first-ever flatwater flip."

While Mark answers their questions about petroglyph sites, rapids, camps, and the weather, I prepare lunch. Tuna and tomatoes weigh down the bottom bread slices, but the wind sends the top slices into the air like Frisbees.

"What is Steer Ridge Rapid like at this water level?" the blue-nosed boater asks. I anchor the sandwiches to the dry-box lid with arches of duct tape, an essential item in every river runner's medicine bundle, until Mark is ready to eat.

"I'm anxious to get back to my futon," the bearded fellow tells his dog.

"When will the wind stop?" a red-noser asks.

Mark looks at his watch. "Friday, three twenty-three p.m." Your tax dollars at work.

Steer Ridge Rapid, formidable at high water, capsized Major Powell's *Emma Dean* in 1869, spilling blankets, guns, barometer, and crew into the river. "We broke many oars," Jack Sumner wrote, "and most of the Ten Commandments. Major Powell said he lost three hundred dollars in bills. I lost my temper and at least a year's growth—didn't have anything else to lose." The men honed new oars from driftwood. Guns and gear still lie beneath waves and silt.

Our raft poises at a standstill above the rapid's tongue, so weak is the current against the upriver wind. As the waves rise, stiff gusts blow their crests into a wall of spray, obscuring the route. Mark waits for a break in the wind, trying to keep the raft off a villainous logjam in the rapid's midriff. He pulls so hard on the oars, they torque into nine-foot-long parentheses. Suddenly the wind pulses. The current sucks the raft into churning whitewater with a whiplash jerk, tosses it into chaotic rolls, and spits it out through the tailwaves.

When the wind abruptly dies, scourges of tiny gnats devour every mammal on the river that is not dead. Although entomologists would probably classify these insects as midges, river runners call them no-see-ums, punkies, winged teeth, or just plain *gnats*, the name most suitable to their annoying nature. They represent the season's advance troops. After gnats come mosquitoes (subdued by drought these past years), then deerflies, all of which amply fill Desolation's bloodsucker niche. The gnats march rudely onto the scalp, remove a teensy square of flesh, and plunge a scalding needle deep into the major learning hemispheres. Then, for about two hours, they pour battery acid into the wound. They slurp up the petrochemical industry's most toxic insecticides as if they were Godiva chocolate. The ideal solution: post a semistarved whiptail lizard on each shoulder, affixed to my earrings with leashes of dental floss.

The tent provides refuge but heats up like a sauna. The wind pumps up again, explodes a stiff gust. Mark leaves the tent too late to add weight to the camp table. It flies through the air and clubs him. The same gust flattens the tent. I hold it down, body plastered against the floor, suffocating in nylon.

Some sell the desert as a place so abstract, empty, and indifferent, it surrenders its passivity to one's own lambent dreams. While you perch on a sunset-drenched butte contemplating eternity, however, Truth is the horrid little bug sinking its thorny mandibles into your lotus-positioned butt. This desert rakes the flesh, its beauty earned only when blood flows and screams rise in high-pitched fury against dust and wind, the relentless abrasion of razor-edged extremes. T. E. Lawrence, homesick for England and edges less defined, wrote from the Sinai Desert of a "fierce, stimulant, barbaric" sunset that revived "the colours of the desert like a draught—as indeed it did each evening, in a new miracle of strength and heat—while my longings were for weakness, chills and grey mistiness, that the world might not be so crystalline clear, so definitely right and wrong."

I have surrendered my entire intellect to twenty insects the size of a pinhead. My skin is a parched slab of 120-grit sandpaper, granules glued to flesh with hand lotion. Tossing aside a couple of scorpions, I crawl into a sleeping bag gritty with sand. Mark returns, hair upswept by the wind in a full Brezhnev.

"Remember the room in that swank Seattle hotel," I ask, "the one with the immaculate white terry-cloth courtesy robes? Down pillows so lofty, your sinking head reached bottom fifty seconds later? The miniature TV in the bathroom?" He strokes my hair, then struggles to remove fingers stuck in the tangle. "Remember the cool caress across bare shoulders of a dress of pure silk?" Another brickfielder sandblasts the tent, drowning the river's soothing voice. When I say I never want to get into the boat again, he knows I am lying.

At Rock Creek, Desolation's slice into the Tavaputs cuts a mile deep, deeper than the Grand Canyon at the Bright Angel Trail. On the topographical maps the 2,700-foot-high inner gorge registers in erratic, wavy hairlines of such brief contour intervals, they nearly merge to a solid color. Above them sits another tier of ramparts. Tall fir trees, unlikely desert denizens, spill over the high rims' north faces only as far as altitude and moisture allow, then give over to juniper, rabbit brush, and a broad alluvial meadow aflame with spring color. Rock Creek flows as clear as glass into the opaque Green River, its water cool enough to grow trout, reliable enough to inspire homesteaders' dreams of permanence, evidenced by mulberry trees bearing fruit for the pie I bake to bless the end of the wind.

Rock Creek Ranch, one of two hardscrabble ranches that operated in Desolation Canyon until the 1940s, existed more by virtue of creek than river. Cattlemen had little use for the river, indeed feared it, its floods and terror. The river compounded the task of crossing cows from one canyon bottom to another, a necessity in a largely vertical country with neither the grass nor the moisture to support many animals. Rock Creek, on the other hand, only several yards wide even in spring runoff, flowed out of the cliffs into an alluvial crescent that was level, sheltered, and irrigable. The homesteaders cleared the crescent of native shrubs and grew fruit, vegetables, hay, and alfalfa, irrigated by diverting water from Rock Creek along a narrow ditch against the canyon wall. The ranch house, hand-masoned from rose-colored sand blocks, lies in ruin now, roofless but for a clay and viga remnant sprouting a healthy thatch of prickly pear cactus. The old corral fences sag with age. Nearly every item of use on the ranch, from garden seed to plow and bedsprings, came here atop a mule, over rugged trails sixty miles from town. Ranchers at Rock Creek and the McPherson spread downriver had little company but their own families and hired hands, Ute hunters, a stray outlaw or bootlegger. Today Rock Creek sees more people in a few summer days than all the river runners who passed during the half century of ranching.

The ranchers' departure left Desolation Canyon without permanent human residents, and there have been none since. Feral cows—inbred, tough as old bison—still gnaw the Ute side of the river. On the west bank drought and trail erosion have made the range on Desolation's federal grazing allotments less desirable. The BLM reserves several allotments exclusively for bighorn sheep, and in others places the immediate riparian corridor off-limits to livestock. For now visitors need not tiptoe through gnawed stumps and muffins of excreta, and desert flora savor a period of recovery from heavy grazing.

While Mark repairs a fence, I pick mulberries. Mormon leaders encouraged the Latter-Day Saints to add mulberries to the horticultural repertoire, not for food but for shade, windbreaks, and diversionary bait. (Birds can easily devour a peach or apricot crop, but they will stay off those trees if they are attracted by nearby mulberries, fruit they seem to prefer.) My bowl full, I walk along the old flume, hoping to visit the Fremont metates thrown in with the rubble along the irrigation ditch. Like the "Indian pictures" on the rock faces around them, these grinding stones were, to the ranchers, merely backdrop and, save to buttress a ditch, seldom useful.

Five mule deer feed in the junipers that edge the ditch. Compared to the hulking ungulates we see in Montana, these desert deer seem as small as greyhounds. My presence does not alarm them; they frequent

Rock Creek like black-belt shoppers at the mall, begging you to bowl apples or apricots across the ground to them when the old orchard is in fruit. The does have borne no fawns this spring nor have they in any of the years I have observed them. Perhaps the does have lived beyond reproductive age. More likely the interminable drought has taxed the vigor of browse and forage, reducing the food supply. To alleviate stress on winter range, wildlife officials have authorized special hunts on the river in the fall. These deer may leave the canyon, chopped up inside coolers.

In search of metates I walk the flume several times, the last time in disbelief. They have vanished. Despite ranger patrols, boater education, antiquities protection laws, and the prosecution of thieves and vandals when they are caught, pieces of the canyon disappear.

Across the meadow Mark walks the river's edge to camp. The geriatric does feed in the clearing between us, lifting their sweet faces in curiosity. They will stare dumbly into the crosshairs this fall, expecting apples. Mark stalks them in his best Masai warrior trot, fencing pliers raised as if to clobber one. Seems like a fair hunt to me.

I stand by the flume, mourning metates, surrounded by a fidgeting chaos of songbirds in the junipers, pinyon jays in the mulberry trees, ground squirrels scampering down the ditch, the deer barely twenty yards away, unafraid, their soft ears pivoting. Here walks St. Francis of Assisi, I think, birds orbiting my ears, lizards on my shoulders, straining at their leashes, their thin gray tails draped in the cusps of my shoulderblades, small furry beasts trailing with no fear, as if some instinct dismissed all threat and made them entirely submissive. Here I am with fat purple berries and my benign entourage of nature. There is Mark, sneaking up on five sleek does with pliers.

In a descent of tender, melodic notes, a canyon wren sings the sun off the escarpment. A deep shadow rises slowly up the rock face in the sun's place. The canyon wren came to this country voiceless, a friend once told me, saw the red-rock canyonlands and invented its distinctive song. The river's surface breaks into nacreous fragments of copper and blue, reflections of sandstone and sky. Sauce simmers on the stove, and my mulberry pie bakes in the Dutch oven. Fresh-cut ribbons of fettucine hang from the raft's bow line until the water boils. We shake sand from tarp and sleeping bags, turn the gnats over to hungry bats, grunt with the pleasure of wind-chapped skin cleaned by solar shower, and sit back in blissful stupor, minds operating at river speed. Impatience and haste go poorly on the river. There is no time for future or past, only an unbearably rich profusion of air, color, and light ingested by a synaesthetic faculty. Color and scents become taste, light becomes music, sounds glide over bare flesh in touches thick with affection.

Above Wire Fence Rapid the river bulges into broad eddies, which of course the English call *edwards*. The rapid lies around the bend, unseen. Lest we be complacent, its growl fills the ears for the half-mile flatwater approach. A second rapid immediately below it, at Three Fords, rates as one of the river's largest. I cinch up my life jacket, relatch dry-box lids, secure oar pins, brace feet against the aluminum frame, and poise the oars in a position that will maximize my stroke. In short, I use all the physics I can muster to keep six hundred pounds of raft, gear and husband right side up.

Desolation's rapids occur at the mouths of lateral canyons, where flash floods wash debris into the main current, constricting the channel into a narrow chute. In high water the river roars over the debris; in low water unwary boaters can pinball through a boulder garden. Water levels rule rapids. Nature, with help from the U.S. Bureau of Reclamation, rules water levels. The undammed Yampa River, not yet ruled by bureaucrats, rules itself, emptying northwestern Colorado runoff into the Green north of Desolation. The Yampa is a leaky pipe in a controlled waterworks bracketed on Utah's northern and southern borders by Flaming Gorge Dam and Glen Canyon Dam.

In 1964 the Bureau of Reclamation dammed the Green at Flaming Gorge for water storage and hydroelectric power, inundating ninety-one miles of river and canyon behind it in a slack-water reservoir. From the foot of the dam downriver through Dinosaur National Monument to the Yampa's mouth—sixty-five river miles—the Green's ecology has also changed. The reservoir acts as a settling basin, reducing the river's turbidity. The dam set a new headwaters on the mainstem, discharging cold, clear water from the lower depths of the reservoir as if the water were snowmelt from the mountains. The cooler river temperatures altered the fauna immediately below the dam. Controlled, stabilized discharges—a river without the muscular floods of spring—also affected the shape of the channel and the vegetation along its banks.

In other words, the predam Green ran warm and silty to opaqueness. It flowed low in winter, swelled during its spring peak to six or more times its normal size, and ripped through the canyons in awesome flood every ten or twenty or hundred years. The clear, cold postdam river neither rages nor floods; it hiccups politely at the push of a button. Bureaucrats, politicians, utility companies, and consumers, as well as weather and snowpack, determine the timing and volume of seasonal peaks. Hydrographs that once showed gentle rolls on either side of a soaring cone (the May and June flows) now chart a rise in spring and nipples in late summer and winter, when peaking power demands draw more river through the turbines to buzz air conditioners or furnaces as far away as New Mexico and California. Artificially stocked trout, fish invoking comfort, cash, control, and a constituency, replaced humpback chubs, squawfish, razorback and flannelmouth suckers, and other natives whose names evoke itches. Between Flaming Gorge Dam and the Yampa River's mouth, some of these natives fall into the category of doom, "rare if not extirpated."

Below the Yampa's mouth, from the Uinta Basin through Desolation Canyon, Flaming Gorge Dam's relation to the river grows more subtle. Diurnal dam discharges—the hiccups—attenuate by the time they reach the Yampa. Inflow from the Yampa and other tributaries then warms the Green again and augments its volume. Native fish reappear, and one of the West's siltiest rivers becomes silt-loaded once more.

Somewhere upstream from everyone's river trip sits a dam. Although its physical influence may grow negligible with distance, symbolically it remains nothing less than apocalyptic. "In the view of conservationists, there is something special about dams, something— as conservation problems go—that is disproportionately and metaphysically sinister," John McPhee wrote in *Encounters with the Archdruid.* For conservationists "the outermost circle of the Devil's world seems to be filled mainly with DDT. Next to it is a moat of burning gasoline. Within that is a ring of pinheads each covered with a million people—and so on past phalanxed bulldozers and bicuspid chain saws into the absolute epicenter of Hell on earth, where stands a dam." Perhaps the reaction to dams is so vehement, McPhee reasons, because "rivers are the ultimate metaphors of existence, and dams destroy rivers. Humiliating nature, a dam is evil—placed and solid."

Precisely 986,644 cubic yards of concrete fixation and metaphor straddle the Green River at Flaming Gorge. The dam's implications in conservationist iconography, however, loom larger than its actual environmental consequences farther downriver, a point well taken here and now, poised in a torrid blush of adrenaline above the roar of Wire Fence and Three Fords Rapids in Desolation Canyon. The ecological changes on the Green River come from many sources—climate cycles, invasions of exotic flora and fauna, and a complex array of human activities. The paramount agent of change in this river landscape is not a dam but a species: *Homo sapiens.*

The wild Yampa joining a wild, damless, "untouched" Green through the narrows of Desolation Canyon, what a river! Years ago, before ranger life, we rode its ghost. After an El Niño winter, in the spring of 1983, as record-breaking snowpack and late spring storms slid off the Rockies; as Bureau of Reclamation engineers soaked their button-downs in sweat, watching the reservoir behind Flaming Gorge Dam rise; while their colleagues downstream at Glen Canyon Dam, who had kept Lake Powell as full as possible as a hedge against drought, began to regret their decision; as water poured into Lake Powell faster than it could be released through Glen Canyon's penstocks and outlet tubes, which were operating at full capacity; as spillway tunnels used for the first time since dam completion in 1963 began to spew red water and boulders rather than clear lake water because the tunnels' three-foot-thick concrete and rebar lining had simply been ripped away, cavitated by a hundred-mile-an-hour jet of raging river, which began to exfoliate the sandstone on either side of the dam abutments as if it were peanut butter; while dam operators installed wooden flashboards atop the spillway gates so the lake would not overtop the dam; as the engorged, ever-rising Lake Powell was held in check by *plywood and epoxy*, Mark and I ran the Green River through Desolation in a thirteen-foot inflated soap dish, a raft designed for fly-fishing in limpid Montana riffles. Cottonwood groves drowned, beaches and eddies vanished, rapids became churning whitewater hurricanes, and snags, telephone poles, and dead livestock roared past the raft. A massive muscle of water—44,800 cubic feet per second (cfs)—moved through Desolation, hellbent for the plywood.

We learned to row whitewater that year, to lay down our beds distant from a river's edge that rose three feet before sleep's first dreams.

The dam wranglers learned that the River could still throw a formidable wrench into the Hydro Empire, but they would meet the challenge with better runoff prediction models and spillway cavitation-control systems, or whatever ingenious devices might be required. While no one can accurately predict the dams' life expectancies (none was designed with a mortality plan), most engineers agree that the dams will outlive their reservoirs, which will eventually fill with silt.

The River resumed its outlaw self that year and the next, also a record breaker. Then came the drought. For the past several years peak flows through Desolation have seldom exceeded 9,000 cfs, whereas peaks during "normal" years usually range from about 14,000 to 20,000 cfs. (One cfs is water a foot deep and a foot wide traveling at one foot per second.) The high-water Green beneath us today runs half its normal spring volume and, accustomed but not resigned to puny peaks, we accept cheap thrills. Desolation's rapids, relatively speaking, are as tame as a narcoleptic ocelot.

You can recheck gear, tighten the last strap, wriggle down harder in your seat, and open and shut your fists on the oar grips, but there is the moment when pure river takes over and you yield to it with a great surge of love and terror. Wire Fence Rapid has a steep drop down a slender tongue of silk, a long, mirror-slick, mesmerizing sheen of descending water. A split second before the raft hits the five-foot wall of roiling lateral waves at the tongue's tip, I am spellbound by an aromatic river of air curling above the water itself, a cool, stony, turbulent smell, the smell of rapids.

Three Fords Rapid, a narrow slot piling water against a sheer cliff, follows quickly. George Bradley, one of Powell's 1869 crew, called it an "old roarer" and ran it in boater's nightmare style: boat swamped, his foot caught under the seat, head dragging though haystack waves, raised now and then for gulps of air. Our run is tame. At its end, when we wipe the tailwaves from our eyes, we are in Gray Canyon.

Desolation and Gray Canyons lie end to end, changing from one to another in an instant. The difference is rock, several million years, and biome. From younger Tertiary strata, depositions of an ancient lake, we have dropped into older, softer marine sediments deposited during the Cretaceous, when a shallow sea covered the Colorado Plateau.

What could be duller than the interminable descent of particles through a shallow, listless interior sea, revealed millions of years later as a sky-high torte of petrified sand? On the contrary, the late Cretaceous period, Gray Canyon's underpinnings, was a time of flux. Deltas migrated, bedrock uplifted, tectonic plates lurched, estuaries, streams, swamps, and bogs into which the last of the dinosaurs plunged headlong. Gray's coal beds attest to the period's abundant flora—sequoia trees, cypresses, palms, and ferns.

Today Gray Canyon's dry, rocky face belies its colorful origins as a humid, semitropical, watery, paleogeographical Gulf Coast. Low-slung, set-back, wedding cake terraces skirted by crumbling fans of talus have replaced sheer, ragged-edged, cloud-raking cliffs. Desolation's walls begin pale beige and turn to red-gold in its heart. Gray Canyon rises uniformly golden brown. Even within his lackluster repertoire of names, Major Powell could not make up his mind about Gray Canyon. For the coal beds he saw here in 1869, he named it Coal Canyon. Two years later, when his crew passed through Powell-less, the name was Lignite Canyon. By 1872 publications record Gray Canyon.

Day has no ceiling, no floors or walls. We float under the escort of Gray's rich, teeming spraddle of proteins, inhabiting an eternity of great blue herons and dark geysers of swallows that erupt from ledges in great circles, spiraling higher and higher, straining to rise. Six snowy egrets, members of an avian tribe once nearly decimated by wetland dewatering and hats, wade the shallows on slender black legs and wacky yellow feet that looked dipped in egg yolks. White comes to the canyon on magpies' vests, a heron's throat, the feathered tarsi of a golden eagle. The egret, the canyon's sole solid-white bird, appears like parentheses around river season, seen on the first and final trips of the year as it migrates along the river corridor.

Beneath the river's mirror, giant minnows swirl in their spawning beds. The Colorado squawfish is North America's largest minnow, a member of the cyprid family, and a voracious omnivore that once topped eighty pounds and lengths of six feet until anglers and fertilizer markets, selecting for the largest fish, gradually reduced the general size class of this stunning predator. Of a four-foot dinner squawfish caught in Gray Canyon by Powell's 1871 party, crewman

Frederick Dellenbaugh noted, "The heart after removal kept up pulsations of twenty beats to the minute for half an hour."

Called "white salmon" for their considerable migrations, squawfish once swam the Colorado River Basin from Wyoming to the Gulf of California. Natural populations are extinct in the heavily developed lower basin, leaving remnant populations in the upper basin. Like humpback chubs, bonytail chubs, and razorback suckers, squawfish are under federal protection as an endangered species.

Mark tends to his chores along the riverbanks, photographing vegetation and archeological sites for a careful record of their condition. The river carries us on exhilarating rides through Range Creek and Rabbit Valley Rapids. Oars poise at the ready above Coal Creek Rapids, a hazardous S curve of whitewater punctuated by Dumpster-sized holes, where the river slicks over submerged boulders, falls into deep troughs, then turns on itself in boat-smashing waves. Below Coal Creek we pull into a beach at the mouth of Poverty Canyon and make camp.

It has been a two-snake day. One snake, a midget faded rattlesnake, surprised us as Mark worked on a trail that river runners use to scout Coal Creek Rapid. The other, a sleek, elegant whipsnake, parks under my lawn chair in camp and stares at my toes, which its heat-addled brain reads as baby mice. Tomorrow we will float the last miles of Gray Canyon, pull into a boat ramp at canyon's end, and be trucked back to town, two grousing neoprimitivists thrust back into the plastic frights of The Spectacle.

River rhythms drowned me a week ago, hardly a day into this trip. By now I am so engulfed, so beyond the normal experience of domesticity, rescue is futile. It has become second nature to stuff our bedrooms into bags each morning and push into the current, to fall over backward in the boat, bodies limp with the heady scent of cliffrose and rapids, to grunt up a rugged side canyon, shins lacerated by thorn and scrub, merely to see the petroglyph of a man with a wolf's head staring across the air at us. It is routine to drop from some high, remote rim observed time after time from the river then finally visited after years of seduction, to stumble back to camp, pluck rattlesnakes from our ankles, and stand at a cookstove, stirring a simmering pot, toes buried amidst the creamy blossoms of a thousand birdcage primroses.

Mark disappears up Poverty Canyon. I hear his call and follow. Poverty's "creek," the paltry collection of seeps and springs only a few yards upcanyon, rations its life zone in a narrow wall of slough grass as tall and dense as bamboo. Where the moisture ends, the jungle ends. I stand in bare rock below the canyon rim, suddenly showered with delicate blue petals, Mark's invitation to join him on top and walk the benches.

Blooming scorpionweed covers the tops of the inner gorge. Desert plants grow widely spaced, guarding their small homesteads of nutrients and moisture. But this scorpionweed, a humble wildflower also known as heliotrope, outblues the rest of spring's exuberant fever by a collective, quixotic display that carpets acres of golden-brown rock. The bloom echoes an explosion on some raw upland of the Cretaceous, millions of years ago, the avant-garde of the angiosperm "spike": the sudden, soundless, widespread, color-bright debut of the earth's first flowering plants. No one will believe us when we say *blue desert*. They will think of shadows or mood or emptiness.

During winters away from Desolation, I fret over Desolation. After this trip there are reasons for solace. The blue benches, a healthy wildflower season, may not bode an end to the drought, but more rain has fallen this spring than last. As usual, egrets appeared, ravens did not. Desolation Canyon remains damless. No one is mining oil shale. No one has turned bighorn sheep management over to the U.S. Air Force. The river rangers continue their steady instruction in the proper care and feeding of Desolation.

Eagles fly here but some have eaten poison. In a few weeks armadas of recreationists will hammer the cottonwood camps, squeeze the daylights out of their wilderness experience. Biologists unveiling the mysteries of native fish edge closer to the possibility of their demise, unsure if the fish can be saved, unsure who exactly these little-known fish are or if we will find out before they are gone. Just how wild is Desolation?

From this chair beside the river, whipsnake lacing gracefully around my ankles like water flowing, it seems impossible that the river changes beyond this bend, that somewhere it straightens its sinuous coils around towering rock and emerges into valleys hemmed by mountains whose peaks bear the snows that give the river its beginning. It seems impossible that the river would not act by its own nature. Yet this canyon paradise is a qualified paradise, the Green River through Desolation Canyon an elongated island of whitewater wedged between two of the West's largest dams. Is the river an outlaw or the northern conduit of an aqueduct extending from Wyoming to Mexico, federally neutered, designer-plumbed by Bechtel Steel and the Bureau of Reclamation?

Some moments, floating the current on my back, losing an entire afternoon to tireless scrutiny of rock, are "wild" enough to obliterate my anxiety about the river, but there is little doubt. I live on a tightly disciplined floodplain in the heart of an energy colony, a system of heroic but aging hydraulics. Their impacts are not always apparent. When you float Desolation, you think, This is how a wild river is. But if you live on the river long enough, if you love it with all the ferocity of a passionate, surrendering affair, with love's innocence and erotica and its dizzying inertia, you will begin to see otherwise. If you memorize a single cottonwood and watch this tree season after season, if you peer over the shoulder of people who are taking the finest of measurements, you may begin to know. The land immediately beyond the river—so harsh, vertical, dry, rugged—is, relatively speaking, wild, wild, land. But the River itself, to borrow a poet's words, is a snake nailed to the earth.

Terra Incognita: Into the Maze

Edward Abbey

IN THIS, THE PENULTIMATE CHAPTER OF *Desert Solitaire,* ABBEY
RECOUNTS WHAT MAY WELL HAVE BEEN THE FIRST DESCENT VIA
ROPE INTO THE MAZE, A LABYRINTH OF CANYONS THAT DRAIN INTO
THE GREEN AND COLORADO RIVERS NEAR THEIR CONFLUENCE.

"Do we really need all that rope?" I ask Waterman, as he
proudly and smugly coils his new nylon and stows it
into his pack, along with slings, carabiners, brakebars
and other hardware. "Who's going to carry it?"

"I'll carry it," he says cheerfully, through a magnificent, sandy
beard; "you can carry the water."

But before we can explore The Maze we have to find out how to
get to it. There's only one man in Moab who claims to have been
there, a garage mechanic named Bundy, so we pay him a visit. Squatting on his heels, he draws us a map in the sand. Gas up at Green
River, he says—it'll be your last chance. Take about twenty gallons
extra. Go south twenty-five miles toward Hanksville. About a mile
past Temple Junction you'll see a little dirt road heading east. Take it.
Keep going about thirty-five, forty miles till you get to an old cabin.
That's French Spring. Better fill your water cans there; might be your
last chance. Then south a few miles toward Land's End brings you out
to the head of Flint Trail. Look it over careful before you try to go
down. If you make it head north six miles past Elaterite Butte to Big
Water Spring—should be water there, though this time of year you
can't always be certain. Keep bearing north and east. Seven miles past
Big Water Spring you come to The Maze overlook and that's the end
of the trail. From there on you could use wings.

We follow his instructions carefully and they turn out to be as
correct as they are precise. We camp the first night in the Green River
Desert, just a few miles off the Hanksville road, rise early and head
east, into the dawn, through the desert toward the hidden river. Behind

us the pale fangs of the San Rafael Reef gleam in the early sunlight; above them stands Temple Mountain—uranium country, poison springs country, headwaters of the Dirty Devil. Around us the Green River Desert rolls away to the north, south, and east, an absolutely treeless plain, not even a juniper in sight, nothing but sand, black-brush, prickly pear, a few sunflowers. Directly eastward we can see the blue and hazy La Sal Mountains, only sixty miles away by line of sight but twice that far by road, with nothing whatever to suggest the fantastic, complex and impassable gulf that falls between here and there. The Colorado River and its tributary the Green, with their vast canyons and labyrinth of drainages, lie below the level of the plateau on which we are approaching them, "under the ledge," as they say in Moab.

The scenery improves as we bounce onward over the winding, dusty road: reddish sand dunes appear, dense growths of sunflowers cradled in their leeward crescents. More and more sunflowers, whole fields of them, acres and acres of gold—perhaps we should call this the Sunflower Desert. We see a few baldface cows, pass a corral and wind-mill, meet a rancher coming out in his pickup truck. Nobody lives in this area but it is utilized nevertheless; the rancher we saw probably has his home in Hanksville or the little town of Green River.

Halfway to the river and the land begins to rise, gradually, much like the approach to the Grand Canyon from the south. What we are going to see is comparable, in fact, to the Grand Canyon—I write this with reluctance—in scale and grandeur, though not so clearly stratified or brilliantly colored. As the land rises the vegetation becomes richer, for the desert almost luxuriant: junipers appear, first as isolated individuals and then in stands, pinyon pines loaded with cones and vivid colonies of sunflowers, chamisa, golden beeweed, scarlet penstemon, skyrocket gilia (as we near 7000 feet), purple asters and a kind of yellow flax. Many of the junipers—the females—are covered with showers of light-blue berries, that hard bitter fruit with the flavor of gin. Between the flowered patches and the clumps of trees are meadows thick with gramagrass and shining Indian ricegrass—and not a cow, horse, deer or buffalo anywhere. *For God's sake, Bob*, I'm thinking, *let's stop this machine, get out there and eat some grass!* But he grinds on in singleminded second gear, bound for Land's End, and glory.

Flocks of pinyon jays fly off, sparrows dart before us, a redtailed hawk soars overhead. We climb higher, the land begins to break away: we head a fork of Happy Canyon, pass close to the box head of Millard Canyon. A fork in the road, with one branch old, rocky and seldom used, the other freshly bulldozed through the woods. No signs. We stop, consult our maps, and take the older road; the new one has probably been made by some oil exploration outfit.

Again the road brings us close to the brink of Millard Canyon and here we see something like a little shrine mounted on a post. We stop. The wooden box contains a register for visitors, brand-new, with less than a dozen entries, put here by the BLM—Bureau of Land Management. "Keep the tourists out," some tourist from Salt Lake City has written. As fellow tourists we heartily agree.

On the [sic] French Spring, where we find two granaries and the old cabin, open and empty. On the wall inside is a large water-stained photograph in color of a naked woman. The cowboy's agony. We can't find the spring but don't look very hard, since all of our water cans are still full.

We drive south down a neck of the plateau between canyons dropping away, vertically, on either side. Through openings in the dwarf forest of pinyon and juniper we catch glimpses of hazy depths, spires, buttes, orange cliffs. A second fork presents itself in the road and again we take the one to the left, the older one less traveled by, and come all at once to the big jump and the head of the Flint Trail. We stop, get out to reconnoiter.

The Flint Trail is actually a jeep track, switchbacking down a talus slope, the only break in the sheer wall of the plateau for a hundred sinuous miles. Originally a horse trail, it was enlarged to jeep size by the uranium hunters, who found nothing down below worth bringing up in trucks, and abandoned it. Now, after the recent rains, which were also responsible for the amazing growth of grass and flowers we have seen, we find the trail marvelously eroded, stripped of all vestiges of soil, trenched and gullied down to bare rock, in places more like a stairway than a road. Even if we can get the Land Rover down this thing, how can we ever get it back up again?

But it doesn't occur to either of us to back away from the attempt. We are determined to get into The Maze. Waterman has great confidence in his machine; and furthermore, as with anything enormously attractive, we are obsessed only with getting *in*; we can worry later about getting out.

Munching pinyon nuts fresh from the trees nearby, we fill the fuel tank and cache the empty jerrycan, also a full one, in the bushes. Pine nuts are delicious, sweeter than hazelnuts but difficult to eat; you have to crack the shells in your teeth and then, because they are smaller than peanut kernels, you have to separate the meat from the shell with your tongue. If one had to spend a winter in Frenchy's cabin, let's say, with nothing to eat but pinyon nuts, it is an interesting question whether or not you could eat them fast enough to keep from starving to death. Have to ask the Indians about this.

Glad to get out of the Land Rover and away from the gasoline fumes, I lead the way on foot down the Flint Trail, moving what rocks I can out of the path. Waterman follows in first gear, low range and four-wheel drive, creeping and lurching downward from rock to rock, in and out of gutters, at a speed too slow to register on the speedometer. The descent is four miles long, in vertical distance about two thousand feet. In places the trail is so narrow that he has to scrape against the inside wall to get through. The curves are banked the wrong way, sliding toward the outer edge, and the turns at the end of each switchback are so tight that we must jockey the Land Rover back and forth to get it around them. But all goes well and in an hour we arrive at the bottom.

Here we pause for a while to rest and to inspect the fragments of low-grade, blackish petrified wood scattered about the base of a butte. To the northeast we can see a little of The Maze, a vermiculate area of pink and white rock beyond and below the ledge we are now on, and on this side of it a number of standing monoliths—Candlestick Spire, Lizard Rock and others unnamed.

Close to the river now, down in the true desert again, the heat begins to come through; we peel off our shirts before going on. Thirteen miles more to the end of the road. We proceed, following the dim tracks through a barren region of slab and sand thinly populated with scattered junipers and the usual scrubby growth of prickly pear, yucca and the alive but lifeless-looking blackbrush. The trail leads up and down hills, in and out of washes and along the spines of ridges, requiring four-wheel drive most of the way.

After what seems like another hour we see ahead the welcome

sight of cottonwoods, leaves of green and gold shimmering down in a draw. We take a side track toward them and discover the remains of an ancient corral, old firepits, and a dozen tiny rivulets of water issuing from a thicket of tamarisk and willow on the canyon wall. This should be Big Water Spring. Although we still have plenty of water in the Land Rover we are mighty glad to see it.

In the shade of the big trees, whose leaves tinkle musically, like gold foil, above our heads, we eat lunch and fill our bellies with cool sweet water, and lie on our backs and sleep and dream. A few flies, the fluttering leaves, the trickle of water give a fine edge and scoring to the deep background of—silence? No—of stillness, peace.

I think of music, and of a musical analogy to what seems to me the unique spirit of desert places. Suppose for example that we can find a certain resemblance between the music of Bach and the sea; the music of Debussy and a forest glade, the music of Beethoven and (of course) great mountains; then who has written of the desert?

Mozart? Hardly the outdoor type, that fellow—much too elegant, symmetrical, formally perfect. Vivaldi, Correlli, Monteverdi?—cathedral interiors only—fluid architecture. Jazz? The best of jazz for all its virtues cannot escape the limitations of its origin: it is *indoor* music, city music, distilled from the melancholy nightclubs and the marijuana smoke of dim, sad, nighttime rooms: a joyless sound, for all its nervous energy.

In the desert I am reminded of something quite different—the bleak, thin-textured work of men like Berg, Schoenberg, Ernst Krenek, and the American Elliot Carter. Quite by accident, no doubt, although both Schoenberg and Krenek lived part of their lives in the Southwest, their music comes closer than any other I know to representing the apartness, the otherness, the strangeness of the desert. Like certain aspects of this music, the desert is also a-tonal, cruel, clear, inhuman, neither romantic nor classical, motionless and emotionless, at one and the same time—another paradox—both agonized and deeply still.

Like death? Perhaps. And perhaps that is why life nowhere appears so brave, so bright, so full of oracle and miracle as in the desert.

Waterman has another problem. As with Newcomb down in Glen Canyon—what is this thing with beards?—he doesn't want to go back. Or says he doesn't. Doesn't want to go back to Aspen. It seems that the U.S. Government—what country is that?—has got another war going somewhere, I forget exactly where, on another continent as usual, and they want Waterman to go over there and fight it for them. For IT, I mean—when did a government ever consist of human beings? And Waterman doesn't want to go, he's afraid he might get killed.

As any true patriot would, I urge him to hide down here under the ledge. Even offer to bring him supplies at regular times, and the news, and anything else he might need. He is tempted—but then remembers his girl. There's a girl back in Denver. I'll bring her too, I tell him. He decides to think it over.

In the meantime we refill the water bag, get back in the Land Rover and drive on. Seven more miles rough as a cob around the crumbling base of Elaterite Butte, some hesitation and backtracking among alternate jeep trails, all of them dead ends, and we finally come out near sundown on the brink of things, nothing beyond but nothingness—a veil, blue with remoteness—and below the edge the northerly portion of the Maze.

We can see deep narrow canyons down in there branching out in all directions, and sandy floors with clumps of trees—oaks? cottonwoods? Dividing one canyon from the next are high thin partitions of nude sandstone, smoothly sculptured and elaborately serpentine, colored in horizontal bands of gray, buff, rose, and maroon. The melted ice-cream effect again—Neapolitan ice cream. On top of one of the walls stand four gigantic monoliths, dark red, angular and square-cornered, capped with remnants of the same hard white rock on which we have brought the Land Rover to a stop. Below these monuments and beyond them the innumerable canyons extend into the base of Elaterite Mesa (which underlies Elaterite Butte) and into the south and southeast as far as we can see. It is like a labyrinth indeed—a labyrinth with the roof removed.

Very interesting. But first things first. Food. We build a little juniper fire and cook our supper. High wind blowing now—drives the sparks from our fire over the rim, into the velvet abyss. We smoke good cheap cigars and watch the colors slowly change and fade upon the canyon walls, the four great monuments, the spires and buttes and mesas beyond.

What shall we name those four unnamed formations standing erect above this end of The Maze? From our vantage point they are the most striking landmarks in the middle ground of the scene before us. We discuss the matter. In a far-fetched way they resemble tombstones, or altars, or chimney stacks, or stone tablets set on end. The waning moon rises in the east, lagging far behind the vanished sun. Altars of the Moon? That sounds grand and dramatic—but then why not Tablets of the Sun, equally so? How about Tombs of Ishtar? Gilgamesh? Vishnu? Shiva the Destroyer?

Why call them anything at all, asks Waterman; why not let them alone? And to that suggestion I instantly agree, of course—why name them? Vanity, vanity, nothing but vanity: the itch for naming things is almost as bad as the itch for possessing things. Let them and leave them alone—they'll survive for a few more thousand years, more or less, without any glorification from us.

But at once another disturbing thought comes to mind: if we don't name them somebody else surely will. Then, says Waterman in effect, let the shame be on their heads. True, I agree, and yet—and yet Rilke said that things don't truly exist until the poet gives them names. Who was Rilke? he asks. Rainer Maria Rilke, I explain, was a German poet who lived off countesses. I thought so, he says; that explains it. Yes, I agree once more, maybe it does; still—we might properly consider the question strictly on its merits. If any, says Waterman. It has some, I insist.

Through naming comes knowing; we grasp an object, mentally, by giving it a name—hension, prehension, apprehension. And thus through language create a whole world, corresponding to the other world out there. Or we trust that it corresponds. Or perhaps, like a German poet, we cease to care, becoming more concerned with the naming than with the things named, the former becomes more real than the latter. And so in the end the world is lost again. No, the world remains—those unique, particular, incorrigibly individual junipers and sandstone monoliths—and it is we who are lost. Again. Round and round, through the endless labyrinth of thought—the maze.

Amazing, says Waterman, going to sleep.

The old moon, like a worn and ancient coin, is still hanging in the west when I awake. All night long the wind has been blowing, haunting my dreams with intimations of disaster, and in the east above the rim and mountains are salmon-colored clouds whipped into long, sleek, fishlike shapes by the wind. Portents: Red skies at morning, sailors take warning. Northeast the sky is vaguely overcast, a pallid gray.

As I start a fire and prepare breakfast the wind stops, suddenly, and the tremendous silence flows back, sealing the canyon country beneath a transparent dome of timelessness. Then sun comes up, a resounding fire, the great golden gong of dawn: Waterman stirs feebly in his bag.

After breakfast we get ready for the descent into The Maze, the first so far as we know since the Indians left seven centuries before—if they were ever here at all. Once again Waterman checks the beautiful rope, all one hundred and fifty feet of it, and his other climbing equipment, while I divide and pack our rations for the day: raisins, shelled nuts, hard chocolate, cheese, dried beef, oranges and water.

The drop-off over the white rim is too far for our rope but about a mile to the east we find a break in the caprock where we can descend to the dark-red stratum below. We are still nearly a thousand feet above the actual floor of The Maze. We traverse the red ledge in a westerly direction and find some notches through which we can climb down to the bulging, rounded, buff-colored rock of the Cutler formation, principal material of The Maze and of the similar Needles area on the east side of the river.

Here we find ourselves rimmed-up, five hundred feet or so above the canyon floor. After further exploring we find a good spot for a rappel, with a pinyon pine to serve as belay. The only trouble is that it is impossible to see from here whether or not there is a feasible route the rest of the way down. If further descent turns out to be impossible, then whoever goes down the rope first is going to be in a tough situation. The wall at this point is somewhat overhanging, requiring a free rappel of forty to fifty feet—easy enough going down but cruel hard work to get back up. I don't know about Waterman but am certain that I could never climb that far up a rope myself. Of course there are various techniques for doing it but none of them is easy. I invite Waterman to go first, he invites me, and we waste about ten minutes in the Alphonse-Gaston routine.

He loses patience first, as I felt sure he would, gets into a sling, hooks up his carabiners, runs the double rope around a brake bar, backs over the edge and slides out of sight. I crawl along a narrow shelf to one side and watch him free himself from the rope and disappear below among the crevices and boulders. Presently he comes back and tells me to come on down, he has found a way clear to the bottom.

So it's my turn to dangle in mid-air. I've never made a free rappel before and am a little nervous about it. As I lean back over the edge I can't help but look down and the sight of Waterman far below looking up at me is frankly kind of sickening.

"What are you waiting for?" he wants to know.

"Are you sure this rope is strong enough?"

"It held me, didn't it?"

"Yes, but I weigh more than you do."

"Well, give it a try anyway."

A very humorous fellow. But there's no honorable way out of this for me. After another minute of equivocation and technical inquiries, I lean back farther, keeping my eyes on the rope, and go down. Nothing to it. Half an hour later we're down on the sandy floor of the canyon and inside The Maze. We've brought the rope with us, of course, and therefore will have to find a different route up to the rim, if there is one. But that problem can be deferred for a while. If necessary we've got enough food for two days.

The air is hot, clear, dry and our canteens nearly empty; we've taken three hours in the descent. The first thing we've got to do is find water. We start walking down the canyon. If we keep going we will reach the Green River, about ten miles away according to our map, just above its confluence with the Colorado. There may, of course, be obstacles; we don't know.

Within half a mile, however, we find cottonwoods and shoals of damp, firm, sand on the canyon floor. I dig a hole as big around as my fist and elbow deep and come to wet gravel; a few more inches and I find water.

There is a stand of wild cane nearby. I cut two stalks, a fat one and a thin one, and punch the pith out of the joints of the bigger one by using the smaller as a ramrod. Happy now, greatly relieved, I recall for Waterman's edification a few appropriate lines from Burns:

> Green grow the rashes, O!
> Green grow the rashes, O!

The lasses they have cozy bores,
The widows all have gashes, O!

Now we've got a siphon, two feet long. I offer it to the thirsty Waterman, he sticks it in the hole and drinks heartily. When he is finished I take it, blow out the sand, and also drink. The water is warm, smelly, but potable and quite refreshing. Feeling much better we sit in the shade of the trees and eat some lunch. I cut a few holes in the drinking straw, creating a sort of crude recorder, and play a few tunes in a barbarous scale never heard before this side of the Atlas Mountains. I stop, Waterman comes back and lies down for a siesta. I go exploring.

At one place on the canyon wall I find three arches or natural bridges, one above another, all spanning the same drainage chute. Going farther up-canyon I come to a fork, the first of many branches in the canyon system. The main or wider canyon turns to the left, revealing vistas of alluvium flats covered with sagebrush, more cottonwoods, more and more branching canyons with deep alcoves high in the walls, likely sites for Indian ruins. But I keep to the right, under the rim of the overlook where we had camped the night before, and scan the walls for a possible route to the top.

I come after a time to a lovely pool in a basin of sand, fed by a trickle of water flowing down the canyon's rocky floor. I drink again, fill my canteen and go on. This canyon, like all the others, forks again and again; I keep to the right-hand branch each time and finally arrive at a dead end, a box, with unscalable walls rising three, four, five hundred feet straight up toward the hot blue sky. I go back to the pool and take a dip in the water.

Lying on my back on the smooth sandstone beside the pool I notice a fingerlike ridge that juts into the canyon from the base of the main wall under the plateau above. If we can climb the ridge to the maroon bench above the Cutler, we might be able to traverse laterally to the opening in the white rim through which we had originally descended. From here it looks as if it might go.

I'm just starting up to investigate the ridge when Waterman appears, tracking me up the canyon floor. He joins me, we climb the ridge together and discover that it does indeed go all the way to the red ledge. There are a couple of tricky pitches with rotten rock and fingerholds of exquisite delicacy but most of the way is easy. We return to the bottom of The Maze to get out packs and the rope, and to do a little more exploring.

It is now late in the afternoon. We don't have much time left before sundown. Our sleeping bags are up on the rim in the Land Rover and we have nothing to eat but nuts and raisins. We decide it best to climb out of The Maze before dark and save further exploration for tomorrow. We go back to the pool and the base of the ridge. On the way Waterman points out to me the glyph of a snake, which I had missed. The Indians had been here. But nobody else, so far as we can tell. Nowhere have we seen a trace of the white man or of his horse or cow—or helicopter. But then we have seen only a tiny corner of The Maze, maybe no more than one per cent. The heart of it remains unknown.

We climb the ridge, scale the bluffs, and traverse without difficulty the sloping red bench for a mile to the east, where we find the notch that leads to the top through the white rimrock. As we proceed we mark our route with pointer stones; this will be known hereafter, for a thousand years, as the Abbey-Waterman trail. Maybe. More likely the BLM or the Park Service will bypass our trail with an electrical chairlift for crippled tourists.

We reach the rim a little before sundown and after a quick supper—for it's cold and windy up here—go early to bed. Above the Orange Cliffs a dismal sunset of bloody sun and gray overcast lingers for a long time on the horizon while the wind howls across our prostrate forms all night long.

In the morning, the wind is still blowing, it's much colder, and the entire sky is dark with storm clouds threatening rain or possibly, judging by the chill in the air, even snow. It would not be the first time that a blizzard hit the high plateaus in mid-September. I try to wake up Waterman: snow, I tell him, it's going to snow. He only curls up tighter in the sack; he doesn't want to go home.

I build a big roaring fire, hang the coffee pot in the flames, dump a pound of bacon into the skillet and stir briskly with a fork. The fierce wind fans the fire and chases sparks, coals, and shreds of juniper bark over the edge of the cliff, ten feet away. A dried-up tumbleweed comes over the rise from the north, dances past and sails into space above The Maze. Ecstasy—and danger; we'll never get the Land Rover up those switchbacks if it storms. A few drops of rain sprinkle the sandstone at my feet and patter gently on Waterman in his bag. He makes no move. Breakfast, I tell him, let's eat! He comes to life.

As we eat we discuss the situation. We each have another day to spare but no more; I have to return to the Arches, he has to register for the fall term at Colorado University, far over on the eastern slope. If we get caught down here by the storm it may be a number of days before we can get out. And we don't have much food left. Of course in an emergency we could always descend again into The Maze, hike down the river, build a raft, float fifty miles down to Hite, and hitch-hike a ride from there back to civilization, if anyone happened to be going that way. We agree, regretfully, to start back at once.

It takes only a few minutes to roll up our sacks and pile our gear into the vehicle; a light rain sizzling in the fire encourages our movements. Soon we are grinding back along the trail, four-wheel drive all the way to Big Water Spring through the grand and beautiful desolation of the middle-bench country—above the inner canyons, under the ledge—where nothing grows but the sword-bladed yucca, the scattered clumps of blackbrush and occasional stunted junipers. Next time I come this way, I think (and may it be soon!) I'm going to bring a boxful of Christmas tree decorations—silver-blue tinsel, red candles, peppermint canes, silver bells, golden stars and frosted baubles—and I'm going to pick out the loneliest, most forlorn of those little junipers and dress it in splendor, gay and glittering, and leave it there shining in the wilderness for a season or two, until the winds and the sun and the birds strip it bare again.

We reach the foot of the Flint Trail. The storm is building up, the wind colder and harder than ever, but luckily for us the heavy rain has not come down. Waterman shifts into low range; I get out and walk along behind to assist on the turns. There is no trouble; getting up proves to be no harder than coming down, through [sic] we do find it necessary to add a little water to the radiator when we arrive on top.

7000 feet up now; we put on jackets and hoods as a fine sleet drives down from the sky and turns the dust into mud. While Waterman pours more gasoline into the tank I load my pockets with pinyon nuts—might need them yet. We go on, past the old cabin at French Spring and through the woods and past the flowery meadows now gray beneath a mist of snow and rain. We stop at the BLM shrine to record our visit.

"First descent into The Maze," writes Waterman in the book, though we cannot be absolutely certain of this. And I write, "For God's sake leave this country alone—Abbey." To which Waterman adds "For Abbey's sake leave this country alone—God." The air is thick with a million fluttering snowflakes; we hurry on through the forty miles of desert, reach the paved road without getting stuck and get back in Moab at dark, just in time for cocktails and dinner, while a great storm, first and biggest of the autumn season, blankets the high country with snow from Denver to Salt Lake City.

Suggested Reading

≋ Native Inhabitants

Conetah, Fred. *A History of the Northern Ute People.* Fort Duchesne, UT: Uintah and Ouray Tribal Publications, 1982.

———. *Stories of Our Ancestors.* Fort Duchesne, UT: Uintah and Ouray Tribal Publications, 1974.

Smith, Anne M. *Ethnography of the Northern Utes.* Santa Fe: Museum of New Mexico Press, 1974.

———. *Ute Tales.* Salt Lake City: University of Utah Press, 1992.

≋ Explorers and Settlers

Barton, John D. *Buckskin Entrepreneur: Antoine Robidoux and the Fur Trade of the Uinta Basin 1824–1844.* Vernal, UT: Oakfield Publishing Co., 1996.

Colbert, Edwin H. *The Great Dinosaur Hunters and Their Discoveries.* Mineola, NY: Dover Publications, 1984.

De Voto, Bernard. *Across the Wide Missouri.* Boston: Houghton Mifflin, 1947.

Goetzmann, William H. *Exploration and Empire.* New York: Alfred A. Knopf, 1966.

Hafen, LeRoy, ed. *The Mountain Men and Fur Traders of the Far West.* Spokane, WA: Arthur Clark, 1968.

McClure, Grace. *The Bassett Women.* Athens: Swallow Press of Ohio University Press, 1985.

Morgan, Dale L. *The West of William H. Ashley.* Denver, CO: Old West Publishing Co., 1964.

Stegner, Wallace. *The Gathering of Zion: The Story of the Mormon Trail.* New York: McGraw-Hill, 1964.

———. *Mormon Country.* Lincoln, NE: Bison Books, 1981.

≋ River Runners

Abbey, Edward. *Down the River.* New York: E. P. Dutton, 1982.

Cassady, Jim, Bill Cross, and Fryar Calhoun. *Western Whitewater from the Rockies to the Pacific: A River Guide for Raft, Kayak, and Canoe.* Berkeley, CA: North Fork Press, 1994.

Darrah, William Culp. *Powell of the Colorado.* Princeton, NJ: Princeton University Press, 1951.

Flavell, George. *The Log of the Panthon: An Account of an 1896 River Voyage from Green River, Wyoming, to Yuma, Arizona through the Grand Canyon.* Boulder, CO: Pruett Publishing, 1987.

Fleck, Richard F., ed. *A Colorado River Reader.* Salt Lake City: University of Utah Press, 2000.

Fletcher, Colin, *River: One Man's Journey Down the Colorado, Source to Sea.* New York: Alfred A. Knopf, 1997.

Goldwater, Barry. *Delightful Journey Down the Green and Colorado Rivers.* Tempe: Arizona Historical Foundation, 1970.

Huser, Vern. *River Reflections.* Chester, CT: Globe Pequot Press, 1985.

Lavender, David. *River Runners of the Grand Canyon.* Grand Canyon, AZ: Grand Canyon Natural History Association, 1951.

Murray, John A. *The River Reader.* Guilford, CT: Nature Conservancy/Lyons Press, 1998.

Stone, Julius. *Canyon Country: The Romance of a Drop of Water and a Grain of Sand.* New York: G. P. Putnam's Sons, 1932.

Webb, Roy. *Riverman: The Story of Bus Hatch.* Rock Springs, WY: Labyrinth Publishing Co., 1989.

≋ THE POLITICS OF WATER

Cosco, John. *Echo Park: Struggle for Preservation.* Boulder, CO: Johnson Books, 1995.

Harvey, Mark. *A Symbol of Wilderness: Echo Park and the American Conservation Movement.* Albuquerque: University of New Mexico Press, 1994.

McPhee, John. *Encounters with the Archdruid.* New York: Farrar, Strauss and Giroux, 1971.

Reisner, Marc. *Cadillac Desert: The American West and Its Disappearing Water.* New York: Viking Penguin, 1986.

Permissions

EDWARD ABBEY, "Terra Incognita: Into the Maze," from *Desert Solitaire: A Season in the Wilderness*, by Edward Abbey. Copyright 1968 by Edward Abbey, renewed 1996 by Clarke Abbey. Reprinted by permission of Don Congdon Associates, Inc.

WILLIAM ASHLEY, from *The Explorations of William H. Ashley and Jedidiah Smith, 1822–1829*, edited by Harrison Clifford Dale (Lincoln: University of Nebraska Press, 1941). Reprinted by permission of the publisher.

GEORGE Y. BRADLEY, from "George Y. Bradley's Journal: May 24–August 30, 1869," edited and introduced by William Culp Darrah, *Utah Historical Quarterly* 15 (1947): 31–72. Reprinted by permission of the Utah State Historical Society.

DAVID BROWER, "Dinosaurs, Parks, and Dams," *Pacific Spectator* 8 (Spring 1954). Reprinted by permission of the heirs of David Brower.

KIT CARSON, from *Kit Carson's Autobiography*, edited by Milo Milton Quaife (Lincoln: University of Nebraska Press, 1966). Reprinted by permission of the publisher.

FREDERICK S. DELLENBAUGH, from *A Canyon Voyage: The Narrative of the Second Powell Expedition* (Tucson: University of Arizona Press, 1996).

Deseret News, "Uinta not what was represented," *Deseret News*, September 25, 1861, 172. Reprinted by permission of the *Deseret News*.

BERNARD DE VOTO, from "Shall We Let Them Ruin Our National Parks?" *Saturday Evening Post* 223, no. 4 (July 22, 1950). Reprinted with permission of the *Saturday Evening Post*, copyright 1950. Copyright renewed BFL & MS, Inc., Indianapolis.

EARL DOUGLASS, "The Dinosaur National Monument," unpublished manuscript, the Earl Douglass Collection, J. Willard Marriott Library Special Collections, University of Utah. Reprinted by permission of the J. Willard Marriott Library.

FRAY FRANCISCO SILVESTRE VÉLEZ DE ESCALANTE, from *The Dominguez-Escalante Journal: Their Expedition Through Colorado, Utah, Arizona, and New Mexico,* edited by Ted J. Warner, translated by Fray Angelico Chavez (Salt Lake City: University of Utah Press, 1995). Reprinted by permission of the publisher.

THOMAS J. FARNHAM, from *An 1839 Wagon Train Journal: Travels in the Great Western Prairies, the Anahuac and Rocky Mountains, and in the Oregon Territory* (New York: Greeley and Melrath, 1843).

PHILIP L. FRADKIN, "Beginnings: Four Streams in Search of a River," from *A River No More: The Colorado River and the West* (Berkeley: University of California Press, 1996). Reprinted by permission of Philip L. Fradkin.

PHILIP L. FRADKIN, "A Recent Year," from *Sagebrush Country: Land and the American West* (Boulder, CO: Johnson Books, 2004). Reprinted by permission of Philip L. Fradkin.

JOHN C. FRÉMONT, from *Report on the Exploring Expedition to the Rocky Mountains* (Washington, DC: Gale and Seaton, 1845).

E. L. KOLB, from *Through the Grand Canyon from Wyoming to Mexico,* by E. L. Kolb (New York: Macmillan, 1914; Tucson: University of Arizona Press, 1989).

WILLIAM LEWIS MANLY, from *Death Valley in '49* (San Jose, CA: Pacific Tree and Vine Co., 1894).

RUSSELL MARTIN, from *A Story That Stands Like a Dam: Glen Canyon and the Struggle for the Soul of the West* (New York: Henry Holt and Company, 1989). Reprinted by permission of Russell Martin.

ELLEN MELOY, "Two-Snake Days," from *Raven's Exile: A Season on the Green River.* Copyright 1994 Ellen Meloy. Reprinted by permission of the University of Arizona Press.

JOHN STRONG NEWBERRY, from *Report of the Exploring Expedition from Santa Fe, New Mexico, to the Junction of the Grand and Green Rivers of the Great Colorado of the West, in 1859* (Washington, DC: Government Printing Office, 1876). Reprinted by permission of University of Michigan Making of America.